Literacy for Diverse Learners:

Finding Common Ground in Today's Classrooms

Literacy for Diverse Learners:

Finding Common Ground in Today's Classrooms

Editors:
Barbara Honchell
and
Melissa Schulz

Christopher-Gordon Publishers, Inc.
Norwood, Massachusetts

Copyright Acknowledgments

Every effort has been made to contact copyright holders for permission to reproduce borrowed material where necessary. We apologize for any oversights and would be happy to rectify them in future printings.

Christopher~Gordon Publishers, Inc.
Bridging Theory and Practice

1502 Providence Highway, Suite 12
Norwood, MA 02062

800-934-8322 • 781-762-5577
www.Christopher-Gordon.com

Printed in the United State of America
10 9 8 7 6 5 4 3 2 1   09 08 07

ISBN: 1-933760-06-0
Library of Congress Catalogue Number: 2006936461

Table of Contents

Foreword

During the 21st century, educators will encounter many challenges; chief among them is how to prepare all students to function in a society that requires increasingly sophisticated uses of literacy. This problem is especially challenging in the face of an ever increasing linguistic and ethnic diversity of the student population. *Literacy for Diverse Learners,* edited by Barbara Honchell and Melissa Schulz, responds to this challenge by providing firsthand knowledge, research, and numerous examples from parents, classroom teachers, teacher educators, and administrators, illustrating effective ways to support the literacy development of diverse students. The book takes an approach to diversity that is distinctive in two ways. First, diversity is broadly defined to include any student that does not fit within the mainstream of children in a classroom; second, a wide range of connected phenomena and issues related to diversity are described and discussed.

In the first section, we meet a first- and sixth-grade European-American child who exemplify diversity because they are having difficulty learning to read and write. As their stories unfold, we learn that Derek and Tammy's classroom teachers turned the children's failure into success. These caring classroom teachers conveyed, through their actions and words, that Derek and Tammy can, and will, learn to read and write. They were tenacious and committed to finding a way to teach them by observing and evaluating the children's strengths, identifying what they could do independently while reading and writing, and using this information to help them to learn something new. The teachers did not stop working to make the children's literacy learning experiences positive and rewarding, which ensured their success.

The six chapters in section 2 focus on classroom practices that support diverse learners. Although different aspects of literacy learning (e.g., reading, writing, children's literature, drama, oral language development for first- and second-language learners) in early childhood, home, and elementary school contexts are addressed, a "constructivist" perspective on thinking, learning, and literacy learning frames and links these chapters. Constructivists view learners as active participants in the learning process, not passive recipients of information delivered by robotic teachers in a preplanned and sequence manner. Social aspects of learning are viewed as relevant in classrooms, homes, communities, and schools. Furthermore, interaction between adults and children have a strong influence on what is learned, how it is learned, and how much is learned.

The last section of *Literacy for Diverse Learners* is a call to action. These three chapters are enlivened and strengthened by vignettes and case studies of efforts to reconceive professional development, leadership, school organization, and school reform. The authors respond to the most frequently asked questions about how to meet the diverse needs of an increasingly complex and everchanging school culture.

- What kind of professional development can schools offer to meet the current needs of an increasingly more diversified school?

- How do we help teachers work as professional development teams to construct learning opportunities tailored to their particular interests around diverse learners?

- How do we develop trusted, responsive leaders to effectively coach and support teachers in academically diverse schools?

- How do we create opportunities for teachers and administrators to build a sense of trust and community to effectively change classrooms and embrace change to improve student achievement of diverse learners?

- What changes in school organization are needed to achieve school- and districtwide reform?

- What are the major barriers to reform and how can they be prevented?

- How can we best address the conflicting political and policy demands for serving diverse students' needs and increasing demands for rigor and common achievement standards for all students?

Though each of the 12 chapters stands on its own merit, when taken together, three recurring and common themes frame the discussions to make *Literacy for Diverse Learners* unique. First, there is a shift away from a deficit model of teaching, whereby diverse students are viewed as lacking basic knowledge and skills that must be remedied through instruction, to putting efforts into redesigning literacy experiences to meet the individual learning strengths and needs of diverse students. Assessing and building on learners' strengths is seen as a philosophical choice that teachers, administrators, and policy makers can make. Contributors to this book reveal, through concrete examples, how skillful teaching of diverse learners comes from the ability to hold high expectations while providing learning opportunities and experiences whereby students can reach those expectations.

The second theme that underpins *Literacy for Diverse Learners* is that as children entering our schools become more diverse, on several levels, traditional practices of teaching them to read and write need to be reexamined.

Teachers, administrators, teacher educators, and policy makers are asked to overcome their reliance on the familiar ways to teach diverse populations, to step outside the narrowness of their traditions, and to use the richness and diversity of children's experiences to better understanding the complexities of the learning process and improve their practice. The most effective teachers readily agree that they learn more while working with struggling students who have diverse needs than from those who learn more easily.

The third theme that emerges while reading this book is the authors' respect for diverse capabilities, perspectives, social, and cultural practices and a feeling that in spite of increased levels of underachievement in the face of growing diversity among students, there are indications that much of this failure is preventable. As revealed in the substantial guidance and practical suggestions for restructuring educational programs and literacy instruction in our schools, contributors to this book are committed to meeting the diverse learning needs of individuals and helping all children to reach their full potential. And they are optimistic that teachers and children can achieve these goals.

Literacy for Diverse Learners provides a broad overview of what matters most and what works in helping diverse students to become proficient readers and writers. The book is a necessary resource and a "must read" for teachers, teacher educators, and policy makers interested in improving literacy education in today's increasingly diverse classrooms.

Carol A. Lyons
Professor Emeritus
Ohio State University

Preface

This book is about teaching literacy to culturally and linguistically diverse children who are in preschool through fifth grade. When we use the term "literacy," we are referring to reading, writing, listening, and speaking practices. We decided to collaborate together on this project while teaching in the same school with a diverse student population. We were teaching Reading Recovery to low-performing first-grade students who were struggling with literacy. Many of our students received additional services, such as English language learner instruction, speech, and language support, or were being considered for special education. While we know that effective literacy instruction must focus on student's individual needs, this can be very challenging for elementary school teachers with 25 students who have a wide range of academic and personal experiences. Schools, administrators, teachers, and literacy coaches need to be prepared to meet diverse needs of all learners while simultaneously holding expectations of excellence in acquiring literacy for all children. This is no small task!

Sometimes, it seems easier to say what a diverse learner isn't rather than what he or she is. Diverse children are not from the mainstream or majority culture. Often, their home, native language, or dialect is not that of the majority. Many diverse learners are unsuccessful in school. While we will attempt to define what we mean by diversity, ultimately, the definition is not nearly as important as the fact that, as educators, we have the responsibility and the ability to teach all the children in our schools. We cannot change the factors that create the diversity, we can only teach to support literacy learning. The aim of this book is not to understand labels or subgroups, but rather effective literacy instruction for all children. This book examines how teachers, administrators, and literacy coaches can become more prepared to address the varied range of academic competence of children who arrive at their school.

Introduction to Section One: Issues of Diversity

The chapters in the first section exemplify and personify diversity for various learners, children who are not from the mainstream or majority because they are at risk for reading and/or writing failure. In this section, Dantas and Kantor take a close look at the school life of one first grader, Derek, who was identified as an "at risk" reader and writer. Derek is a European-American, red-haired, talkative, and lively child who entered first grade from a working-class community. Important to Derek's school literacy journey was his teacher's ability to open up "official" classroom spaces that gave Derek greater access to social membership in groups inside and outside of the classroom.

Also in this section, Barbara Honchell introduces us to Tammy, who is a dark-haired, quiet, and delightful child who wanted to please her teachers but appeared to lack self-confidence in reading. Tammy, like Derek, is a European-American child from a working-class community. Tammy is unsuccessful with reading in spite of excellent classroom reading instruction and Title 1 reading services. Tammy is an older diverse learner who was failing to read at the beginning of sixth grade. Her teacher helped Tammy integrate her isolated item knowledge (letter and word knowledge) into an integrated, working, systematic approach to reading. Tammy's story provides us with information about older, diverse learners who are trying to become literate.

Finally in this section, Ellison will shed light on the truth and misconceptions about second-language learning. We will meet several Spanish-speaking students, Consuelo and Paco, who are very different from each other. Paco comes to the classroom with very limited knowledge of both English and Spanish language. While Consuelo is a literate Spanish-speaking student, he is trying to learn English as a second language. The educational journeys and opportunities for academic success are in sharp contrast from one another.

Chapter 1

Defining Diverse
Literacy Learners

Barbara Honchell and Melisa M. Schulz

We were working together in a school that took pride in its diverse population. In fact, 37 languages were spoken within the student population. In the spring, the first graders all presented a schoolwide program, where the children performed the well-known song "It's a Small World" in their native language. It was the first time we saw the wealth of language diversity honored, but the honoring seemed somewhat artificial in nature when compared to the daily whole-group instruction using basal readers we observed and the general approach to supporting diverse learners being that of "pull out" rather that "push in." These observations were not intended to be critical observations but rather representative of the way that many schools were dealing with the issues of diversity, which were becoming more apparent on a yearly basis. This particular school was working with many diverse languages, but we had seen the schools attempting to enhance instruction for diverse learners as related to other aspects of diversity, such as special education inclusion, racial differences in previously all-white schools, and also a wide array of other subgroups that were becoming more visible as the federal government began addressing academic progress of children by groups when considering the status of the schools.

For us, the issue was very personal as we were teaching Reading Recovery lessons with first-grade children who are notable for their individual needs as literacy learners. We were both working with children receiving other special services, such as English language learning (ELL) instruction, speech, and language support, or were being considered for referral to special education. For us, we viewed this in terms of each child we were teaching. It was in this context that we began to talk with each other about other schools and other children we had experienced as teachers and began to puzzle together what we knew about diversity in the hopes of meeting the needs of the children like Marcus, Bilal, Ashley, and Suzanna we were teaching.

Introduction

Every day, children walk through the school door with a wide range of academic abilities and personal experiences. Schools need to be prepared to meet the diverse needs of all learners who walk through that door. This book is about teaching literacy to culturally and linguistically diverse children who are in preschool through fifth grade. When we use the term "literacy," we are referring to reading, writing, listening, and speaking practices. Sometimes, it seems easier to say what a diverse learner isn't rather than what he or she is. Diverse children are not from the mainstream or majority culture. Often, their home, native language, or dialect is not that of the majority. Many of these diverse learners are unsuccessful in school. While we will attempt to define what we mean by diversity, ultimately, the definition is not nearly as important as the fact that, as educators, we have the responsibility and the ability to teach all the children in our schools. We cannot change the factors that create the diversity, we can only teach to support literacy learning. The aim of this book is not to understand labels or subgroups, but rather effective literacy instruction for all children.

    This book examines how teachers can become more prepared to address the varied range of academic competence of children who arrive at their school. There has been a significant amount of research examining what makes literacy instruction effective for diverse learners. This book will survey the research literature and provide additional information that will enhance future literacy instruction of diverse learners in general classrooms in mainstream schools. Our intention is to create a resource for classroom teachers, literacy coaches, administrators, and curriculum designers to better understand the

evolving process of literacy learning for diverse learners in contemporary classrooms in America. As we said to each other as we began our shared exploration of this topic, the world is an ever-changing place and so is school, since
school mirrors the larger community in which it exists; however, schools sometimes reflect the communities that existed 25 years ago rather than the current
ones. When visiting a classroom just the other day, this poster was displayed
on the wall and seems an appropriate way to define diversity before looking at
the numbers or research:

*D*ifferent

*I*ndividual

*V*aluing

*E*ach other

*R*egardless of

*S*kin

*I*ntellect

*T*alents or

*Y*ears

Demographics of Diverse Learners

There are a growing number of diverse learners who enter the public schools.
As an example, the current U.S. Census Data (U.S. Bureau of the Census, 2000)
indicate that the number of African-American people living in the United States
has increased by 22%, while the number of Hispanic/Latino people has increased by 58%. There are several terms that are frequently used by teachers,
administrators, and researchers to describe "diverse" learners. Some of the
terms include: linguistically diverse learners, limited English proficient learners, English language learners, or exceptional learners. The list goes on and on.
Many educators think about these children as the subgroups who must reach
grade-level performance for their school to stay out of trouble. Others think of
these children as diverse learners who go together to create a rich classroom
environment in which we all learn together. I overheard a teacher attempt to
explain this idea to a child by saying, "If we all liked the same kind of ice cream,
there would only need to be one flavor, but that would be really boring." This
is a much more important issue than ice cream flavors, because the futures of
many children are at stake due to the achievement gaps that often accompany
diversity.

An Increase in the Literacy Achievement Variation

When young children enter school, teachers assess their literacy skills. Some skills include letter recognition, knowledge of letter and sound relationships, word knowledge, writing vocabulary, concepts of print, and text reading level. Mounting evidence continues to document an achievement gap between students. The variation is obvious as early as kindergarten on measures of letter recognition and letter sound relationships between whites and Hispanic children (West, Denton, & Reaney, 2000). Another similar gap is found along economic lines (West, Denton, & Germino Hausken 2000; Denton, West, & Walston, 2003). Evidence from longitudinal research suggests that while the differences among children's literacy progress are apparent early on, they become even more pronounced after four years. It is unlikely that children will change their classroom ranking from first to fourth grade. In short, children who are struggling in first grade will continue to struggle in fourth grade and children who are making average progress will be average in fourth grade as well (Juel, 1988). Children who lack an understanding of what they need to do to help them become more successful often lack basic literacy understanding in comparison to their classmates. However, there is mounting evidence that it is possible to alter this pattern with high-quality instruction (Rodgers & Gómez-Bellengé, 2003). Their classmates continue to demonstrate academic progress while they remain behind. It is possible to undercut literacy failure for diverse learners, and the goal of this book is to provide recommendations for teachers so they can achieve this goal.

Meeting Diverse Learner's Literacy Needs

Teachers, administrators, and researchers are aware of the achievement differences between students; however, the problem is even more apparent in schools, which serve communities with cultural and language identities that are different from the mainstream culture. The focus for this book is on general classrooms in such schools. Diverse children often lack access to the same social, economic, and political power as children and families from mainstream communities. Diverse children from marginalized, nonmainstream communities encounter increased difficulty with literacy acquisition and do not achieve the same level of literacy competence as other mainstream children.

More than 20 years have passed since Shirley Brice Heath's (1983) landmark work, *Ways with Words*, documented the impact upon children when their literacy practices at home are unrecognized by the school community. It is ironic that Heath's work was done in North Carolina, the state where many of our contributors live and work. A robust literature has developed the notion of the highly contextualized nature of literacy across many cultures and socio-economic communities (Hale, 2001; Taylor & Dorsey-Gaines, 1988; Tomlinson, 1999; Yatvin, 1991). This diversity highlights the need for schools to understand how to reach students from cultural, socioeconomic, and linguistic backgrounds that differ from the mainstream. In short, not all families share the same reading, writing, listening, and speaking practices, but schools often carry out mainstream literacy instruction as though they do. In the next section, we provide an overview of two perspectives frequently adopted by educational researchers and educators in general.

Intervention and Prevention Perspective

Educational researchers have taken two distinct directions in their attempts to better understand the diversity and to make a difference in the lives of diverse children and families. One perspective of diverse children and their families is that they are "at risk" in school because they are deficient. Reflecting this deficit-oriented image, some parent-involvement programs are designed as if parents are to blame for their children's literacy problems. A significant amount of research exists to refute the belief that poor, undereducated, and language-minority children come from literacy-impoverished home environments (Auerbach, 1989; Auerbach, 1995; Danzinger & Lin, 2000; Purcell-Gates, 1995). Most marginalized families not only value literacy, they often believe that it is essential for success in school and society, and they work hard to help their children become academically successful (Compton-Lilly, 2003; Taylor & Dorsey-Gaines, 1988).

In a study of literacy values of Mexican Americans, Ortiz (1992) found that parents were very concerned with their children's academic achievement and spent significant amounts of time reading and writing with their children. On the other hand, some educators and researchers view the situation of diversity as the "problem" of the child. When the child is unable to work successfully within the confines of the classroom instructional program, remediation in the form of compensatory education or retention (approximately 6% of children annually) is considered to be the best option so the child will be "ready" to actively participate in the classroom instruction (Walmsley & Allington, 1995; Allington & McGill-Franzen, 1995). In other words, from this perspective, the children must fit into the school and its curriculum rather than the school organizing itself to embrace diversity. Another perspective that is evident in the research literature is the multiple literacies perspective. This perspective views diversity through a different, and in our outlook, perhaps more proactive, positive lens.

Multiple Literacies Perspective

Another perspective of diverse children and their families is for educators to recognize the resources that all families bring to the school community. In this book, the contributors are aligned with the multiple literacies perspective. As Moll and Greenburg (1990) explain, that regardless of educational background, homes of poor and language-minority families are rich "funds of knowledge" that are often unrecognized and untapped by the school community. Educators who use a sociocultural perspective call for more meaningful strategies for working with families based on research conducted with diverse families (Heath, 1983; Purcell-Gates, 1995; Taylor & Dorsey-Gaines, 1988). Many classroom teachers are from economically middle-class families and bring those "funds of knowledge" to the classroom. If these teachers completed a short quiz with items to check, such as "I know how to get my children into Little League, piano lessons, soccer, etc." or "I know how to get a library card," they would likely score quite high. On the other hand, if the quiz consisted of items to check such as "I know how to keep my clothes from being stolen at the laundromat" or "I know how to read a corporate financial statement and analyze my own financial statements," teachers would not likely score as well (Payne, 2001). Teachers often are not knowledgeable about either the world of poverty or wealth. This is not necessarily an issue of socioeconomics, although this is often a visible aspect of diversity. For educators who recognize the resources or "funds of knowledge" of *all* families, communication and trust are enhanced and the classroom is perceived as more accessible by more families. The school expands itself to include and appreciate the richness a diverse community creates.

Methods of Instruction for Diverse Learners

Researchers such as Cummins and Moll have recommended educational reform to successfully alter the relationships between teachers and students and between schools and communities. According to Cummins (1986):

"The required changes involve personal redefinitions of the way classroom teachers interact with the children and the communities they serve. In other words, legislative and policy reforms may be necessary conditions for effective change, but they are not sufficient. Implementation of change is dependent upon the extent to which educators, both collectively and individually, redefine their roles with respect to minority students and communities" (p. 19).

Moll conducted a study that was part of a larger project on "effective" schooling in three elementary schools and seven classrooms in a major metropolitan area in the southeastern part of the United States. Based on Moll's research findings, teachers who have "personally redefined" themselves and who are outstanding teachers of English language learners have three related qualities. First, expert teachers are theoretically equipped; the teachers are capable of explaining the "how" and "why" of their teaching and they are able to independently determine what support and guidance is necessary to provide each learner with the help to become successful. Second, expert teachers are able to use their professional judgment to implement curriculum that is the most effective at meeting their learners' academic needs. Autonomy is diminishing for educators in the current school environment, which pressures teachers and learners to act as passive givers and receivers of a scripted curriculum. Teachers are highly successful when an educational philosophy across the whole school supports teacher autonomy in making curricular and pedagogical decisions in response to the diverse needs of each learner within the classroom (Moll, 1988). Third, expert teachers meet regularly with colleagues and university professors to discuss teaching issues, and these peers become a support group that provides encouragement and professional teaching advice and support. The following diagram illustrates and highlights the three areas of knowledge for expert teachers that facilitate response to literacy learners:

Expert Teachers **Respond to Learners' Needs Guided by:**		
Conceptual Knowledge and Theoretical Understanding of Instruction	**Curriculum and Process Knowledge**	**Sociocultural Knowledge**
• differentiation of instruction based on authentic assessment	• awareness of the curriculum for instruction for multiple grade levels	• effective tiers, lessons, and products to support all learners
• integration of student's varied experience and knowledge into instruction	• awareness of the interests and experiences of students related to the curriculum	• offers large-group, small-group, and individual instruction as meets the needs of the learner
• scaffolding of learning through sensitive observation and response	• ability to tailor instruction to the academic needs of the learner	• awareness of multiple intelligences
• understanding of many forms of instruction	• use varied supplementary materials	• effectively accessing the learning profiles for all students
• variation in the implementation of instructional strategies to meet student needs	• developing tasks that respect the knowledge base of the learner	• advantaging the cultural backgrounds of the students

Characteristics of Effective Instruction

The research literature highlights three characteristics that need to be in place for highly effective teaching to occur (Moll, 1988). First, highly effective teachers incorporate differentiated instruction that provides learners with the opportunity to use reading, writing, and oral language in multiple ways across multiple academic content areas. These interactions are of broad enough scope that all children can actively participate, rather than tasks with right and wrong responses. The teachers scaffold the students' literacy attempts to encourage student risk taking and discovery (Boyle & Peregoy, 1990; Peregoy & Boyle, 1993; Gibbons, 2002). Second, the teachers believe that all children have funds of knowledge to share (Moll & Greenburg, 1990), and by incorporating students' experiences within lessons, the students have increased motivation to learn. As one teacher explains it, "The richer the content, the more the students had something they connected to." Thus, children can participate in complex tasks with high levels of success. Third, the teachers have autonomy in their teaching. Moll (1988) explains:

"This autonomy was not only reflected in their teaching, but in the children's learning. The students, to a great extent, had options about their learning: They could select projects, books, tasks, and assignments, and they routinely helped each other, as well as younger students, with their assignments" (p. 471).

Learning through Collaboration

Teachers who have a strong theoretical understanding of effective teaching and learning produce instruction that is highly effective for diverse learners. The theory of learning on which this book is based focuses on the work of Lev Vygotsky (1978, 1986), a Russian psychologist whose work became widely translated in the late 1960s. Vygotsky's most profound ideas are centered on the role of assisted performance (teaching). Vygotsky sees the development of the mind (learning) as coconstructed activity that occurs through the participation with others in goal-directed activity. Teachers and students are active participants, and learning is a collaborative undertaking. Vygotsky uses the phrase the "zone of proximal development," which is the distance between what a student can do alone and what the child can do jointly with the support of a more knowledgeable person. For instance, if a child engages in a complex activity, such as writing, with the help and support of others at first, he or she may be more capable of independent writing later by him- or herself. When a teacher gives the child the right support at the right time, it is more likely he or she will be successful with the writing task.

Scaffolding

The term *scaffolding* was first used by Wood, Bruner, and Ross (1976), who carefully analyzed the interactions between parents and children. The researchers defined scaffolding as a process that "enables a child or novice to solve a task or achieve a goal that would be beyond his unassisted efforts" (Wood, Bruner, & Ross, 1976, p. 90). Scaffolding involves providing support to learners so they move toward new skills, concepts, or levels of understanding. Scaffolding is temporary assistance. For instance, when a worker builds a scaffold to work on part of a building temporarily, it will later be removed when the work is completed. As Vygotsky (1978) has said, what a child can do with support today, he or she can do alone tomorrow. This book offers numerous suggestions for scaffolding learning for diverse learners who are either learning English as a second language or for children who are chronologically placed in the right grade level, but their academic ability is delayed.

Teachers who are able to provide teaching and learning (scaffolding) opportunities in the general classroom will be more equipped to meet the wide range of academic abilities present today. Individualized, small-group, and large-group teaching and learning contexts have great potential in the general classroom. For example, there are two teaching approaches used in the general classroom, shared writing and interactive writing, that allow the teacher to scaffold diverse children's writing attempts within the context of the whole group. Shared writing is one method of whole-group writing instruction that provides students with the opportunity to observe and participate in the writing process without the responsibility of having to write independently. Shared writing is beneficial for beginning readers and writers, especially English language learners who may have limited writing experiences in English as a second language. Interactive writing is another method of whole-group writing instruction that can be very meaningful for diverse learners who are struggling academically with their grade-level literacy curriculum or for English language learners who are just learning to write in a second language. During interactive writing, the children take part in the writing process and "share the pen" with the teacher. These are just two of the many teaching practices explored in detail in this book, since we have focused the entire second section on teaching to support diverse literacy learners.

Conversational versus Academic Proficiency with Language

Teachers who understand and have developed a sound theoretical knowledge base are more equipped to meet the needs of all students' academic needs in their general classrooms. There is a common misconception that many educators have regarding English language learners. An English language learner may appear to handle the demands of functioning in an English-only classroom well because he or she can talk to the teacher one on one, talk with a friend in the school hallway, or likes to play with other classmates on the school playground. Researchers have found that even though English language learners can develop conversational language rapidly, usually taking 1–2 years, the same English language learners may take between 5–7 years to develop academic learning that is the same as their native English-speaking classmates (Collier, 1989; Cummins, 1996, 2000; McKay et al., 1997). In short, English language learners need to gain more language proficiency each and every year to catch up and close the gap with their native English-speaking classmates. Connections can also be made between English language learners and English speakers with a dialect different from American standard English; language proficiency can influence the literacy success for children with many different, yet related, language variations. In the next section, we will address the advantages to individualized instruction for diverse learners in the general classroom.

Individualized Student-Centered Instruction

Instruction is very effective for diverse learners when teachers offer flexible instruction that is tailored to meet diverse learner's individual, academic needs. Selecting reading materials with an appropriate reading level is a critical factor in effective literacy instruction for diverse learners. Specifically, Fountas and Pinnell (1999, p. 1) maintain, "Matching books to readers depends on three interrelated sets of understandings, all of which are critical to effective teaching:

- knowing the readers
- knowing the texts
- understanding the reading process"

Matching children with the right book is critical, and its importance cannot be underestimated. Reading engagement is the ultimate goal in reading. For students to become engaged in reading, teachers need to provide children with books they can read for an extended period of time that are interesting to them. This may be a daunting task for general classroom teachers who have a large number of students in their classroom. In order for the goal to be achieved, teachers can organize their classroom so that they have time for individual reading conferences with children. As Sharon Taberski (2000) describes in her book, *On Solid Ground*, reading conferences are very important at the beginning of the school year when teachers are just learning each student's individual reading ability. Taberski recommends scheduling conferences 5 days a week for 1 hour a day. Taberski (2000) maintains that, "These initial conferences help me assess each child's stage in reading, identify some skills and strategies to focus on, and find some books best suited for independent reading" (p. 37). During individual reading conferences, teachers can observe how children handle books, determine what type of reading strategies the student is using at difficulty, and what he or she needs to learn about reading. Teachers need to know their readers and their personal reading interests; reading conferences provide the right context within the general classroom so this can take place. As the year progresses, the classroom teacher can reduce the number of individual reading conferences and increase the number of guided reading groups he or she conducts in the classroom.

Another useful instructional technique for diverse learners in the general classroom is to provide them with books and corresponding audiotapes. Diverse learners need many opportunities to both hear the spoken word and see its graphic representation. Studies conducted with learning-disabled children found that children benefit from the simultaneous listening to and reading of audiotaped books (Conte & Humphreys, 1989; Janiak, 1983). Paired reading is useful for diverse learners. Li and Nes (2001) maintain that when an English language learner is paired with a more "skilled reader" who reads a portion of the text aloud and the English language learner reads along simultaneously, the English language learner's fluency and pronunciation are improved. In the next section, we will introduce the importance of teacher autonomy and teacher collaboration. This will be discussed further in the third section of the book, which focuses on school organization, professional development, and administrative support for effective instruction.

Teachers Have Autonomy

Teachers who are able to use their professional judgment to implement curriculum that is focused on meeting their students' individual and diverse needs, while holding students to high standards for individual achievement, will be more successful at closing the achievement gap for diverse learners. All aspects of teaching, including adding to knowledge about topics of deliberation through professional development, cannot be overlooked. Teachers can become actively involved in professional development in the school and district plane, within school teams, and at the individual level when their theory and practice match, thus allowing for focused decision making about instruction and the professional development needed to enhance quality instruction. It is through effective individual teachers and well-organized schools that the best situation for diverse literacy learners is established.

School Organization for Diverse Learners

For those readers who were educated in the public schools of the 1950s and 60s, if you reflect upon the school experiences, it is likely that you do not remember children in your classrooms much different than you. Schools and families were more like the television programs we now see on the TV Land channel, such as "Leave it to Beaver" or "Our Miss Brooks," than it is in the schools of today. But if we reflect on medicine or transportation, we have seen similar changes. Today's children don't know about the mumps or measles, and we are no longer driving cars with fins and two-toned paint. Thank goodness for both. Schools and classrooms have some common features from the past but are also organized in some very different ways. Today, all children come to school regardless of gender, socioeconomic status, or physical or mental disabilities. Our schools belong to all these children!

Many of the classrooms of today are grounded in "best practice" education, using instructional techniques discussed in section two of this book. One of the biggest changes afoot in education today is the understanding that these practices cannot be implemented on a random basis and that each teacher cannot have his or her own version of "best practice." Rather, the school team must pull together to offer children a seamless approach to learning based on sound educational principles. Teachers must work together with knowledgeable leadership to organize the school in order to provide literacy instruction that brings the curriculum to the child, rather than expecting the children to be ready for some preconceived curriculum. The fact of the matter is that in schools where everyone believes in children's potential as learners and who accept responsibility for children's learning, there is a greater likelihood that children are offered more and better instruction. This belief must go way beyond the sign at the entrance to the school that reads, "ALL CHILDREN CAN LEARN."

Conclusion

Diverse learners should not be denied the right to become full members of the school community. Students will arrive at the school door with a varied range of academic competence and out-of-school experiences. Teachers need to be prepared to meet the diversity represented in the student population and embrace the richness it offers to the school and the classroom, rather than to view diversity as a problem to solve.

Overview of the Remainder of the Book

This edited book is organized into three sections:

1. understanding the issue of diversity and its impact on literacy learning for all children

2. instructional practices for classroom and special education teachers that will support the literacy development for culturally and linguistically diverse learners

3. aspects of school organization that will support the literacy learning of culturally and linguistically diverse learners

Each author has based his or her chapter on research and practical application of the research with preschool to Grade 5 children and teachers. You may want to read the entire book or explore selected chapters, depending on your particular interests. We do recommend that you explore the first section in detail, so that the examples of particular diverse literacy learners will stay with you as you read about particular topics. Hopefully, particular children you have taught will become your own relevant examples, and you will read with Bilal or Dequan in mind.

The chapters in the first section exemplify and personify diversity for various literacy learners, children who are not from the mainstream or majority culture. We offer several examples for you, in order for you to help you look at diversity from multiple perspectives and to understand the broad base for our definition of diversity. The second section offers an array of instructional elements for teachers to use in various preschool and elementary school instructional settings with the intent of suggesting many possible ways to include diverse in learners in effective learning engagements that thrive in environments that are rich and valuing of differences. The final section focuses on planning for organization, professional development, and administrative support required for effective instruction. Opportunities for learning need to be organized from a school vision that is centered on a theory of literacy learning that embraces what all children and families have to offer the school community. While individual teachers can provide this kind of learning environment in a single school year, the best learning situation is one in which the school and the school district recognize, appreciate, and actively explore diversity as a basis for decision making.

References

Allington, R. L., & McGill-Franzen, A. (1995). Flunking: Throwing good money after bad. In R. L. Allington & S. A. Walmsley, *No quick fix*. New York: Teachers College Press.

Auerbach, E. R. (1989). Towards a social-contextual approach to family literacy. *Harvard Educational Review, 59,* 165–181.

Auerbach, E. (1995). Deconstructing the discourse of strengths in family literacy. *Journal of Reading Behavior, 27*(4), 643–661.

Boyle, O. F., & Peregoy, S. F. (1990). Literacy scaffolds: Strategies for first- and second language readers and writers. *The Reading Teacher, 44,* 144–200.

Collier, V. P. (1989). How long? A synthesis of research on academic achievement in a second language. *TESOL Quarterly, 23*(3), 509–531.

Compton-Lilly, C. (2003). *Reading families: The literate lives of urban children.* New York: Teachers College Press.

Conte, R., & Humphreys, R. (1989). Repeated readings using audiotaped materials enhance oral reading in children with reading difficulties. *Journal of Communication Disorders, 22,* 65–79.

Cummins, J. (1986). Empowering minority students: A framework for intervention. *Harvard Educational Review, 56*(1), 18–36.

Cummins, J. (1996). *Negotiating identities: Education empowerment in a diverse society.* Ontario, CA: California Association for Bilingual Education.

Cummins, J. (2000). *Language, power, and pedagogy: Bilingual children in the crossfire.* Cleveland, UK: Multilingual Matters.

Danzinger, S., & Lin, C. L. (2000). *Coping with poverty: The social contexts of neighborhood, work, and family in the African-American community.* Ann Arbor, MI: University of Michigan Press.

Denton, K., West, J., & Walston, J. (2003). Reading: Young children's achievement and classroom experiences. Retrieved February 9, 2004, from the National Center for Education Statistics Web site: http://nces.ed.gov/pubs2003/2003070.pdf

Fountas, I. C., & Pinnell, G. S. (1999). *Matching books to readers.* Portsmouth, NH: Heinemann.

Gibbons, P. (2002). *Scaffolding language scaffolding learning: Teaching second-language learners in the mainstream classroom.* Portsmouth, NH: Heinemann.

Hale, J. (2001). *Learning while black: Creating educational excellence for African-American children.* Baltimore: Johns Hopkins University Press.

Heath, S. B. (1983). *Ways with words: Language, life, and working communities and classrooms.* New York: Cambridge University Press.

Janiak, R. (1983). Listening/reading: An effective learning combination. *Academic Therapy, 19,* 205–211.

Juel, C. (1988). Learning to read and write: A longitudinal study of fifty-four children from first through fourth grades. *Journal of Educational Psychology, 80,* 437–447.

Li, D., & Nes, S. L. (2001). Using paired reading to help ESL students become fluent and accurate readers. *Reading Improvement, 38*(2), 50–61.

McKay, P., Davies, A., Devlin, B., Clayton, J., Oliver, R., & Zammit, S. (1997). *The bilingual interface project report.* Canberra, AU: Department of Employment, Education, Training, and Youth Affairs.

Moll, L. C. (1988). Some key issues in teaching Latino students. *Language Arts, 65,* 465–475.

Moll, L. C., & Greenburg, J. B. (1990). Creating zones of possibilities: Combining social contexts for instruction. In L. C. Moll (Ed.), *Vygotsky in education* (pp. 319–348). New York: Cambridge University Press.

Ortiz, R. (1992). *The unpackaging of generation and social class factors: A study on literacy activities and education values of Mexican-American fathers.* Unpublished doctoral dissertation, University of California at Los Angeles.

Payne, R. (2001). *A framework for understanding poverty.* Highlands, TX: aha! Process, Inc.

Peregoy, S. F., & Boyle, O. F. (1993). *Reading, writing, and learning in ESL.* New York: Longman.

Purcell-Gates, V. (1995). *Other people's words: The cycle of low literacy.* Cambridge, MA: Harvard University Press.

Taberski, S. (2000). *On solid ground: Strategies for teaching reading K–3.* Portsmouth, NH: Heinemann.

Taylor, D., & Dorsey-Gaines, C. (1988). *Growing up literate: Learning from inner-city families.* Portsmouth, NH: Heinemann.

Tomlinson, C. A. (1999). *The differentiated classroom: Responding to the needs of all learners.* Alexandria, VA: ASCD.

U.S. Bureau of the Census. (2000). *Statistical Abstract of the United States: 2000.*

Vygotsky, L. (1978). *Mind in society: The development of higher psychological processes.* London: Harvard University Press.

Vygotsky, L. (1986). *Thought and language.* Cambridge, MA: Harvard University Press.

Walmsley, S. A., & Allington, R. L. (1995). Redefining and reforming instructional support programs for at-risk students. In R. L. Allington & S. A. Walmsley, *No quick fix.* New York: Teachers College Press.

West, J., Denton, K., & Germino Hausken, E. (2000). Kindergartners' educational progress in reading: A study of language minority and nonlanguage minority children. *Education Statistics Quarterly, 2*(1), 7–13.

West, J., Denton, K., & Reaney, L. M. (2000). The kindergarten year: Findings from the early childhood longitudinal study, kindergarten class of 1998–99. *Education Statistics Quarterly, 2*(4), 25–30.

Wood, D., Bruner, J., & Ross, G. (1976). The role of tutoring in problem solving. *Journal of Child Psychology and Psychiatry, 17*(2), 89–100.

Yatvin, J. (1991). *Developing a whole language program for a whole school.* Newark, DL: International Reading Association.

Chapter 2

Opening Up Learning Opportunities in a Diverse Classroom Context:

One Struggling Reader's Literacy Journey

Maria Luiza Dantas and Rebecca Kantor

It is March, and the school day has just started. Mrs. Boyd's[1] first graders take turns completing the activities planned for their morning "quiet work time": math computers, coloring a dinosaur handout at the art table (part of the Dinosaur unit), journal writing, and math tubs. Derek approaches Malu [first author] with excitement to show her his Cub Scout book. He points to the paragraphs on one page that he needs to have memorized for his next Cub Scout meeting, and he asks Malu to check if he can say them correctly. He then shows the book to Mrs. Boyd and practices reading with her, too. After reading to Mrs. Boyd, Derek sits at the art table with Jack, John, Edward, Karla, and Kari. They are all coloring the dinosaur handout except for Derek, who shares his new book with Jack, John, and Edward. Later on, before the end of the morning quiet work time, Mrs. Boyd asks Derek if he wants to practice with her what he needs to have memorized for the Cub Scouts.

---

[1] The teacher and all children's names are pseudonyms.

Introduction

In the scenario above, we see that despite all of the literacy requirements and challenges facing Mrs. Boyd and her students, she chooses to open up opportunities for Derek's, and each of her student's, literacy learning within a classroom context of diverse learners. Demanding school literacy journeys challenge children and intersect with other important developmental passages. For Derek, who has been identified as a "struggling reader," and all other children, the process of becoming a reader intersects with processes of gaining access to different social worlds as a first grader and membership in social groups inside and outside of school. Bringing the Cub Scout book to the classroom was a significant event in Derek's process of becoming a reader. Until this day, Derek had not demonstrated much excitement and eagerness in reading a book in class or to his teacher and peers. Based on his low reading scores in assessments at the beginning of the year, Derek had been referred to the school's early reading intervention (ERI) program, a daily "pull out" program.

Within the tapestry of diverse learners in first-grade classrooms, we find a number of children like Derek who are identified as "struggling readers" and referred to ERI programs. Being a low-achieving reader often positions a student with lower social status in the classroom that increases the risk of an achievement gap by reducing the quality of classroom engagement and, therefore, the experience of reading instruction. For other students, learning to read can be a smooth process in which they acquire particular positions with status in the classroom (e.g., being a good reader; being asked to read with a peer; advancement to chapter books). In these ways, learning to read impacts students' social and emotional development, as well as their academic success (Lyons, 2003).

In our view, the process of learning to read is one of the important social forces in children's identity construction (including their identities as readers); children need, but do not always have empowering experiences with, agency within the social contexts and literacy practices available to them in the classroom. Thus, opening up opportunities for literacy learning in a diverse classroom implies "expanding repertoires of practice" (Comber, 2004) that positively impact upon children's range of reading competencies and abilities, their emotional well-being, and their identities related to gender, race, ethnicity, family/community cultures, and socioeconomic and linguistic background. In this chapter, we examine Mrs. Boyd's role in opening up opportunities for Derek to become an active learner and participant in the classroom. The practical, instructional recognition that Derek's literacy journey as a first grader intersected with social worlds, such as the Cub Scout community, his classroom peer culture, the interaction patterns and structure of classroom literacy events, permitted decision making, and agency (Dyson, 2001) despite his status as a struggling reader and his membership in the ERI program, which meant daily absence from his classroom life. To reveal Derek's experiences, we examine Derek's agency within different "subject positionings" or ways of being (Walkerdine, 1990) within the landscape of his first-grade journey and discuss ways teachers can tap into a struggling reader's potential and diverse interests.

Literacy for Diverse Learners: The Case of Struggling Readers

The process of learning to read is public, especially in the first grade. Children struggling to learn to read are at risk of silencing themselves, disengaging from the learning process, falling behind academically, and carrying a lower social status as a poor reader. The child's status or "symbolic capital" (Christian & Bloome, 2004) carries with it consequences to his or her interactions with peers during literacy events (either child-initiated or child-directed), which shape his or her literacy history and impact upon the construction of his or her reading identities. Struggling readers wrestle with low self-esteem and poor self-concepts that affect their personal initiative and willingness to take risks required in the process of learning to read (Clay, 1991; Lyons, 2003). Parents, especially mothers, are also at risk of being blamed for their children's lack of educational achievement and experience emotional burdens as they attend to the demands placed on parents of students who do not do well in school in addition to attending to their own schedules (Dudley-Marling, 2001). Furthermore, boys are more at risk of being identified as struggling readers than girls, who often do better than boys in academic or school literacies (Comber, 2004).

How can teachers then open up social and learning spaces in the classroom for students who become identified as "struggling readers"? Teachers' knowledge and expertise in intervention is critical to struggling readers' success and ability to catch up to grade-level curriculum (Clay, 1991; Ganske, Monroe, & Strickland, 2003; Lyons, 2003). However, students' academic success goes beyond literacy interventions in and out of the classroom, and particularly, programs with emphasis on skill-and-drill exercises. Intrinsic to the intervention and instructional process is students' social and emotional development, as well as their perceived agency as a learner, reader, and peer. In the case of children identified as low achieving and referred to intervention services, teachers need to carefully expand their own repertoires of practice so that students can take on different roles and positionings in the classroom. According to Comber (2004), improving boys' engagement with school literacies entails:

"(teachers) expanding their repertoires of practice and (making) a pedagogical shift from the regulation of boys in and through lessons, to an opening up of active positions for them to take up. The resultant changed activity structures and roles in literacy lessons may trigger and sustain boys' interest" (p. 115).

School offers a unique space for the construction of children's reading identities as they are able to explore with and develop their abilities in different contexts, purposes, and audiences. In Derek's case, Mrs. Boyd facilitated social and learning spaces in the classroom, in which he was able to position himself as an expert and acquire status that officially acknowledged his construction of self and learner as a multifaceted process.

Reading Identities and Positionings in a Diverse Classroom

Children construct, take up, and are labeled and positioned within different reading identities in their literacy history and school career. Reading identities, such as "good reader," "struggling reader," "fast reader," "slow reader," or "nonfiction reader," impact students' perception of competence and self-efficacy. As Alvermann (2001) notes, "Readers locked into 'special' identifications know all too well which side of the enabling or disabling binary they occupy and the consequences such identities carry" (p. 677). Learning to read becomes a defeating and invalidating process. Struggling readers tend to "engage in passive failure and learned helplessness" (Johnston & Winograd, 1985, as cited in Heron, 2003, p. 569). Collins' (2003) case study of one child's struggle to be seen as competent illustrates the impact of ability profiling and school failure. There is an intrinsic connection between social identity and learning to read that goes beyond remedial programs' focus on skills, abilities, attitudes, and motivation.

Sociocultural studies argue for "culturally responsive teaching" (Au & Jordan, 1981; Ladson-Billings, 1994), that is, instructional and curricular approaches that build upon and support students' cultural "funds of knowledge" (Moll, Amanti, Neff, & González, 1992), that is, their linguistic, sociocultural, and intellectual capital. However, bridging students' cultural funds of knowledge from home into the school curriculum and implementing reading interventions may not be sufficient to support struggling readers if teachers disregard the mediating role of students' symbolic capital in the classroom, that is, their "privileged social status and social position within a particular situation" (Christian & Bloome, 2004, p. 367). Children's reading identities are also constructed in socially situated practices (Gee, 2003), including peer-culture worlds that have been shown to be remarkably complex (Corsaro, 1985; Kantor, Elgas, & Fernie, 1993). Dyson's (1995, 2001) work on situated literacy sheds light on the complexity of children's negotiations between "official" and "unofficial" worlds of the classroom. Derek's example, in the beginning of this chapter, illustrates the social nature of literacy learning and the interconnectedness between school and outside school literacy practices, as well as the multiple roles and purposes reading can serve in children's lives. What can be a significant event to one child may not be to another. It also illustrates how teachers can open up opportunities for learning and taking up higher status positions for students who might be excluded from classroom dialogues. In such social and learning contexts, students acquire a sense of agency or capacity to act upon the world (Holland, Lachicotte, Skinner, & Cain, 1998). In other words:

> "Teachers do not simply present learning tasks and knowledge and magically students become readers and writers. Rather, teachers and students together create a 'culture' in the classroom that helps students make sense of what is occurring in the classroom, what they are expected to do, what it means, how they are to go about the process of learning, and who they are in the classroom as learners, readers, and writers" (Christian & Bloome, 2004, p. 366).

Context: Derek, His Teacher, Their Classroom, and School Community

Derek's story is part of a larger, year-long ethnographic study, which examines literacy learning and teaching processes in a first-grade classroom (Dantas, 1999). This chapter focuses on Derek's trajectory over the year and across contexts, including the classroom, school, ERI program, home, and community. Derek is one of the focal students who were identified in collaboration with the teacher. A "purposeful sampling" approach (Patton, 1990) guided the selection of an information-rich classroom setting and selected participants representing a rich, but not extreme, example of teacher expertise in early literacy education, and focal students representing diverse literacy backgrounds and levels of ability according to school assessments.

Derek, a European-American, red-haired, talkative, and lively young boy, entered Highwood Elementary as a kindergartener. He was interested in, and knowledgeable about, nature, science, and mathematics. He scored below grade level in reading and writing in the beginning of the year (see Table 2:1) and received additional instruction in these areas through the school's ERI program. Derek lived with his mother, father, and younger brother in a predominantly white, working-class community. Both parents worked at their small copy-service business, and they struggled financially throughout the school year. Derek's mother was a former high school teacher who was actively involved in the school's Parent and Teacher Association (PTA). His parents wanted Derek to be at Highwood Elementary, and they drove him to school every day, since they lived outside the school's attendance area.

Table 2:1　The Students' Scores on Districtwide Reading and Writing Assessments

Student	Letter Identification		Writing Vocabulary		Sentence Dictation		Text Reading Level		Writing Rubric [a]	
	Fall	Spring	Fall	Spring	Fall	Spring	Fall	Spring	Fall	Spring
Karla	54	54	16	88	31	37	05	24	02	03
Kiera	53	54	18	108	36	37	24	24	03	04
Laurie	53	54	23	58	34	37	09	24	02	04
Ellen	45	54	05	60	17	37	03	24	01	03
Bobby	51	54	12	51	18	36	02	14	01	03
Alice	39	—	08	—	13	—	A	—	01	—
Edward	53	54	08	47	17	34	B	12	01	03
Tyler	44	54	04	39	07	36	01	14	01	03
Nathan	30	54	03	47	09	35	A	09	01	02
Juanita	26	—	03	—	03	—	B	—	01	—
Jack	34	52	02	24	01	34	02	03	01	02
Tracy	53	54	07	30	28	37	03	24	02	03
John	39	54	01	35	02	35	A	12	01	02
Kristen	—	54	—	30	—	37	—	14	—	03
Joel	54	54	12	54	27	37	07	24	02	03
Kevin	—	54	—	40	—	36	—	12	—	03
Katia	45	54	07	40	04	31	B	08	01	03
Luana	17	—	05	—	04	—	A	—	01	—
Craig	42	54	05	30	18	30	02	06	01	02
Derek	41	54	02	39	01	37	A	16	01	02
Diane	48	54	12	40	10	33	01	12	01	02
Ryan	40	54	04	43	0	37	02	10	01	03
Tom	53	54	09	28	18	37	03	14	02	03
Kim	53	54	12	62	23	37	03	24	02	03
Sandy	52	54	16	52	30	36	05	24	02	03
Joe	52	54	13	46	24	36	03	14	02	02
Shelly	04	—	01	—	05	—	B	—	01	—

Note. Compare the data above to the following maximum scores for each test: Letter Identification = 54; Writing Vocabulary = 41+; Sentence Dictation or Hearing and Recording Sounds in Words = 37; Text Reading Level = 34; and District's Writing Rubric = 4.

[a] These are Mrs. Boyd's scoring of the students' writing samples, which were later scored by a second reader (and in some cases, a third reader) in the district.

Mrs. Boyd, a European-American woman in her late forties, had been teaching for 14 years at Highwood Elementary when she engaged in this research project. She had lived in the school's community for over 20 years, and she began her teaching career at Highwood Elementary after raising her three children. Two of her children had attended Highwood before she started to work as a teacher. We invited Mrs. Boyd to participate in this study due to her teaching expertise and strong language arts curriculum. Mrs. Boyd saw the research project as an opportunity for professional development and reflection on her teaching.

The school, a professional-development site affiliated with a large Midwestern university, had a history of child-centered education and a focus on integrated and literature-based curriculum. Highwood Elementary was located in a small city (19,000 population). The school philosophy also emphasized an integrated approach to learning and teaching through the development of thematic units. The building of a new school had impacted Highwood's student population. The school's new attendance area served a more socially and economically diverse community, including families with limited knowledge of the school's educational philosophy. Faculty concerns involved limited family involvement and supporting students with a wider range of needs and literacy backgrounds.

Mrs. Boyd's students, as well as the school population, were predominantly European American from lower- to middle-income families. Of Mrs. Boyd's group of 26 students, 3 were African American and 1 was biracial. The students' literacy backgrounds varied, and 20 students were below the district's expected reading level in the beginning of first grade, and the 8 lower-achieving students were referred to the school's ERI program.

The school presented an open-space architecture aimed at fostering a collaborative relationship among the teaching faculty (see Figure 2:1). Mrs. Boyd's

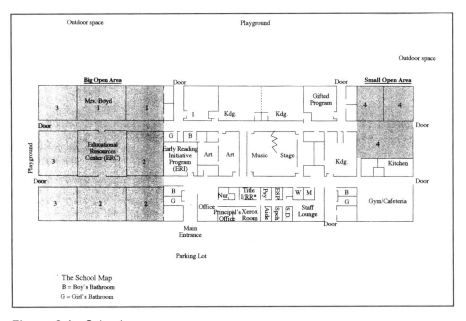

Figure 2:1   School map.

classroom (see Figure 2:2) was located in one of the school's two open areas. Her classroom shared a large space with eight classrooms that were separated by bookcases and display boards, as well as other furniture and school equipment (i.e., desks, computers, and file cabinets). The furniture was low enough that it was easy to see what was happening in other classrooms; however, during classroom time, teachers and students became so involved in their own spaces that it seemed as if they had real walls in between their classrooms.

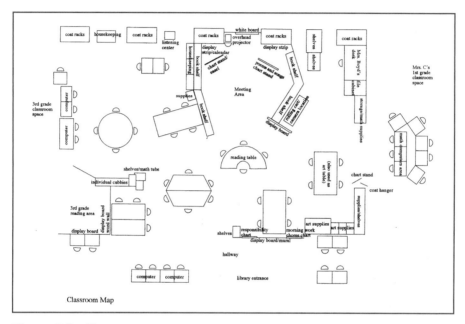

Figure 2:2 Classroom map.

Documenting Derek's Literacy Journey as a First Grader

We gathered detailed documentation of literacy learning opportunities available in the classroom and Derek's home context via observations, field notes, teacher and student interviews, one home visit and parent interviews, examination of teaching materials and student artifacts, and school-, district-, and state-level documents. This ethnographic approach allowed us to identify classroom routines and literacy events, interaction patterns, and individual and group expectations of reading achievement and purposes (Frank, 1999; Green, Dixon, & Zaharlick, 2003).

The concept of social and learning spaces, subjectivity, and multiple identities or ways of being guided our analysis and interpretation of Derek's and Mrs. Boyd's trajectory over the year. In a particular classroom and school setting, students have access to, create, and/or are expected to participate in multiple social and learning spaces (e.g., peer-group activities, reading intervention programs, classroom routines, etc.). These spaces are situated in the classroom history and practices. Students' successful participation involves their ability to take on multiple identities as a learner, reader, classroom and school member, etc. Central to successful participation is the process of decentering the self, or subjectivity, in ongoing negotiation of contradictions and power relations (Weedon, 1987). For example, Derek wrestled with time constraints to meet his own expectations of being socially accepted among peers and to please his teacher. Terms such as being a "better reader" carried power with his teacher and parents, and being a "fast worker" allowed him time to bond and become a part of the boys' peer culture.

In the next sections, we describe Derek's literacy journey as he gained entry in the social dialogues of what it meant to be a reader by the standards of parents, peers, his teacher, classroom and school curricula, and district curriculum and standards. We first look at Derek's exploration of social and learning spaces, and then the process of taking on different reading identities. Second, we describe Mrs. Boyd's role in opening up and creating official spaces for different repertoires of practice.

Snapshots of a "Struggling Reader": Derek's Exploration of Learning and Social Spaces and Identity Work

Not surprisingly, particular events, people and personal interests, skills, and background impacted Derek's exploration of learning and social spaces in first grade. However, his status as a "struggling reader" was only one part of his social worlds as a young boy, older brother, first grader, Boy Scout, peer, builder, scientist, nature lover, etc. The difference for Derek was the possibility of turning these social worlds into official learning spaces, recognized by Mrs. Boyd as part of his literacy curriculum and instructional process. Intrinsic to meeting Derek's diverse needs was the recognition of his learning potential across social spaces.

As previously mentioned, Derek started the year with low reading and writing scores in the required district assessments. Concurrently, Derek was among the first group of students in the state to be impacted by a mandate on a fourth-grade reading guarantee, which influenced district-level changes on proficiency expectations and a high level of anxiety for teachers and parents. In two events for parents, the Information Night and the Literacy Night, Mrs. Boyd addressed these expectations:

Learning to read this year is an important issue. (Information Night, September 1998) . . . By the end of the year . . ., [the] children are expected to be able to read like a Level 14. And . . . you may say, "What do you mean by Level 14?" *Goodnight Moon* (Brown, 1997) is the book that, by the end of the year, expectations are, hopefully the children will be able to read. We know that not everyone will be here. It's our goal to move your children as far, as long as we can with it. It's a big goal. Next year, they're increasing it . . . [to] two more levels. So it makes it even more difficult. So it's all part of getting ready for the proficiency test. (Literacy Night, January 1999)

The state mandate meant that students who failed the reading portion of standardized tests in fourth grade would be retained. As Mrs. Boyd explained, the district's text reading–proficiency expectations for first graders by the end of the year had changed from Level 12 to 14, and in the following year, to Level 16 (based on the criteria set by Scott Foresman Special Practice books, 1979). Derek's mother was highly concerned about Derek's ability to meet the school's reading-proficiency expectations and worked closely with him throughout the year to meet the teacher's monthly homework schedule and other assignments.

Derek's scores were among the lowest in the classroom, in particular, his text reading level (see Table 2:1). He was part of a group of eight students (including Craig, Jack, John, Katia, Nathan, Tyler, and Ryan) whose scores qualified for the first round of group interventions implemented by the district's ERI program. The school also offered individual Reading Recovery interventions and adapted small-group interventions guided by the Reading Recovery teacher. Juanita and Shelley were selected for the first one and Luana for the latter. Some students moved or were discontinued/graduated from intervention services during the year, and other students were selected (e.g., Alice and Kevin for Reading Recovery, and Diane and Edward for ERI). Derek graduated from the ERI in March.

Derek's classroom, school, family, and community contexts serve as snapshots and broad categories of the multiple dimensions of Derek's social worlds. At home, Derek's mother regularly exposed him to books. He was involved in his church's Sunday school and Adventure Club, and Cub Scouts. At school, Derek often played computer games and followed "how to" books to build complicated cars and other structures. Developing friendships and being accepted by his peers, as well as meeting his teacher and parents' expectations, were concerns that guided Derek's interactions in the classroom over the school year. To meet his teacher and parents' expectations of being a good student, Derek followed classroom routines and completed assigned reading activities. In Figure 2:3, we show snapshots of multiple dimensions into Derek's identity work.

Multiple Identities & Memberships Enacted through Literate Practices	
Multiple Identities	**Social Worlds and Learning Spaces**
Peer and Friend	Home Context, August: "… Deep down inside I think [Derek] loves the social aspect of school … [He] … is also concerned because his favorite friends from kind. [kindergarten] are in other classes and a child he "clashed" with will be with him again. He tends to be shy with his peers until they seek him out…. He is generally happy and loves a good joke" (Derek's Parents' Response to Mrs. Boyd's Parent Survey). Classroom Interactions, September–November: Becoming a friend by exchanging phone numbers and sharing stories of his home experiences (Classroom Observations). Classroom Interactions, September–May: Derek often concluded his individual work quickly to be able to use the math tubs, particularly the interlocking cubes, and interact with a group of boys. Derek shared with his peers his experiences as a Cub Scout and home projects, such as a handmade flashlight (Classroom Observations).
Student	Home Context, August: "[Derek] is highly independent and seems to need to "test" authority before offering his respect. He has been in a school situation for 3 full years (2 preschool—1 kind.) and believes in the importance of "being a good kid" in school. He is generally happy and <u>loves</u> a <u>good</u> joke. He is <u>very</u> creative and really enjoys art class" [underlines in the original] (Derek's Parents' Response to Mrs. Boyd's Parent Survey). Classroom Interactions, October: The biggest thing with [Derek] is he is capable of letter-sound relationships when writing. He needs to be nudged along (Mrs. Boyd's Journal Entry). Classroom Interactions, November: Mrs. Boyd felt that the home visit to Derek made a difference in relation to his participation in the classroom. Despite Derek's playfulness in the classroom, he also took classroom work assignments seriously (Informal Conversation with Mrs. Boyd).
Science/Nature Expert	Home Context, August: "[Derek] … is fascinated by nature—weather, the animal world, all natural sciences" (Derek's Parents' Response to Mrs. Boyd's Parent Survey). Classroom Interactions, February: "[Derek] is enjoying this unit—his knowledge about penguins is amazing and he doesn't hesitate to make sure I have all the facts straight or to verbalize it in another way" (Mrs. Boyd's Journal Entry). Classroom Interactions, March: In the Rainforest unit, he brought to the classroom his volcano kit, which was used as part of a whole-group experiment led by Mrs. Boyd (Classroom Observations).
Beginning Reader/ Early Reading Intervention (ERI) Student/ Chapter Book Reader	Home Context, September: During his grandmother's visit, Derek read her one of his ERI books entitled The Ghost (Cowley, 1983). Student-led Conference, February: During Derek's student-led conference with Mrs. Boyd and his mother in February, he set as his reading goal for the rest of the year to read chapter books. Mrs. Boyd wrote with Derek in the conference form: In reading, I would like to get better *at reading chapter books. We* [Mrs. Boyd and Derek] *talked about how he'd need to know more words. He feels better about reading now.* [in italics what Mrs. Boyd wrote with Derek] Classroom Interactions, March: Completing a Cub Scouts assignment at the classroom: reading and memorizing a sequence of paragraphs from the Cub Scouts book of general guidelines (Classroom Observations). Classroom Interactions, March: "I'm ahead on reading now. My mom said that I'm the only one that can read a book [in my reading group] and that my reading teacher told her that I'll be out of reading group soon" (Informal Conversation with Derek). Classroom Interactions, May: "I'm reading chapters now… I finished one yesterday" (Informal Conversation with Derek).

Figure 2:3   Snapshots into Derek's identity work.

Derek's emerging sense of self as reader and learner was embedded in the various contexts of his social worlds. Derek's reading road to literacy development was impacted and shaped by social worlds in which reading practices were an important part of the membership process. These social worlds comprised learning spaces that afforded situated sets of opportunities for practice of literate actions. For example, exchanging phone numbers with classmates was part of his classroom social world. Though Derek did not demonstrate interest in reading "school" books, his interest in acquiring membership in Cub Scouts and the classroom's chapter book peer culture fostered his engagement in new reading spaces—importantly, Derek's opportunity to bring into classroom spaces his expertise in science and nature and out-of-school experiences. The cumulative effect of these experiences resulted in a broader and active sense of self as learner and reader.

Promoting Literacy: Meeting the Needs of Diverse Learners

In Mrs. Boyd's classroom, meeting the needs of diverse learners meant creating visible, workable spaces for multiple (reading) identities. The above snapshots of Derek's identity work shows classroom spaces in which he was able to share his expertise in science and nature and out-of-school experiences. Important to Derek's school literacy journey was Mrs. Boyd's ability to open up "official" classroom spaces for his social worlds outside the classroom, and in this way, make visible some of Derek's multiple identities as a reader and learner beyond his position as a low reader. Opening up "official" classroom spaces involved Mrs. Boyd's use of multiple lenses to assess Derek's identities as learner and reader throughout the year. These lenses or assessment tools included: formal assessments, such as Clay's (1993) Observation Survey and Text Reading Level, the district's writing rubric, ongoing running records and reading conferences, beginning-of-the-year parent survey, classroom/school observations, ongoing informal conversations with parents, communication with other teachers who worked or were also working with Derek, one home visit, and active participation in school events for families. For example, Mrs. Boyd's beginning-of-the-year survey provided the following insights into Derek's interests, expectations, and concerns: Derek excels at any type of spatial or mechanical learning. He seems to enjoy numbers (math); especially enjoying money! He is fascinated by nature: weather, the animal world, and all natural sciences. He loves using any type of tools (except pencils, crayons, etc). Derek tells us that he does not want to go to school because it is boring and he has to do "work." He is also concerned because his favorite friends from kind. [kindergarten] are in other classes and a child he "clashed" with will be with him again. He tends to be shy with his peers until they seek him out. Deep down inside I think he loves the social aspect of school and he <u>loves</u> to "show off" new knowledge at home. (He can't wait to try out the new climbing wall—ironic because he has a mild fear of heights.) [underlines and parentheses in the original] (Response to Parent Survey, August 1998)

Mrs. Boyd's home visit to Derek's house was another important lens into Derek's out-of-school experiences and her own process of relationship building with parents: "It [the home visits] does give one so much more insight into a child's background—what they are bringing with them to school, etc. I believe it gives each of the parents the feeling that the teacher is truly interested in their child and them. It gives one the sense that the teacher is a friend . . ." (e-mail communication, December 1998).

Derek's information and experiences were accommodated into the instructional and curriculum process. The home visit provide the following insights into Derek's background: his interest in Lego toys, putting together elaborate cars (often with his father) by looking at the pictures and following the directions, watching nature videos and TV shows, camping trips with the family, refrigerator as the location for classroom handouts (including weekly newsletter and homework, and list of high-frequency words for first grade). Mrs. Boyd's range of learnings afforded Derek to take on multiple positionings and identities as science and nature expert, storyteller, peer, Cub Scout, good student, active participant in classroom conversations, etc. For example, as Mrs. Boyd describes, he actively participated in whole-group conversations during the Penguin unit: "[Derek] is enjoying this unit—his knowledge about penguins is amazing and he doesn't hesitate to make sure I have all the facts straight or to verbalize it in another way" (Dialogue journal, February 1999).

Thus, Derek's story of becoming a reader in first grade intersected with his teacher's own process of curriculum construction and decision making. Despite state mandates and the push for reading proficiency, as defined by particular standards and a single road to reading, for both Derek and Mrs. Boyd, literacy learning and the process of becoming a reader took place in multiple and interrelated local contexts and spaces in and out of the classroom. These spaces continually impacted Mrs. Boyd's ability to see Derek's multiple identities as learner and reader. Being a struggling learner was just one piece of the puzzle.

The richness of Derek's multiple interests and reading identities illustrates that there is an availability of diverse spaces for learning, but they are not always found in what is defined as the official curriculum. Furthermore, like Mrs. Boyd, teachers can tap into a struggling reader's potential and diverse interests and allow for a richer sense of self as learner and reader. Derek's mother reported on his reading growth that one of the best things that happened "throughout the course of the year he believed that he could do it" (Derek's mother, personal interview, May 1999).

Widening Our Literacy Lenses: What Derek's Journey Tells Us about Struggling Readers

Like Derek, struggling readers have to negotiate diverse identities in order to become successful in the classroom and meet multiple social demands. Important to Derek's school literacy journey was his teacher's ability to open up "official" classroom spaces for the experiences and knowledge of his social worlds from outside of the classroom where reading practices were an important part of the membership process and Derek experienced greater success. Mrs. Boyd made visible some of the multiple aspects of Derek's identity as a reader and does not limit him to the label of a "struggling reader." Derek's story illustrates the situated nature of reading learning (Green & Bloome, 1997). That is, it shows that a child's identity as a learner, reader, and first grader is constituted across contexts, within a process of interpreting, reinterpreting, and re-creating what becomes constituted as "local spaces" and literacy stories.

Derek's local identities were reformulated across time through his social construction of interactional spaces during classroom literacy practices. Derek's situated literate actions within classroom literate practices involved a process of historically interpreting and reinterpreting the social, cultural, and political world and his place in it. The analysis of Derek's experiences as a first grader make visible his re-creation of classroom space(s) by negotiating identities (as a student, 7-year-old, peer, son) within the constraints and demands of classroom routines, roles and expectations, and institutional and power relations. Importantly, Derek's ability to negotiate multiple demands (i.e., district demands regarding higher proficiency scores for reading and writing, his teacher's curriculum expectations, and his parents' close attention to his school and district requirements, etc.) within the local classroom space illustrates the process of identity construction as fluid, dialogic, and dynamic. Derek's identity work shaped, and was shaped by, social spaces in the classroom, school, Boy Scout group, home, etc. Social and emotional motives promoted Derek's learning. For example, learning to read became a goal-oriented activity as he defined his learning goal as the ability to read a chapter book.

Conclusion

Some teachers know little about their students' sociocultural "funds of knowledge" (Moll et al., 1992) and how to incorporate these experiences in the school curriculum. Teachers' ability to act as "kid watchers" (Goodman, 1997) and creatively coconstruct curricular experiences with their students can open up "official" classroom spaces in which children's diversity and multiple identities can be resources for new opportunities for literacy learning.

The learning spaces available or present in Derek's experiences as a first grader were situated within intermingling contexts; that is, his actions, participation and interactions at home, his community, school, and in the classroom created particular "consequential progressions" historically, socially, culturally, and politically situated (Putney et al., 2000). In this way, Derek's actions and interactions were not complete or autonomous, and they could only be read in relation to, and juxtaposed with, other contexts and texts that were simultaneously occurring over time. Central to Derek's experiences as a first grader was Mrs. Boyd's ability to open up "repertoires of practices" (Comber, 2004) in which he acted upon his multiple identities as reader and learner.

Mrs. Boyd's ability to bridge the "unofficial" into the "official" curriculum made visible Derek's agency and decision making as he gained entry to social dialogues that defined what it meant to be a reader, learner, and peer according to the standards of parents, peers, classroom and school curricula, and district curriculum. For example, reading became a personal goal when Derek realized that school reading gave him greater access to social membership in groups inside and outside of the classroom (e.g., chapter book peer culture and Boy Scouts). Derek's experiences illustrate the process of learning to read as an important social force in children's identity construction (including their identities as readers), and teachers' unique role in creating spaces for empowering experiences that positively impact upon children's sense of self as learner, reader, and their range of reading competencies and abilities across literacy practices in and out of the classroom. The tapestry of diverse learners in first-grade classrooms offer opportunities to all students, including students identified as "struggling readers," to become and see themselves as active learners and participant in the classroom. The interconnectedness between school and outside of school learning and literacy practices and the power of labels as limiting what we can see challenge teachers to broaden their assessment tools and set of lenses to learn about their diverse students' interests, academic abilities, experiences, and funds of knowledge. Without a broader understanding of the multiple roles and purposes reading can have in children's lives, as well as the richness of their lives, teachers are "at risk" of categorizing students under particular labels. In the long run, particular labels restrict students' repertoire of practices rather than create social and learning spaces in which students like Derek can demonstrate and develop their interests, abilities, and multiple identities beyond the category of a struggling reader.

References

Alvermann, D. E. (2001). Reading adolescents' reading identities: Looking back to see ahead. *Journal of Adolescent & Adult Literacy, 44*(8), 676–690.

Au, K., & Jordan, C. (1981). Teaching reading to Hawaiian children: Finding a culturally appropriate solution. In H. Trueba, G. Guthrie, & K. Au (Eds.), *Culture and the bilingual classroom: Studies in classroom ethnography* (pp. 139–152). Rowley, MA: Newbury House.

Brown, M. W. (1947). *Goodnight moon.* New York: Harper Row.

Christian, B., & Bloome, D. (2004). Learning to read is who you are. *Reading & Writing Quarterly, 20*(4), 365–384.

Clay, M. M. (1991). *Becoming literate: The construction of inner control.* Portsmouth, NH: Heinemann.

Clay, M. M. (1993). *An observation survey of early literacy achievement.* Portsmouth, NH: Heinemann.

Collins, K. M. (2003). *Ability profiling and school failure: One child's struggle to be seen as competent.* Mahwah, NJ: Lawrence Erlbaum.

Comber, B. (2004). Three little boys and their literacy trajectories. *Australian Journal of Language and Literacy, 27*(2), 114–127.

Corsaro, W. (1985). *Friendship and peer culture in the early years.* Norwood, NJ: Ablex Publishing.

Dantas, M. L. (1999). Negotiating literacy teaching and learning across contexts and overtime in a first-grade classroom. Unpublished dissertation. Ohio State University at Columbus.

Dudley-Marling, C. (2001). School trouble: A mother's burden. *Gender and Education, 13*(2), 183–197.

Dyson, A. H. (1995). Writing children: Reinventing the development of childhood literacy. *Written Communication, 12*(1), 4–46.

Dyson, A. H. (2001). Where are the childhoods in childhood literacy? An exploration in outer (school) space. *Journal of Early Childhood Literacy, 1*(1), 9–39.

Frank, C. (1999). *Ethnographic eyes: A teacher's guide to classroom observation.* Portsmouth, NH: Heinemann.

Ganske, K., Monroe, J., & Strickland, D. (2003). Questions teachers ask about struggling readers and writers. *The Reading Teacher, 57*(2), 118–128.

Gee, J. (2003). Opportunity to learn: A language-based perspective on assessment. *Assessment in Education: Principles, Policy, & Practice, 10*(1), 27–47.

Goodman, Y. M. (1997). Multiple roads to literacy. In D. Taylor (Ed.), *Many families, many literacies: An international declaration of principles.* Portsmouth, NH: Heinemann.

Green, J., & Bloome, D. (1997). Ethnography and ethnographers of and in education: A situated perspective. In J. Flood, S. Heath, & D. Lapp (Eds.), *Handbook of research on teaching literacy through the communicative and visual arts* (pp. 181–202). New York: Macmillan.

Green, J. L., Dixon, C. N., & Zaharlick, A. (2003). Ethnography as a logic of inquiry. In J. Flood, D. Lapp, J. R. Squire, & J. M. Jensen (Eds.), *Handbook of research on the teaching of English language arts* (2nd ed., pp. 201–224). Lawrence Erlbaum.

Heron, A. H. (2003). A study of agency: Multiple constructions of choice and decision making in an inquiry-based summer school program for struggling readers. *Journal of Adolescent & Adult Literacy, 46*(7), 568–579.

Holland, D., Lachicotte, W., Skinner, D., & Cain, C. (1998). *Identity and agency in cultural worlds*. Cambridge, MA: Harvard University Press.

Kantor, R., Elgas, P. M., & Fernie, D. E. (1993). Cultural knowledge and social competence within a preschool peer culture group. *Early Childhood Research Quarterly, 8*, 125–147.

Ladson-Billings, G. (1994). *The dreamkeepers: Successful teachers of African American children*. San Francisco: Jossey-Bass Publishers.

Lyons, C. A. (2003). *Teaching struggling readers: How to use brain-based research to maximize learning.* Portsmouth, NH: Heinemann.

Moll, L., Amanti, C., Neff, D., & González, N. (1992). Funds of knowledge for teaching: Using a qualitative approach to connect homes and classrooms. *Theory Into Practice, 31*(2), 132–141.

Patton, M. Q. (1990). *Qualitative evaluation and research methods* (2nd ed.). Newbury Park, CA: Sage Publications.

Putney, L., Green, J., Dixon, C., Duran, R., & Yeager, B. (2000). Consequential progressions: Exploring collective-individual development in a bilingual classroom. In P. Smagorinsky & C. Lee (Eds.), *Constructing meaning through collaborative inquiry: Vygotskian perspectives on literacy research* (pp. 86–126). Cambridge, MA: Cambridge University Press.

Walkerdine, V. (1990). *Schoolgirl fictions*. London: Verson.

Weedon, C. (1987). *Feminist practice & poststructuralist theory*. Malden, MA: Blackwell Publishing.

Older, Unsuccessful Readers: Diversity Personified

Barbara Honchell

At the time of this study, Tammy was a sixth-grade student at a K–8 school. She qualified for service in the Title 1 program because she scored a two in reading on the End-of-Grade testing and was reading 2 years below grade level. During conversations with the Title 1 teacher, Tammy's classroom teachers indicated that although they thought she had untapped potential, they couldn't really say why Tammy was experiencing difficulty with reading.

Tammy was a quiet, yet delightful, child. She was a willing participant in a one-on-one intervention. She wanted to please and worked hard at school. Tammy was not a risk taker and appeared to lack self-confidence. While reading, she would wait for the teacher to tell her what to do at difficulty rather than take a chance. According to interviews and surveys at the beginning of her lessons, Tammy liked animals and enjoyed "American Girl" books and *Teen* magazine.

Tammy participated in 50 one-on-one lessons during a semester. Tammy made good progress in text-reading level, from reading at a fourth-grade reading level to a sixth-grade reading level. On exit surveys, she indicated that she enjoyed the lessons and thought she had learned a lot. She liked being alone with the teacher so that "other kids didn't hear me read." In addition, the data show that Tammy made significant growth in reading achievement as a result of an intervention developed to support older at-risk readers through individual strategy instruction.

Introduction

School administrators and teachers are concerned about the number of older at-risk students, such as Tammy, who not able to take advantage of good classroom instruction because of difficulty with the reading process. Since many classrooms are organized around the concepts of an average group of students or grade-level performance, students who have not reached grade-level performance in reading often experience difficulty with most classroom assignments, which require reading. A diverse learner who is not able to actively participate in learning within this "average" group becomes a cause for concern. Remedial reading programs exist in many schools in the United States to address what is perceived by many to be a problem. These programs have not met the expectations of many people who support the concept of additional assistance for readers experiencing difficulty with learning (Allington & Cunningham, 1996; Cooley, 1981; Kaestle & Smith, 1982). In the past 30 years, special programs have been designed to focus on students in the remedial reading and reading lab class. There is little evidence that any of these programs have changed the academic lives of the students who participate in them (Cunningham & Allington, 1994). There are many reasons that this is true (Johnston & Allington, 1991). Several include:

- A special program lowers the perceived level of responsibility of the "regular" teacher to meet the needs of the students who participate.

- Special classes meet during the school day, and the students who participate miss instruction in the classroom that is also needed.

- Often, the special program teacher is a teacher assistant with minimal training.

Cunningham and Allington (1994) conclude that even though these programs are based on years of research and experience, the programs often contribute to the problem.

   For whatever reasons, interventions that have been offered have not been successful for many of these students (Morris, Ervin, & Conrad, 1996). Commonly, students tend to regard their continued reading failure as something over which they have no control. They express their problems as the fault of the system, the teacher, the parents, or difficult material. Assuming responsibility for their own learning and becoming independent readers seems an unattainable goal, too lofty even to be considered when weighed against past performance (Walmsley & Allington, 1995).

   This chapter will present an in-depth study of an elementary student as an example of many who participated in an individual reading intervention modeled after Reading Recovery® for older, diverse readers who were unable to benefit from either classroom or small-group interventions previously offered to them. The children who participated in this intervention are examples of "diversity personified." They were not selected because of any educational or societal label. They were selected because they were unsuccessful in the classroom, largely because they were reading 2 years or more below grade level. Tammy is white and comes from a lower-middle-class intact family. She speaks English as her first language and has never been retained, and yet in an academic sense, she was not in the mainstream of her classroom. The challenge was to attempt to understand Tammy as a learner and help her become a more successful reader.

How Could Reading Recovery Link to Older Readers?

Reading Recovery has had a great success rate with beginning readers who are in the bottom 20% of their first-grade class. Reading Recovery is a trademark name for this early intervention. Many children move from the bottom of the first grade to average in the class in 12–15 weeks of instruction (Askew & Frasier, 1997; Clay, 1987; Lyons, Pinnell, & DeFord, 1993; Rowe, 1997). Upon successful completion of the intervention, most children progress in reading with the rest of the class without additional support (DeFord, Pinnell, Lyons, & Place, 1990; Lyons, Pinnell, & DeFord, 1993; Rowe, 1997). The teacher's work with the students is a model of individualized, assisted performance. The theory behind Reading Recovery revolves around general cognitive processes initiated by the child to get the message from the text (Clay, 1982, 1985). These processes include the use of strategies such as self-monitoring, searching, cross-checking, then confirming or self-correcting. With these strategies at their disposal, children can work on text independently, thus gaining confidence in themselves as readers and writers. These are the same strategies Clay identified that high-progress readers use almost automatically as they learn to read (Clay, 1991). It is my observation when teaching older at-risk readers that, often, these older readers have many bits and pieces of knowledge about reading but have no problem-solving process to allow them to use what they know. Often, older, struggling readers may be so dependent on someone else to tell him or her how to work in the text they no longer attempt to use what they do know. Once these students begin to have some success with independent problem solving in a supported one-on-one situation with a noticing teacher, they may begin to try the strategies that appear to be essential for any reader.

Changing the processes used by older readers is likely to take longer than younger students because the older readers have been habituating ineffective ways of dealing with text and have practiced dependence for longer periods of time (Clay, 1993a). Because it takes longer to facilitate change with older readers, school districts may have been reluctant to invest the time and energy necessary to change older readers' behaviors. However, when students are taught effective problem-solving strategies and develop a balance in sampling text information, change occurs for them in both reading technique and attitudes toward reading (Lee & Neal, 1992–1993; Lowe & Walters, 1991). So the question becomes, as educators, are we willing to invest in the literacy futures of older and very diverse readers who have yet to experience success as readers in a manner that truly meets their needs? First, I will present the theoretical underpinnings for such an investment, and then I will offer Tammy as an example of a student whose reading life was changed because of the opportunity to develop useful reading strategies.

Skills and/or Strategies

One specific overarching problem is that the instruction offered in many remedial reading programs has traditionally focused on skills in isolation (Allington, Stuetzel, Shake, & Lamarche, 1986). Students often complete skill lessons in workbooks or worksheets with the teacher serving as manager of the class but offering little direct instruction. Frequently, students demonstrate mastery of skills without exhibiting use of enhanced skill knowledge in classroom reading lessons because the lack of congruence between the special class and the regular class often leads to confusion for students who are already struggling to learn to read (Allington et al., 1986).

Since the skills approach to teaching at-risk readers has not had the anticipated effect, it is appropriate to look at other ways to support struggling readers. Much information is available on the importance of the learner being "strategic" (Duffy et al., 1987; Garner, 1992; Paris, Lipson, & Wixson, 1994; Paris, Wasik, & Turner, 1991). What are the issues connected with the development of strategies and the reasons that strategy development could be useful to those who have often been called "special readers"?

According to the *American Heritage Dictionary* (1994), a strategy is a plan of action or the method to accomplish an objective. If we narrow this concept to focus toward reading strategies, reading strategies could be explained as by Clay (1993b):

"When we operate or work on a problem, we are engaged in a conscious search for solutions. In reading, we sometimes consciously search for a word or a meaning or a correction, but most of the time our active search is a fast reaction of the brain that seems to be automatic and not conscious. Perhaps strategies is a better name for these fast reactions used while reading" (p. 39).

A Vygotskian Perspective on Learning Strategies

Lev Vygotsky, a Russian educator, developed a theory of learning that focuses on the interactions between the adult and child in a learning situation (Vygotsky, 1978). According to Vygotsky, every child, except the most severely disabled, has, by nature, the ability to perceive, attend, and remember. As the learner is able to control and regulate these abilities through interactions with supportive others, problem-solving skills develop. The purpose of teaching and the role of the teacher take on added importance when viewed from a Vygotskian perspective (Lyons, 1993) because learning and development are very closely tied. As we consider the needs of diverse learners, an individualized intervention may offer a window into the potential literacy success of students who are not successful in traditional classroom or small-group instructional settings.

The development of reading strategies takes place through "scaffolding" of instruction (Tharp & Gallimore, 1988). The interactions between the student and the teacher in a literacy situation are ideally collaborative in nature, with the teacher providing just enough support to enable success in reading. The teacher values the student's intentions and approximations as indications of tentative knowledge about reading and risk taking. For example, if a student reads "school" for "building," the teacher might say, "I like the way you were thinking about where this story takes place, but reread and see if everything makes sense and looks right as you are reading." The interaction is focused in the student's zone of proximal development, with a gradual withdrawal of support as the student internalizes the needed strategy and becomes independent with its use. The goal is for the child to develop independence necessary to take the action to read in most situations. In order for some students to develop these strategies for applying skills, individual instruction is a necessary component of their learning opportunities.

Some General Information about Strategic Activity

Paris, Lipson, and Wixson (1994) indicate that there are three elements that define strategic behavior: a capable person, a goal, and an action that the person can actually perform and selects to perform. Thus, strategic activity cannot be an accident. The learner must make a conscious choice about the use of the strategy. Strategies are skills under consideration for action or use by the learner to accomplish a particular task. Being strategic, because it takes time and thought, can be difficult for the dependent learner, and frequently, older at-risk readers are very dependent upon the teacher as learners.

Psychologists have identified the three kinds of knowledge learners must have in order to be strategic (Bruner, 1972; Resnick, 1983). These are declarative, procedural, and conditional knowledge. Declarative knowledge involves knowing "that" conditions and situations exist. For a beginning reader, declarative knowledge includes such things as knowing that letters make words and that words go left to right across a page in English, and that periods can end sentences. Declarative knowledge also includes ideas of the reader like "I read slowly," or "Reading is hard for me." Procedural knowledge involves the "how" of reading. It describes the access to reading behavior the learner has when reading. Procedural knowledge includes the skills the reader has learned and can select to use for strategies. Conditional knowledge is the "when and why" of applying action by choice to a skill and actually using that skill for reading. Conditional knowledge is taking procedural knowledge and using it by choice. It is the application phase of the learning. "My teacher has taught me that rereading when something doesn't make sense will help me in situations like this. I think that I will use that strategy here because I think it will work."

The actual decision to use procedural knowledge involves both skill and "will." Will is defined as the motivation to behave in a particular way. Will can be motivated by many things, including pleasing the teacher, earning a prize, or internal desire. This is the pragmatic aspect of strategic behavior. Traditional reading instruction has often focused on the skills of reading without considering the effort and the decisions required to develop strategic processing (Paris, Lipson, & Wixson, 1994) to link skill and will.

Factors Affecting Strategy Development

Bandura (1986), Schunk (1995), and Zimmerman (1995) identified two aspects of self-efficacy that are particularly important to strategy development. They are motivation and self-regulation. Motivation is the mechanism within a learner that begins, controls, and maintains behavior. Self-regulation is the element of thinking that notices if and when knowledge is being used. As you will see, self-efficacy was an important issue for Tammy. I first discuss the nature of self-efficacy and then discuss these two aspects of self-efficacy (motivation and self-regulation) that are critical to strategy development.

Self-Efficacy

Self-efficacy is defined as "people's judgments of their capabilities to organize and execute courses of action required to attain designated types of performances" (Bandura, 1986, p. 391). Self-efficacy influences learning, motivation, and achievement. It affects choice of activities, effort given to an activity, and persistence to work at the activity (Schunk, 1995; Zimmerman, 1995). For example, a learner with high self-efficacy toward reading is likely to look forward to opportunities to participate in guided reading group, try a new reading strategy, such as rereading to confirm, and reread several times if unsure of the meaning of a passage. Of course, self-efficacy is not the only influence in learning situations, but it plays an important role in strategy acquisition, particularly for readers who have already experienced repeated failure in reading (Schunk, 1995).

Motivation

Motivation, as an element of self-efficacy, relates positively to the use of reading/learning strategies. Motivation can be defined as the internal mechanism that initiates, sustains, and directs active behavior (Guthrie & Wigfield, 2000). "Reading motivation is the individual's personal goals, values, and beliefs with regard to the topics, processes, and outcomes of reading" (Guthrie & Wigfield, 2000, p. 405). This affective link to strategy usage is extremely important. Learners are unlikely to become involved in thought processes unless they are motivated internally to accomplish a goal (Garner, 1992). A person's judgment (self-efficacy) about his or her capability related to an action has a link to the internal mechanism that initiates, sustains, and directs that action (motivation).

Self-Regulation

Self-regulation, or self-control, is an essential part of being strategic (Garner, 1992). It is an aspect of the metacognitive knowledge base, the thinking processes. There are three elements to metacognition. The learner needs to be aware if he or she does not understand, know where the problem lies, and have the skill and will to fix the difficulty. In the case of metacognitive knowledge about strategies, it is important to be aware that knowledge is not use. A learner can know the strategy and not use it, even though the strategy would assist learning (Garner, 1992).

In the case of reading, sometimes the reader is aware that he or she does not understand the message but does not have the motivation to expend the energy to remedy the situation. Sometimes, the reader is aware of the confusion but does not have the metacognitive base to provide the appropriate strategy. The awareness that something is wrong with the reading is as important as the awareness that all is well. When readers detect problems, they can adjust processing strategies flexibly by searching for information and checking information sources against each other and correct, if necessary.

The Nature of Strategic Activity

Strategic activity has metacognitive, cognitive, and affective components. The metacognitive element is the conscious or tacit awareness of the need for strategic action. The cognitive aspect is engaging the strategy to make ongoing progress to the goal. The affective element is the motivation to engage in the strategy with its accompanying time and effort required.

According to Paris, Lipson, and Wixson (1994), it is essential that students become independent, self-directed learners. Self-controlled learners demonstrate the following abilities: planning, evaluating, self-regulating of skills, and an ongoing interest in learning. This self-control, or the ability to be strategic, is rooted in development but is impacted by instruction. Being a strategic reader is thus a developmental and instructional issue. The major distinction between someone who is good at any activity and a person who is not good is controlled strategic behavior in that area. Most children learn to be strategic between the ages of 5 and 12; thus, school and strategic development are closely related (Paris, Lipson, & Wixson, 1994).

Strategies and Reading

Bruner (1957) defined a strategy as a "decision process" involving a search for cues that will code the stimulus into appropriate categories. Strategies are the operations we use. In reading, strategies are the processes the reader uses to find and use internal and external information useful in bringing meaning to what he or she is reading, to draw on existing language competencies, to detect errors, and to correct errors (Clay, 1991). Although strategies cannot be seen physically, the observation of behavior can indicate that strategic processing is occurring in the brain. As readers become expert, as they become "strategic," their reading is characterized by quick selection of the strategy that fits the particular situation rather than by the volume of strategies used. The use of strategies can become so automatic that the strategies are not observable except when the reader loses meaning or text is particularly difficult.

The reader's use of strategies is most effective when based on monitoring for meaning or comprehension. This awareness of meaning and resulting self-monitoring is all a part of the planning aspect of strategic processing (Garner,

1992). Poor readers need to develop this deliberate use of planning and acting, particularly as they read for meaning. They are more likely to self-correct for structure and visual errors (Garner, 1992). In order to read strategically, the reader must be conscious of the purpose for the reading and which available skill options to activate. The good news is that readers who do not use fundamental strategies spontaneously can be taught to do so (Garner, 1992).

When Does a Reader Need to be Strategic?

There are three times in reading when strategic action is of essential importance: when learning to read, when the reader is "in trouble" because meaning is lost, and when the text is difficult (Paris, Lipson, & Wixson, 1994). These are the times that reading behaviors can be observed that signal-reading strategies are being used. For the novice reader, strategies applied during reading are open for inspection because they are at the conscious and deliberate phase of use (Paris, Wasik, & Turner, 1991). Researchers have set out to record what children did as they read as a way to understand the nature of strategic reading. This is one of the features of this study, using both running records and lesson records as observational tools.

Clay (1982) describes her early work on error and self-corrections in relation to Bruner (1957; Bruner, Oliver, & Greenfield, 1966). Bruner's theory of perception as a decision process provides one framework for the discussion of error-correction behavior. The decision process would pass through the stages of noticing conflict, cue searching, preliminary categorizing of the problem, confirming check, and final categorizing or correcting. Bruner suggests that when there is a conflict between two systems of representing reality (the actual text and the child's reading of the text), the child may then search further to resolve the conflict. Clay along with Ken and Yetta Goodman (1982) identified some specific reading strategies that are particularly useful in resolving such a conflicting reading situation.

When reading continuous text, students must engage in what Clay calls "reading work" (Clay, 1993b) by using their theories of the world and theories of written language. They solve problems and behave strategically. Good readers operate on problems, search for relationships that order print, and thus make the print simpler to use. Students not progressing in reading may have tried some problem-solving strategies that failed to bring order to their understanding of reading and are likely to become passive in their approach to text, resulting in a lack of action (Clay, 1991). It is important for students to have a set of operations that will allow them to read increasingly difficult text for the precise words and meaning of the author. Clay uses the term *strategies* to apply to these fast operations used to read successfully. Students practice these strategies as they read the writings of others and their own writing. The origins of Clay's theories are historically present in her detailed study of literacy progress made by children in the first 2 years of school (Clay, 1967). In this study, Clay describes the progress made by typical children making good learning gains and then points to the need for additional support for some children in order for them to make learning gains.

Strategies Needed to Solve Problems When Reading

Through careful observation of good readers, Clay (1979, 1982, 1993b) has identified specific behaviors/strategies that are needed to read texts. She has divided these behaviors into two groups. The early behaviors provide the reader with a way to check that he or she is attending to the right part of the page. These are directional movement, one-to-one matching, locating known words, and locating an unknown word.

The higher strategies that Clay (1993b) describes, as used by successful readers, are:

- monitoring or checking on oneself
- cross-checking information or comparing one source of information to another
- searching for cues with structure, meaning, or visual (letter)
- self-correcting using many sources of information and/or good quality substitutions (errors)

Skilled, meaning-focused readers monitor their own reading or check on themselves; search for information in word sequences, in meaning, and in letter sequences; discover new things independently and then cross-check cues one with the other; repeat to confirm or self-correct; and solve new words by these means (Clay, 1993b). The strategies tend to be used in this progression, although the way strategies are used is situational. Certainly, monitoring precedes all other strategies. If the reader has not noticed any inconsistency, he or she cannot address the issue. A self-correction occurs because the reader first notices that something doesn't look right, make sense, or sound right. The thought processes of the reader lead to searching or checking, depending on which is appropriate in the situation.

So with this background on strategies and the factors that influence strategy development, let us now return to Tammy, as an example of an older reader whose learning is generally influenced by the affective factors discussed by Bandura (1986) and Schunk (1995) and whom, we will learn, is also in great need of the reading strategies defined by Clay.

Tammy: Not a Risk Taker

Scores and Analysis from Pretest

Tammy completed a series of initial assessments. Table 3:1 summarizes the assessments that provide information about her item knowledge.

Table 3:1   Summary of Item Assessments

Assessment	Score
Letter identification	53/54
Word test	
Initial basic sight vocabulary	0/20
Advanced basic sight vocabulary	97/100
Concepts about print	22/24
Writing vocabulary	103
Hearing sounds in words	60/64

The item-focused assessments showed that Tammy had good letter knowledge (53/54) (scores for sounds and words were not reported by the teacher) and her sight word knowledge was very strong (97/100). She understood how the English print system works (22/24), and she could write many words quickly (103 in 10 minutes). Tammy heard sounds and produced the letters in a dictation (60/64).

Tammy had three running records for the initial assessment, one at the instructional level and two at the hard level. There were no samples of easy reading. Table 3:2 summarizes the level-one analysis (the simple mathematical calculations) of her running records for text reading.

Table 3:2   Level-One Analysis of Text Reading

Text level	% of accuracy	Self-correction rate
26 (fourth grade)	91% (instructional)	1:4
28 (fifth grade)	87% (hard)	1:9
104 (fourth grade)	87% (hard)	1:4

This initial information indicated that Tammy was reading at the fourth-grade reading level as a sixth-grade student. At her instructional level, she corrected one in four errors, and at a hard level of text, she corrected one in nine errors. On a second fourth-grade passage, Tammy's reading below the instructional level indicates that some material on the fourth-grade level was too hard for her.

The second level of analysis (analysis of cue sources) of the running records revealed a clear pattern of a reader who used visual information without regard for meaning and structure. A typical example of Tammy's reading from the initial assessments in *The Waterbed Mystery* (Skarry, 1976) is "It looks as if someone has been promise/purposely/pitching/punching the waterbeds. Twins/Twice in the past few days were/we've found holes in the/two beds." (Tammy's production is presented as word provided by Tammy/text.)

At the third level of analysis (analysis of reading behaviors), the running records show no examples of monitoring or searching on Levels 26 or 28. On the second fourth-grade passage, a result of some minimal amount of monitoring (repeats and appeals with a resulting telling of the word) and searching (multiple attempts) was a self-correction rate that matched Level 26. The behaviors recorded at the errors did not reveal any clues as to why the teacher used two passages at the fourth-grade reading level. It was documented that Tammy was actually reading lower than fourth grade on some passages. There is no example of easy text from the assessment.

Lessons

As stated earlier, Tammy participated in 50 individual lessons taught by a teacher who had participated in professional development focused on strategy-based instruction. The lessons for the students in this study were based on the individual needs of the learners and demonstrate that it is possible to significantly impact the reading of older readers with one-on-one instruction that focuses on personal needs of learners. The 45-minute lesson structure occurred as follows:

1. Reading to the student by the teacher: The teacher read material to the student that was of interest, but that the student may not be able to read fluently him or herself. The teacher modeled strategies that the student needed to see used. The teacher observed and noted the student's response to the text in terms of content, meaning, and use of the strategies that were modeled. This component was specifically included to renew an interest in reading. An added benefit of this component was that students often wrote about the material read to them during this portion of the lesson, since the material to be read was often chosen because of its high interest level (7 minutes).

2. Familiar reading by the student of previously read material: The student read to the teacher from his or her previously read set of materials. These were selections from previous lessons that had been introduced and used for running records earlier. The teacher observed and noted use of strategies to guide the teaching during the lesson (8 minutes).

3. Running record with follow-up teaching point: The teacher took a running record on the previous day's new reading material while the student read orally. The teacher then selected an example of a strategy that could be taught or praised from the running record. Discussion of meaning of the reading followed the oral reading. The running record was analyzed after the lesson for accuracy, use of cues, and strategies and patterns of literacy development (10 minutes).

4. Working with letters and words: The teacher demonstrated how a particular type of word works through demonstration with magnetic letters on a white board. The student participated in the manipulation of the letters. Concepts demonstrated might include some phonetic principle, use of endings, or other word relationships that would be useful in reading and writing. The concept was selected because of something that occurred and was noted in a previous lesson during reading or writing that indicated partial understanding of the concept but need for more information (3 minutes).

5. Writing: After a short conversation between the student and the teacher, the student generated a sentence or two about any topic of interest and wrote the sentences with as much teacher support as needed to produce a readable text. The teacher and the student worked together on the practice page to generate unknown or partially known words needed for the text. This assisted interaction with writing supported the development of reading knowledge, thus expanding the student's capacity to perform within the zone of proximal development (10 minutes).

6. Reading of new material: The teacher introduced a carefully chosen new reading selection that would be used for the running record the next day. The student read the selection as independently as possible. The teacher supported with suggestions of strategies to try or information that the student might need to problem solve in the text. The focus was on reading for meaning with balance between the use of the cue sources and use of strategies on the run in text (10 minutes).

The lesson format described was developed over 3 years of work with students. But the lesson format was secondary to the interactions between the teacher and the student that are based on the teachers' skilled observations and response to the student. The lesson merely provided a context for the strategy teaching. The key factors that have been identified as essential to the success of Reading Recovery (Clay & Watson, 1982), that is, the teacher training to be an observer and noter of reading behavior that will support learning and the focus on independent problem solving for students, are the same. Now, I will present a detailed discussion of Tammy's strategy development through her individual series of lessons.

Tammy's Lessons

One of the key features of Tammy's lessons was the teacher's ability to select text at an appropriate level of difficulty. Selection of text for reading is always challenging, but particularly so for diverse learners, since their background knowledge, repertoire of skills, and use of strategies is often unique. Figure 3:1 summarizes the percent of accuracy for the text used during each lesson. Figure 3:1 indicates that all but 7 of the 50 books read during Tammy's lessons were either at the instructional or easy level (90% or better) when self-correcting was not figured into the accuracy rate. There was only one running record below 90% accuracy (hard) when self-correcting of reading was figured into the percent of accuracy (Lesson 45). It is important to notice the effect of self-correcting on reading level for Tammy. Self-correcting brought all but one text to the instructional or easy level of reading.

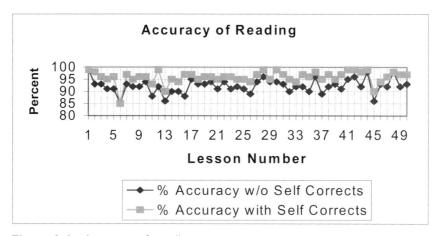

Figure 3:1 Accuracy of reading.

Strategy Usage during Lessons

The three strategies of interest, monitoring, searching and checking, and self-correcting will be examined by analyzing the running records for each lesson.

Monitoring

Tammy's monitoring, primarily noticing if her reading made sense, and secondarily, if it looked and sounded right, was excellent. Tammy monitored 50% of her errors or better on 47 of her 50 lessons. Figure 3:2 shows this high level of monitoring.

Monitoring is a key strategy that allows the other strategies of searching and self-correcting to develop. Tammy generally monitored by rereading. For example, during the book *Orange Attack* (Buxton, 1994), Tammy read, "Join us in our fights against the Blue Army and your/their deadly froze/freeze-guns!" She reread the entire sentence, a noticing behavior, even though she could not fix the errors. On occasion, there were examples of monitoring through an appeal for the word to be provided by the teacher. For example, during the book *What a Plant!* (Latham, 1993), Tammy read, "There are also some plants that really/relee/A/T/rely on animals in different ways." (*A* means the student appeals for help. *T* means the teacher told the word to the student.)

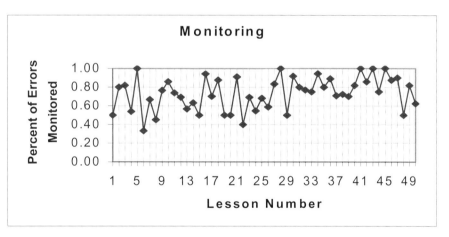

Figure 3:2 Use of monitoring.

Searching and Checking

Tammy also showed use of searching and checking, although not to the same degree that she was able to monitor. Figure 3:3 summarizes Tammy's searching documented on the running records. Tammy was searching and checking inconsistently. Usually, between 10% and 40% of the errors showed multiple attempts, the indicator for searching and checking. Tammy only had five running records, with no examples of searching. However, her use of searching for more information to solve problems was not consistent.

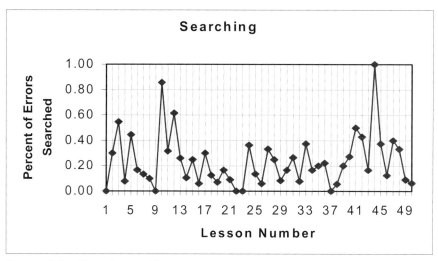

Figure 3:3   Use of searching.

Self-Correcting

Tammy self-corrected between 13% and 87% of her errors on all running records. While the percent of self-corrects was inconsistent, the use of the strategy was present during every lesson. Clay (1991) considers a good self-correction rate as 30%–40%, as documented in her initial study of good readers. Tammy corrected at a rate of 40% or higher on 39 of her 50 lessons. Figure 3:4 shows the daily use of this strategy. A second look at the display offered in Figure 3:1 (Accuracy of Reading) shows the impact of this self-correcting behavior shown in Figure 3:4. Thirty-four of Tammy's running records moved from the instructional reading level to the easy reading level (95%–100% accuracy) when self-correcting is figured into the accuracy rate (see Figure 3:1). The text was certainly at an appropriate level of difficulty to allow her to work effectively.

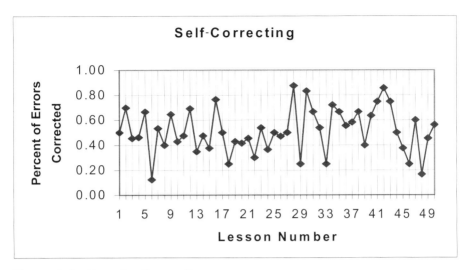

Figure 3:4 Use of self-correcting.

Integration of the Strategies

Given Tammy's active use of strategies, it is important to see what the strategy use looked like in combination. Figure 3:5 shows the use of all three strategies of interest on one graph. This graph very clearly indicates the use of the three strategies, with more examples of monitoring than any other strategy. Tammy's running records showed many examples of monitoring or noticing dissonance. Tammy was able to correct some of the errors she noticed and overtly searched

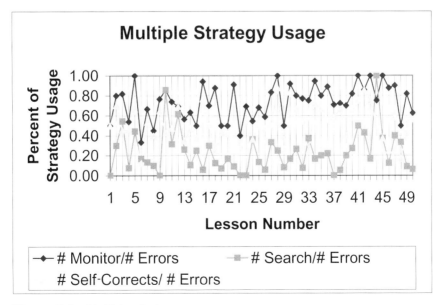

Figure 3:5 Multiple strategy use.

for some of the corrections. Figure 3:5 shows the layers of Tammy's work with monitoring at the highest level, self-correcting at the middle level, and searching and checking at the lowest level. She was able to search and check some errors without showing her work overtly, resulting in that strategy appearing to be least actively used.

Scores and Analysis from Post-test

Tammy completed the selected assessments from the modified Observation Survey, along with five running records. The running records from the assessment are of particular importance for Tammy, since she was not reading professionally leveled texts. Tammy had five running records for her final assessment, ranging in accuracy from 88% to 97%. Table 3:3 summarizes the first level of analysis (simple mathematical calculations).

Table 3:3   Level-One Analysis of Text Reading

Text level	% of accuracy	Self-correction rate
24 (third grade)	97% (easy)	1:2
26 (fourth grade)	93% (instructional)	1:4
28 (fifth grade)	91% (instructional)	1:3
30 (sixth grade)	95% (instructional)	1:2.3
32 (seventh grade)	88% (hard)	1:8

Note that Tammy read three texts at the instructional level, with varying degrees of success. All were read with a good self-correction rate. The guidelines for administration of the running record (Clay, 1993a) indicate that it is the highest level where the reader scores 90%–94%, that is, the reader's instructional level.

Level-two analyses (analysis of cue sources) of these running records show that Tammy used a balance of cue sources, meaning, structure, and visual information when reading. She noticed errors that did not make sense and used more detailed visual information to correct.

Level-three analyses (analysis of reading behaviors) indicate that Tammy would reread to correct and confirm accuracy of reading. There were many examples of searching, such as "de-tect-or/doctor T" for detective and "shar-/sa-phoning R2 T" for siphoning on *The Waterbed Mystery* (Skarry, 1976). There were also many examples of self-correcting, such as "to/the sc and Carl/Carol sc," also from *The Waterbed Mystery* (Skarry, 1976).

Summary of Tammy's Reading

Tammy demonstrated strategy work, particularly monitoring, throughout her reading lessons, reading a variety of texts at the easy and instructional reading level. She used all strategies, to some extent, showing many examples of monitoring, by rereading or waiting for the teacher to tell the unknown word. She also demonstrated many examples of self-correcting, often combined with rereading. There were some examples of searching with multiple attempts, though not to the same extent as monitoring and self-correcting. Tammy increased her text reading level from fourth to sixth grade from initial to final assessment. She reached grade-level performance in this one-to-one reading situation. Now, it is necessary to explore the strategy attention by the teacher that may have influenced Tammy's use of strategies and increase in text reading level that were documented on the postassessment.

The Teacher Perspective

The information about teacher attention to strategies was documented by reviewing the teacher's lesson records for comments about her own attention to strategies, both in terms of what she observed and also what she taught. Tammy's teacher, Mrs. Sherman, provided careful documentation on her lesson records and used reflection from one lesson to the next to focus her planning. Tammy's lesson records were well documented, with evidence of strategy attention, particularly for monitoring and searching. Mrs. Sherman often noted that Tammy needed to use meaning to guide her reading and was concerned about an overreliance on visual information.

Monitoring

Figure 3:6 provides a visual display of the teacher's cumulative attention to monitoring. Mrs. Sherman attended to monitoring from the beginning of Tammy's program. Not only did Mrs. Sherman attend to monitoring consistently, but also Tammy used this strategy on a consistent basis, particularly after Lesson 31. It seems Tammy understood that the teacher valued this noticing of error even when she could not correct. Tammy reread often to confirm accuracy and at sign of uncertainty. The teacher would encourage Tammy to notice when her reading did not make sense and at least try to figure out why it didn't make sense.

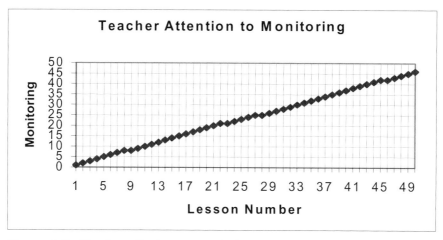

Figure 3:6   Teacher attention to monitoring.

Searching and Checking

Mrs. Sherman showed a pattern for attending to searching that is similar to the pattern for monitoring, as seen in Figure 3:7. The teacher regularly encouraged Tammy to look for more information, once she noticed a discrepancy. Lesson 4 established the baseline for teacher attention to searching and checking. A return look at Figure 3:3, which showed student use of searching, indicates that while Tammy did not attend to searching as often as the teacher did, there were examples of searching on all but four running records.

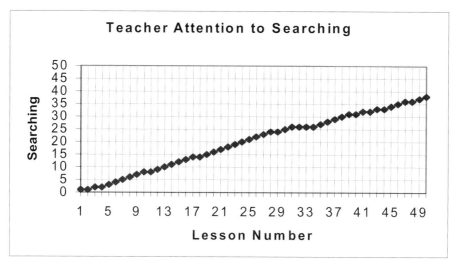

Figure 3:7   Teacher attention to searching.

Self-Correcting

The final strategy of interest is self-correcting. Figure 3:8 shows a lack of attention to self-correcting by the teacher. Lesson 5 established the baseline for attention to self-correcting by the teacher. At one point in the lessons, beginning at Lesson 21, the teacher did not attend to self-correcting on 10 consecutive lesson records. At Lesson 41, the teacher commented on the lesson record that Tammy could not seem to use more than one strategy at a time to self-correct. This graphic indicates that the teacher did not take the strategy work through to its final step of self-correcting by making consistent comments that a reader monitors and searches for information to be able to correct errors when reading isn't meaningful.

Figure 3:4, showing Tammy's use of self-correcting, demonstrates that even though the teacher did not often comment on self-correcting as the purpose for the other strategy work, Tammy seemed to know that her work did not end with the monitoring and searching.

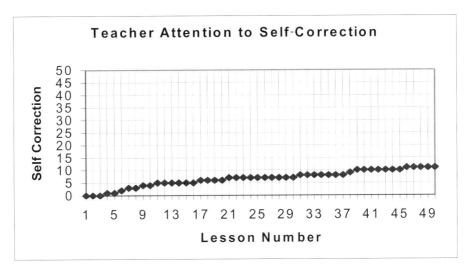

Figure 3:8 Teacher attention to self-correction.

Interpretation

Tammy was using some strategies to read text on the initial assessment and throughout her lessons. Her use of strategies did not really increase during the lessons. Tammy's teacher consistently attended to two of the three strategies of interest. Only monitoring was consistently used and attended by both.

The relationship between teacher attention to strategies and student use of strategies presents an interesting picture for this dyad. Tammy used monitoring and self-correcting on the initial assessments and during every lesson. Use of monitoring, more consistently than any of the other strategies, established the noticing behavior that is so important to successful strategy usage (Clay, 1993b). Tammy's frequent monitoring matched the consistent attention to monitoring by her teacher. In addition, Tammy was self-correcting on the initial assessments and during lessons even without consistent teacher attention to the strategy. Finally, Tammy showed searching and checking at a much lower level than the other strategies. However, this does not match teacher attention to searching and checking.

The only match between the teacher attention and the student use of strategies was for monitoring. However, Tammy was able to maintain a consistent level of strategy work with all strategies on more difficult text during the final assessment. Tammy improved her text reading to grade-level performance. There are several possible reasons Tammy was able to work in this manner.

One reason Tammy was able to maintain consistent use of strategies might be that during her lessons, Tammy was able to practice her strategies during all the reading opportunities the lesson offered. The lesson format allowed for familiar reading, reading during the running record, reading stories she had written herself, and reading of new text. Mrs. Sherman did an excellent job of keeping reading at the instructional or easy level. As a result, Tammy was reading text that allowed her to use strategies and not be overwhelmed with too many problems to solve. The sixth-grade classroom materials may not have offered the opportunity to practice that Tammy needed.

Another possibility is that the teacher's attention to strategies and problem solving, in general, even though the teacher was not attending to self-correcting consistently, encouraged Tammy to use strategies while reading. This could be enough attention to maintain the level of strategy usage that Tammy was using from the initial assessment and during lessons.

Self-efficacy (Bandura, 1986), Tammy's judgments about herself as a reader, particularly from classroom experiences, may have influenced her risk taking in other reading situations. The classroom teacher indicated, during an initial interview, that Tammy did not read in the room and did not actively participate in classroom reading activities. However, it was clear from initial running records that Tammy could use some strategies to read in the one-on-one situation. The final assessment documents that Tammy could read grade-level material. But it is important to remember that Tammy was not confident as a reader. On an exit survey, Tammy indicated that she liked the one-on-one learning situation so her peers would not hear her read. She was willing to read, reread for more information, and make multiple attempts with the teacher one-on-one situation that supported her efforts to use strategies when reading.

The key to Tammy's future success may be the application of the strategies in other reading situations and becoming a risk taker in the classroom as she was in one-on-one lessons. It is possible that Tammy will need even more practice to internalize the strategies and generalize their use. Mrs. Sherman was concerned about whether Tammy could use the strategies without support, that is, whether the use of strategies had moved to the zone of actual development (Vygotsky, 1978). The final assessment, when the teacher was in the role of observer, indicated that Tammy will be able to use strategies independently. There is a suggestion that Tammy's beliefs about herself as a reader improved during the lessons. Trying out different ways to figure out a word or to check for meaning at difficulty in any situation requires a certain self-assurance that Tammy developed in her lessons. Hopefully, she can now move forward and participate in classroom instruction about other aspects of reading with a noticing, supportive teacher.

Conclusion

The detailed study of this student example is an attempt to understand how strategy instruction, as offered through one-on-one instruction, could benefit older readers. The student intervention was modeled after Reading Recovery. The hope was that older readers could acquire independent problem-solving strategies that would allow them to read more complex text effectively with appropriate support from a knowledgeable teacher. The ultimate goal of the reading project was to explore a system to offer older at-risk readers the opportunity to extend their understanding of the reading process to include strategy acquisition as a tool to support their literacy development through one-on-one dialogue and interaction with a teacher who could support strategy development.

The representative, yet unique, outcome of Tammy's literacy journey during this intervention leads to the suggestion that in order to support the literacy development of at-risk students, regardless of their ages, the opportunity for a one-on-one tutorial is an option to explore. Clay (1991, 1993b) addresses the same need for individual instruction in Reading Recovery, rather than even small-group instruction:

"With problem readers, it is not enough for the teacher to have rapport, to generate interesting tasks, and generally be a good teacher. The teacher must be able to design a superbly sequenced programme

determined by the child's performance, and to make skilled decisions moment by moment during the lesson" (Clay, 1993b, p. 9).

In order to have the "superbly sequenced programme" for a student, a one-
on-one teaching/learning opportunity has promise. The teacher in this study
was known to have the three qualities of a good teacher (rapport with students, the ability to generate interesting tasks, and to generally be a "good"
teacher) that Clay (1993) indicates as "not enough." However, the opportunity to teach for strategies in a one-on-one situation seems to offer the opportunity for growth in strategy use and text reading level that will allow for
successful participation in classroom situations for more learners. Paris, Wasik,
and Turner (1991) assert, "Strategic reading is a prime characteristic of expert
readers because it is woven into the fabric of children's cognitive development
and is necessary for success in school" (p. 609). The data showed startling
change in instructional reading level during a relatively short intervention for
Tammy. Based on this research and understanding the habituated nature of
the reading of older at-risk readers, I would assert that it is possible, though
challenging, to help older students become more strategic readers and positively change the trajectory of their text reading level.

References

Allington, R. L., & Cunningham, P. M. (1996). *Schools that work: Where all children
read and write.* New York: Harper Collins College Publishers.

Allington, R. L., Stuetzel, H., Shake, M., & Lamarche, S. (1986). What is remedial
reading? A descriptive study. *Reading Research and Instruction, 29,* 15–30.

American Heritage Dictionary (3rd ed.). (1994). Boston: Houghton Mifflin.

Askew, B. J., & Frasier, D. F. (1997). Sustained effects of Reading Recovery intervention on the cognitive behaviors of second-grade children and the perceptions of
their teachers. In S. L. Swartz & A. F. Klein, (Eds.), *Research in Reading Recovery*
(pp. 18–38). Portsmouth, NH: Heinemann.

Bandura, A. (1986). *Social foundations of thought and action: A social cognitive theory.*
Englewood Cliffs, NJ: Prentice-Hall.

Bruner, J. S. (1957). On perceptual readiness. *Psychological Review, 64,* 123–152.

Bruner, J. S. (1972). Nature and uses of immaturity. *American Psychologist, 27,* 687–
708.

Bruner, J. S., Oliver, R. R., & Greenfield, P. M. (1966). *Studies in cognitive growth: A
collaboration at the center for cognitive studies.* New York: John Wiley & Sons.

Buxton, J. (1994). *Orange attack.* Wellington, New Zealand: Learning Media Ltd.

Clay, M. M. (1967). The reading behavior of five-year-old children: A research report. *New Zealand Journal of Educational Studies, 2,* 11–31.

Clay, M. M. (1979). *Reading: The patterning of complex behavior* (2nd ed.). Auckland, New Zealand: Heinemann Publishers.

Clay, M. M. (1982). *Observing young readers: Selected papers.* Portsmouth, NH: Heinemann.

Clay, M. M. (1985). *The early detection of reading difficulties* (3rd ed.). Auckland, New Zealand: Heinemann.

Clay, M. M. (1987). Implementing Reading Recovery: Systematic adaptations to an educational innovation. *New Zealand Journal of Educational Studies, 22,* 35–58.

Clay, M. M. (1991). *Becoming literate: The construction of inner control.* Portsmouth, NH: Heinemann.

Clay, M. M. (1993a). *An observation survey of early literacy achievement.* Portsmouth, NH: Heinemann.

Clay, M. M. (1993b). *Reading Recovery: A guidebook for teachers in training.* Portsmouth, NH: Heinemann.

Clay, M. M., & Watson, B. (1982). An inservice program for Reading Recovery teachers. In M.M. Clay, *Observing young readers: Selected papers* (pp. 192–200). Portsmouth, NH: Heinemann.

Cooley, W. W. (1981). Effectiveness in compensatory education. *Educational Leadership, 38,* 298–301.

Cunningham, P. M., & Allington, R. L. (1994). *Classrooms that work: They can all read and write.* New York: Harper Collins College Publishers.

DeFord, D. E., Pinnell, G. S., Lyons, C., & Place, A. W. (1990). *The Reading Recovery follow-up study* (Technical Report, Vol. III). Columbus, OH: Ohio State University.

Duffy, G. D., Roehler, L. R., Sivan, E., Rackliffe, G., Book, C., Meloth, M., Vavrus, L., Wesselman, R., Putman, J., & Bassiri, D. (1987). Effects of explaining the reason associated with using strategies. *Reading Research Quarterly, 22,* 347–368.

Garner, R. (1992). Metacognition and self-monitoring strategies. In S. J. Samuels & A. E. Farstrup (Eds.), *What research says about reading instruction* (2nd ed.) (pp. 236–251). Newark, DE: International Reading Association.

Guthrie, J. T., & Wigfield, A. (2000). Engagement and motivation in reading. In M. L. Kamil, P. B. Mosenthal, P. D. Pearson, & R. Barr (Eds.), *Handbook of reading research* (pp. 403–422). Mahwah, NJ: Lawrence Erlbaum.

Johnston, P. H., & Allington, R. L. (1991). Remediation. In R. Barr, M. L. Kamil, P. Mosenthal, & P. D. Pearson (Eds.), *Handbook of reading research, Vol. 2* (pp. 984–1012). New York: Longman.

Kaestle, C. F., & Smith, M. S. (1982). The historical context of the federal role in education. *Harvard Educational Review, 52,* 383–408.

Latham, C. (1993). *What a plant!* Bothell, WA: The Wright Group.

Lee, N. G., & Neal, J. C. (1992–1993). Reading Rescue: Intervention for a student "at promise." *Journal of Reading, 36,* 276–282.

Lowe, K., & Walters, J. (1991). The unsuccessful reader negotiating new perceptions. In E. Furniss & P. Green, (Eds.), *The literacy agenda: Issues for the 90's* (pp. 114–136). Portsmouth, NH: Heinemann.

Lyons, C. A., Pinnell, G. S., & DeFord, D. E. (1993). *Partners in learning: Teachers and children in Reading Recovery.* Portsmouth, NH: Heinemann.

Lyons, C. A. (1993). Interpreting teacher/student interactions in Reading Recovery from a Vygotskian perspective. *The Running Record, 5,* 1–9.

Morris, D., Ervin, C., & Conrad, K. (1996). A case study of middle school reading disability. *Reading Teacher, 49,* 368–379.

Paris, S. G., Lipson, M. Y., & Wixson, K. K. (1994). Becoming a strategic reader. In R. B. Ruddell, M. R. Ruddell, & H. Singer (Eds.), *Theoretical models and processes of reading* (4th ed.) (pp. 778–811). Newark, DE: International Reading Association.

Paris, S. G., Wasik, B. A., & Turner, J. C. (1991). The development of strategic readers. In P. D. Pearson, M. Kamil, R. Barr, & P. Mosenthal (Eds.), *Handbook of reading research* (Vol. 1) (pp. 609–640). White Plains, NY: Longman.

Resnick, L. B. (1983). Toward a cognitive theory of instruction. In S. Paris, G. Olson, & H. Stevenson (Eds.), *Learning and motivation in the classroom.* Hillsdale, NJ: Erlbaum.

Rowe, K. J. (1997). Factors affecting students' progress in reading: Key finding from a longitudinal study. In S. L. Swartz & A. F. Klein (Eds.), *Research in Reading Recovery.* Portsmouth, NH: Heinemann.

Schunk, D. H. (1995). Self-efficacy and education and instruction. In J. E. Maddux (Ed.), *Self-efficacy, adaptation, and adjustment: Theory, research, and application* (pp. 281–303). New York: Plenum Press.

Skarry, P. (1976). The waterbed mystery. In *Excursions* (pp. 84–85). Glenview, IL: Scott Foresman and Company.

Tharp, R. G., & Gallimore, R. (1988). *Rousing minds to life: Teaching, learning, and schooling in social context.* Melbourne, Australia: Cambridge University Press.

Vygotsky, L. S. (1978). *Mind in society: The development of higher psychological processes.* Cambridge, MA: Harvard University Press.

Walmsley, S. A., & Allington, R. L. (1995). Redefining and reforming instructional support programs for at-risk students. In R. L. Allington & S. A. Walmsley (Eds.), *No quick fix: Rethinking literacy programs in America's elementary schools* (pp. 19–44). New York: Teacher College Press.

Zimmerman, B. J. (1995). Self-efficacy and educational development. In A. Bandura (Ed.), *Self-efficacy in changing societies* (pp. 202–231). New York: Cambridge University Press.

Introduction to Section Two: Classroom Practices to Support Diverse Learners

This second section of the book offers an array of instructional elements for teachers to use in various preschool and elementary school instructional settings, with the intent of suggesting many possible ways to include diverse learners in effective learning engagements that thrive in environments that are rich and valuing of differences. The intent is to suggest to the reader a theoretical and classroom context for supporting the literacy learning of diverse children, then to provide examples of instructional techniques for the teacher that are consistent with the theory and useful in guiding literacy growth of the diverse learner.

First in this section is a chapter by Brad Walker, which offers a view of balanced literacy that highlights the teacher's ability to create a knowing, trusting, and empowering context for literacy learning. He suggests that three aspects of the classroom environment—physical, emotional, and instructional—be thoughtfully considered when building the classroom community. Walker cautions us to broaden our view of balanced literacy beyond the components of a framework to a situation that is based on knowing and appreciating the differences in all learners.

Second in this section, Hengameh Kermani shares conceptual understanding regarding the importance of preschool literacy learning from the emergent literacy perspective, with the
intent of helping us to see how this theory is connected to the
language and literacy development of young learners. She suggests to caregivers and preschool teachers that there are practical activities that are life centered and that will enrich and
support language and literacy development at home or in the
school setting. The suggestions will nurture the development
of young children from any background, but are particularly
relevant for enhancing opportunities for children in a group
setting when differences in children could be perceived as a
stumbling block rather than representative of the array of young
learners developing at their own pace and in their own way.

In the next chapter, Melissa Schulz introduces us to second-
grade children from two different cultural and linguistic backgrounds that are a part of a study she conducted in the context
of a changing school community experiencing an influx of children who came from similar middle-class socioeconomic backgrounds but very different cultural backgrounds. She explores
ways to learn about and use the cultural diversity of students'
home environments to create a rich classroom that supports
literacy learning for everyone by knowing the learner and the
family setting.

The last two chapters in this section focus on two powerful
classroom tools for supporting diverse learners in powerful
ways. First, Denise N. Morgan explores the use of writing for
diverse literacy learners, in that by writing about experiences
outside of school, all children in the classroom have opportunities to learn, grow, and appreciate the value of our diverse culture. Writing is a way to honor and recognize what children
bring to school. Writing extends learning through both the stories there are to tell and the understanding of the English print
system that may not yet be understood by young learners.

The last chapter, by Kathy R. Fox, also focuses on dual literacy learning but from the view of children's literature rather
than writing. Fox helps us to see the relationship between the

literacy-related value of reading aloud to children and the cultural value offered by the exploration of literature. She asserts that we can use multicultural literature, in particular, to help children see that we are more alike than we are different.

Chapter 4

Balanced Literacy
for Diverse Learners

Bradford Walker

"Can you help my son, David?"

"Help him with what?"

"With reading. He is going into ninth grade, and he can't read."

"Can't read anything?"

"Well, he is struggling."

"What are you doing now to help him?"

"We have hired a private tutor. It doesn't seem to be working."

"What is the tutor doing?"

"The tutor is asking him to memorize lists of vocabulary words. It isn't helping."

"Well, I could probably better give you suggestions if I could read with your son. "Could we plan a time to get together?"

This conversation took place between a concerned mother and a reading specialist. David's mother took him to the meeting. The specialist initially did written conversation with David and soon learned that David was, indeed, a struggling and reluctant user of print (see Figure 4:1).

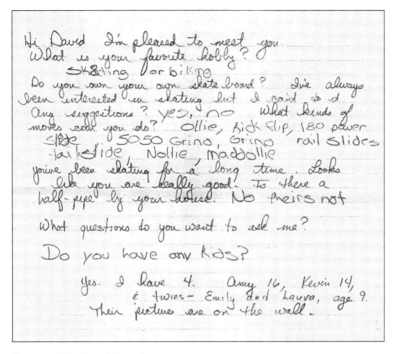

Figure 4:1   David's written conversation.

When children struggle, it is too easy to simply say, "He struggles because he doesn't have a large enough vocabulary," or, "His problem is a lack of understanding of phonics," or, "He is not progressing because his parents didn't read to him as a child." Instead of jumping to conclusions, the reading specialist continued to come to know David as a reader by asking questions and engaging in literacy tasks. The following are examples of her work.

She asked David the Burke Interview Questions (Harste, Short, & Burke, 1995). "David, when you are reading and you come to something you don't understand, what do you usually do?"

David responded, "Sound it out."

"Do you do anything else?"

"Ask the teacher."

"What if you are at home?"

"Ask my mom."

"What if you are alone?"

"I quit."

"Anything else you usually do when you are reading and you come to something you don't understand?"

"No."

The reading specialist continued, "Who is the best reader you know and why?"

"My mom. Because she knows all the words."

"Think about your mom. When she is reading, does she ever come to something she doesn't understand?"

"No."

Fortunately, David's mother was in the room with the reading specialist and said, "Oh, but David, I do. All the time."

David looked at his mother with big eyes and asked, "You do?"

His mother replied, "Yes, let me show you what I do."

David was a ninth-grade student who had a very limited number of strategies he could employ when he came to things he didn't understand while reading. He also had a crippling view of what the reading process was all about. He thought that good readers knew all the words and never came to something they didn't understand. Every time he read, he saw words he didn't know and came to things he didn't understand.

As the reading specialist continued to work with David, she had him read a short story by Tomie DePaola (1983) entitled, "The Legend of the Blue Bonnet." Below (Table 4:1) is a list of some of the miscues that David made as he read.

Table 4:1   David's Miscues

Text	David's Response
drought	drōt
Comanche	Cămōkē, Cŭmōkē, Cŭmănəkē
famine	feminine, fămīne
cared	carried
setting	settling
looked	took
valued	vald
possession	procession
tipis	tips, tīpīs
filled	flied

As she discussed the story with David after he had read it, the reading specialist learned that David knew that Comanche was the name of a Native-American tribe. She wondered why he didn't come up with that in his three attempts at the word as he read. The book is filled with pictures showing Native Americans. The other miscue that caught the specialist's eye was tipis. The sentence which contained the word was, "I'm sure it is not my new bow that the Great Spirits want," a warrior said. "Or my special blanket, a woman added; as everyone went to their tipis to talk and think over what the Great Spirits had asked." The picture showed several tipis with the people returning to them. Again, the specialist wondered why David didn't think, "Tips, tipis? That doesn't make sense. Oh, it's tipis."

At another time, David read *Faithful Elephants,* by Yukio Tsuchiya (1988). The specialist prepared a cloze exercise and asked David to read the paragraphs and tell her words or phrases that would go in the blanks. He was unable to do it.

It is easy to jump to conclusions. Considering the miscues, one might suggest that the best way to help David is to put him through a phonics program. Others might suggest that he needs more vocabulary exercises. Others might suggest that he needs comprehension help. Still others might lament the point that David is far below grade level—how did he ever get this far in the system?

What is needed is to truly come to know David as a reader and then begin to use all that we know about reading and how we learn to read to create engagements that will help him come to the understandings essential to proficient reading ability and to own the strategies that successful readers use. What is needed is a balanced perspective from which to support our students as they grow in literacy.

Introduction

More than ensuring that students simply receive instruction in a variety of preidentified areas constituting a literacy program, balanced literacy for diverse learners requires an in-depth understanding of the literacy processes, how children learn, the learners themselves, the environments which best support literacy growth, and the ways teachers can best help children as they move toward proficiency. Balanced literacy for diverse learners must take place under an overarching umbrella, providing teachers with a perspective of knowing, trusting, and empowering students. If not, efforts to provide balanced literacy can quickly become a program; a set of isolated experiences done to students in order to support literacy growth, rather than a total experience with literacy for meaningful purposes in an environment that supports risk taking, sharing, self-evaluation and reflection, and collaboration. A sense of community must be created, and confidence in the process, and in the abilities of teachers and students, must be evident.

If we are to be successful in our efforts to support literacy growth for diverse learners, we must bring to bear the total strength of all that we know about literacy and how to help children grow in their literacy proficiency. This includes all we know about literacy development, including deep understanding of the literacy processes, knowing our students, knowing how they learn and how to best support that learning, creating effective engagements that support growth, interacting with students in positive, supportive ways, and creating the kinds of environments in which this can all happen effectively. We utilize the vast body of knowledge that has been created over time.

Synonyms of "balanced" are stable, secure, and steady. Balanced literacy is a total package. It is not an approach. It is not a collection of nifty strategies that we guarantee will work. It is an implementation of all we know about how to effectively support literacy and literacy learning. It is more than just ensuring that students simply receive instruction in a variety of preidentified areas constituting a literacy program. Rather, it is a complete experience to include the necessary engagements within a supportive environment. To say one is using a balanced literacy approach suggests a shortsighted view of our responsibilities as educators. We might be more accurate to say that we are working from a balanced perspective. This suggests that we don't look to do a variety of things with our students but that we look at the whole child and at the whole literacy process.

Balanced literacy is so much more than a method or an approach. In many ways, it can be compared to preparing food. The end result of the preparation can be a delicious meal with all the tastes and presentations working together for one impressive, wonderful dining experience, or it can be a set of isolated tastes and presentations that create a negative experience—in which we may choose never to engage again—all based on the chef. The chef is the master who can take the raw ingredients and create the kind of experience that we value. So, to say that we are balanced in our literacy efforts because we teach phonics and we teach phonemic awareness and we have kids read real text and we work on comprehension is not nearly enough. That stance misses the power of a balanced literacy perspective. To say that we are balanced and that we are doing our part as educators is a surface-level look at what needs to be in place in order for success. We can do all the right kinds of teaching—introducing our students to the right kinds of strategies, but until we can put it all together in a balanced effort and orchestrate it as each child needs, when he or she needs it, we will not be successful with diverse learners. The following chart attempts to summarize this information.

Balanced Literacy	
What it is	**What it isn't**
▪ stable, steady work of a reading professional who is an expert in the field and brings all she knows to bear as she supports children as they learn	▪ method of teaching children to read
▪ perspective from which to work that allows us to know children as literate beings and identify possible next best steps in an effort to help them grow	▪ collection of nifty strategies and engagements
▪ something you live, not just do	▪ smorgasbord of activities from which we keep choosing until something works
▪ a philosophical stance toward teaching and learning literacy	▪ an excuse to not push the envelop on our ways of thinking about literacy
▪ ability to orchestrate all strategies, engagements, environments, interaction, etc., based on what we know about our students in effective support of their growth	▪ a way to try to appease the phonics wars and make peace with colleagues
▪ working to facilitate growth of the whole child as a literate being	▪ a way to cover our actions so we don't have to answer to failure
▪ working under the umbrella of knowing the true significance of what literacy can do in our lives, committed to ensure that our students have this blessing of literacy in their lives	▪ simply ensuring that we do phonics, as well as whole language, with a little bit of phonemic awareness thrown in
▪ understanding what proficiency is and creating a steady, consistent program of experiences that will best help students reach proficiency	▪ program of predetermined skills and activities; goals and objectives that cover all the aspects we now include in literacy
▪ knowing literacy and knowing kids and creating learning engagements that will make it happen	▪ making sure we cover the "five domains" of reading instruction
▪ making curricular decisions based on our students	▪ allowing curricular decisions to be made by individuals distant from our classroom and ignorant about our specific children

Pressley et al. (2002) have suggested that teachers who are successful in helping to produce proficient readers and writers are teachers who can take all the aspects of literacy learning and incorporate the teaching and learning engagements into an authentic experience. These teachers seem to be able to do this on the fly—noticing, and then taking advantage of, the numerous "teachable moments" that happen in our classrooms. This chapter argues that the success reported in the Pressley et al. (2002) studies happens because teachers are organized and prepared to utilize the power of a balanced literacy experience. These teachers can take advantage of the many teachable moments that occur because they know the process, they know their students, and they are working from a balanced literacy perspective of strength and have the knowledge base and ability to make it work.

Balanced literacy demands that certain elements be in place as part of our work with students. These elements include:

- understanding, and then ensuring, that the principles of language learning are in place and are part of the philosophical structure undergirding our efforts

- establishing a community of learners in our classrooms

- understanding and using essential/significant concepts of literacy teaching and learning

- conducting meaningful assessment

- developing exciting, inviting learning environments

Let's look at these elements, define them, and identify ways in which they can be implemented in our work with children.

Principles of Language Learning

Balanced literacy suggests that literacy learning in schools happens in an environment in which sound principles of learning are implemented. Teachers understand these principles and their significance in supporting children in their literacy growth, and they work hard to ensure that their work is built upon them. They organize their classrooms so that the principles are in place. They ensure that their interactions with students and the engagements that are created are also consistent with these principles. The principles illustrate a way of doing business in the classroom. Effective teachers strive to be consistent with these principles. The principles determine how we view our students and how we view ourselves and our roles as literacy educators.

Two structures that help us understand these significant principles are Cambourne's (1988) elements of learning and Burke's (Harste, Short, & Burke,

1995) Authoring Cycle. Both models attempt to illustrate the significance of the principles, as well as identify specific ways in which they are implemented in our classrooms.

Cambourne's Elements of Learning

Brian Cambourne (1988) researched elements that seemed to facilitate very young children learning to speak. The same elements highlight principles that will facilitate learning at any age, including diverse learners. Cambourne suggests that immersion, demonstration, expectation, responsibility, use, approximation, and response are elements that are conducive to learning language. This author argues that these same elements are essential elements for all learning and must be part of the foundation for our work in supporting literacy. Each of the elements will be defined, and examples will illustrate how they might guide what we do in the classroom.

Immersion

Cambourne (1988, pp. 67–68) suggests that "learners need to be immersed in text of all kinds." Children are best able to learn to talk or read or write when they are surrounded with a variety of texts inviting them to use the texts for a variety of reasons. In our classrooms, we will be more effective when we can flood the environment with text as Harste (1995) puts it. Do our classrooms truly include a variety of texts that invite our students into literate engagements because they want to learn or understand? Do our classrooms create situations in which students cannot resist the invitation to use literacy to get their needs met, to conduct the business of the class, and to explore questions they have created? Most classrooms have textbooks and library books, but do we also have magazines, newspapers, notes, letters, charts and graphs, journals, pictures, e-mail, and, perhaps, text messaging? Many classrooms have large rooms filled with leveled texts, but do we also have significant amounts of other kinds of texts to be able to say that our students are immersed with text of all kinds and that it is organized in ways that make it inviting and possible with which to engage.

Another important aspect of immersion is that in a child's world of learning to speak, the immersion is done in a context of meaning. Everywhere the child looks, he or she can see the meaningful context in which language is used. The two are matched. As we create immersion in our classrooms, we must be careful to ensure that meaningful contexts are part of that immersion. To have students use literacy to perform tasks that are not meaningful creates inauthentic engagements and is not supportive of learning.

Demonstration

"Learners need to receive many demonstrations of how texts are constructed and used" (Cambourne, 1988, pp. 67–68). Children are supported in their learning to talk because they are usually in a position from which they can see numerous demonstrations of others using language for a variety of purposes. Children see and hear others using language to get their needs met. Additionally, these demonstrations are always seen within a meaningful context. Children can see the context in which language is used, as well as the myriad ways in which it is used. Because the demonstrations happen in a meaningful context, children are better able to understand it and to see how they might be able to utilize language in similar contexts. Do our classrooms take advantage of the numerous demonstrations that can naturally be part of any classroom? Do students see other students reading a variety of texts for a variety of purposes? Do they see other students writing in a variety of genres for a variety of purposes? Do they see other significant people in their lives reading and writing, speaking and listening? What about their teacher, other teachers, or the principal? What about the librarian, the custodians, parents, or people in the community? Demonstrations must also show students successful literacy strategies that they might like to incorporate, as well as successful ways to problem solve as they learn and as they learn to read and write. Demonstrations must also help children come to know what literacy will do for them (Graves, 1991).

An elementary school principal decided that he was going to substitute in every classroom in his school as a way to get to know his teachers and students. When a teacher would call in requesting a substitute teacher because they were sick, he quickly checked his calendar. If he had no meetings or other commitments that couldn't be rescheduled, he would volunteer to be the substitute. The very first classroom he substituted in was one of the first-grade classrooms in the school. As he was ready to begin the day, Lorelie, one of the first graders, asked, "What are you doing here?" He replied, "I'm going to be the teacher today." Her candid response was a great invitation to reflection. She said, "I didn't know a principal could be a teacher."

This principal thought long and hard about her response. He decided that if his students looked at him in this way, he had better change the way he did things. He wondered if his students would also say, "I didn't know a principal was a reader, a writer, a learner." He began to visit classrooms more often. He visited to work with students—to set the demonstration that he was a learner, a reader, and a writer.

A middle school teacher reported being concerned with several students who seemed to have totally given up on learning. In discussing the problem, her team of teachers had decided that perhaps these 4 or 5 students could benefit from creating time to just read good literature and discuss it in natural, meaningful ways. The language arts teacher created some time in her schedule to go get these students, have them select the books they wanted to read, and then discuss them in the ways the students desired, letting their questions and interests guide the discussion. One of the boys identified was actually under house arrest. He wore an ankle bracelet so that law-enforcement authorities could always know where he was. He went to his first meeting kicking and screaming. He had already been in enough "pull-out programs" in his school career. The teacher persisted, and soon the young man realized that this was different. He had ownership, and he was being empowered. The teachers learned that the new structure was being successful a few months later. This boy was returning to his classroom from the lunchroom. He noticed a boy coming to lunch who was carrying a copy of one of the Harry Potter books in his arms. The reluctant reader went up to the boy carrying the Harry Potter book.

"You reading that book?" he asked.

"Yes, I am," replied the other boy.

"It's a great read, isn't it," responded our student.

Demonstrations can come from everywhere. We should ensure that we are identifying, and then taking advantage of, all of the demonstrations that surround us.

Demonstrations can also come from the books that children read. A first-grade teacher was moving around the room as her children wrote. She sat down next to one student to conduct a writing conference. As the child read his piece, she noticed that he had used a hyphen in one of the sentences. The hyphen was used correctly. Knowing that she hadn't taught that convention to her students, she asked the little boy how he had learned how to use a hyphen. The student answered very nonchalantly. "Oh, I saw it in a book I was reading."

Expectation

"Expectations of those to whom learners are bonded are powerful coercers of behavior." (Cambourne, 1988, pp. 67–68). Most adults treat children as if they are going to be successful in learning to talk. In fact, it happens so naturally, that we just assume that children are going to be successful. Because of these natural expectations, children are not overly concerned about learning to speak. They just jump in and make it happen. The expectation that it will happen helps them, and it also helps those around them to interact with them in supportive ways. When a child attempts to use language to ask a question or explain an observation, we treat them as capable, competent language learners and carry on the conversation even in the face of inaccurate or unconventional choices of words or grammar. Their attempts to use language are often met with more language than they might have expected because we continue on with the conversation. This sends a very clear message to the child that we approve of their trying to use language, that we will help them as needed, and that we hope they will continue to use language, because interacting with them is such a pleasurable experience for all of us. What about our classrooms? Do we go about our work from the perspective that we know all our children will learn to read and write? Do they know our feelings? Do we treat our students as the capable, competent language learners they are? Do they know of our trust and confidence in them as learners? Do they benefit from our excitement that stems from knowing they will be successful? Having high expectations for our students is one thing, treating them as capable, competent learners is a necessary addition to that stance. Working tirelessly to ensure that they are successful in their attempts at literacy growth completes the action, showing our true expectations and trust in them.

A teacher was preparing for midterm progress reports that were to be sent home to parents. She liked to hold a quick learning conference with her students before she sent the information home. As she began the conference with a new student to the school, she asked the girl what grade she thought she had earned in their reading class. The girl said, "A 'D'. I always make Ds in my reading class." In fact, that was the exact grade the teacher was planning to give her on the report. Instead, however, the teacher replied to this student, "That's interesting; I was planning to give you a 'B.'" The girl earned a B for the rest of the semester.

Responsibility

Cambourne (1988, pp. 68–68) suggests that "learners need to make their own decisions about when, how, and what 'bits' to learn in any learning task. Learners who lose the ability to make decisions are 'depowered.'" As much as we like to think that we can control what our students learn, when they learn it, and how they learn it, this belief can be inhibiting of the very learning we hope to support. All learners have the responsibility and the choice to attend to whatever aspect of the learning engagement they desire. We cannot control that. Even though we might be talking to an infant, they might be attending to the music coming from the radio, to the soothing words of their mother who is talking to a neighbor at the other side of the room, or to the sounds of our words, not to the words themselves. It is the same in the classroom. Understanding the need for responsibility invites us to think differently about time on task and on the flow of the lessons we teach. We must understand this as a natural part of the learning process and use it in ways that empower the learners. Providing ownership is an effective way of helping learners become the kind of problem solvers and independent learners we want them to be. They must learn to take responsibility for their learning. Choice in materials to read, choice in the ways to interact with others about the texts read, and choice in the questions to structure continued learning are all decisions learners must make and for which they must accept responsibility. Planning for a variety of invitations, all of which will engage our learners in literacy, can be very motivating.

Giving ownership requires a great deal of "letting go" on the part of educators. We are often not comfortable with this. Every lesson plan ought to include a section on ideas for giving ownership. Educators should ask, "Where can I let go?" "Where can I present choice as a matter of supporting ownership and the taking of responsibility?" People who work one-on-one with students in helping them learn to read quickly learn the difference between saying, "Let's read this story today," and, "Which one of these five books would you like to read today?" Allowing students to choose from a variety of books on the same topic, for example, will also help them feel more excited to read. At times when reading the same book as a class is desirable, students should have a choice in how they would like to respond to the text and how they would like to share what they have learned. Given ownership, children feel empowered and in control of their learning. To give ownership also shows students that we trust them and that we value what they can do.

Use

"Learners need time and opportunity to use, employ, and practice their developing control in functional, realistic, nonartificial ways" (Cambourne, 1988, pp. 67–68). Children learning to talk practice their skills in real ways—they talk for authentic purposes. They use language to get their needs met. The authentic purpose takes precedence. Children don't approach an adult and say, "Can we talk so that I can practice my speaking?" They just jump in and talk because it is natural and necessary to getting their needs met. We might ask how much time is spent in our classroom for using literacy for real reasons. We send a clear message by the amount of time we create, the ways we do or don't guard that time, and the authenticity of it. If students know they are reading silently, for example, to practice their skills as readers, they get one message. If they know that we have created time for them to explore the world through reading because we value learning and because we want to learn with them, they receive a totally different message. If we are constantly telling students to practice and to read so they will get better at reading, we might very well be sabotaging our own efforts. There are so many authentic reasons to read. We should help students understand what reading can do for them, not allow reading in school to deteriorate to simply a means of getting good grades or good scores on the end-of-grade test. Reading isn't really a subject in and of itself. It is a tool for learning and exploring. A group of fourth graders were asked to write what reading meant to them. Before they began the assignment, one fourth grader said, "Do you mean real reading or school reading?" What an insightful question. There should be little, if any, difference between the reading students do in school and the reading they do outside of school.

In a similar vein, the time spent using language must somehow be safe time. It must be time in which the ever-present grades are put on hold. Learners need safe time or rough-draft time to use language and to experiment with its many aspects, knowing that they won't be marked down because of mistakes and that they won't be evaluated. They need to interact with us in meaningful ways, because we all want to communicate and learn together.

Durkin (1987) shocked the reading community years ago with her research in which she tried to document just how much time students spent in schools actually reading. Her report that children in elementary schools spent an average of 8–10 minutes a day of actual reading provided an opportunity for deep soul searching and reflection. Even though her study took place several years ago, we might benefit from asking similar questions today. We seem to spend a great deal of time each day in reading instruction. How much time do our students spend each day actually reading for authentic purposes?

Approximation

"Learners must be free to approximate the desired model—mistakes are essential for learning to occur" (Cambourne, 1988, pp. 67–68). Smith (2004) suggests that when the consequences of being wrong are too great, learners will stop trying so that they simply will not be wrong. As children learn to speak, their miscues or approximations are encouraged and almost celebrated. We continue to treat them as capable, competent speakers and carry on the conversation. These children are not marked down, given special minilessons, or sent to remedial training and extra practice. Miscues are expected and encouraged as natural parts of the learning process. Risk taking is a requirement for learning. If students are not willing to take risks, they will be less effective learners. Do our classrooms encourage trying and risk taking? What are the consequences for being wrong in our classrooms? Do our students have rough-draft time for reading, writing, speaking? In other words, we know the value of time to write a rough draft of a paper. That value is lessened greatly if the rough draft is somehow graded. We take away from the author, the opportunity to experiment with words, and identify those that perfectly help create the tone he or she wants. We destroy the opportunity to experiment with different ways to paint the picture desired. Likewise, in reading and speaking. Do our students have time to explore strategies and possible connections and understanding and problem solving without being penalized when they come up short, according to our conventions? Perhaps we could be more effective in supporting literacy growth if we created more rough-draft time for students and allowed them the opportunity to problem solve in an ungraded, unpunished situation.

In an effort to support the learning of her students, a second-grade teacher had assigned her students to use each of their spelling words in a sentence. Laura (see Figure 4:3) seemed to enjoy this assignment because she loved to write. Her sentences were always very colorful and included a great deal of detail. The voice she used as she wrote was good evidence that she was enjoying this opportunity to write. Her sentences often stretched to two or three as she attempted to finish a conversation or explain an idea she had started in her sentence to use one of her spelling words. The second-grade teacher was excited to see this type of writing. She very much enjoyed reading Laura's sentences as she graded the assignment. Feeling the need to use this assignment to help students learn in as many areas as possible, she marked down for mistakes in punctuation, grammar, and the spelling of all words, not just the spelling words which were the focus for the week. Laura would often get an S or S+ for her sentences and the correct writing of the spelling words but would receive an N (Needs improvement) for punctuation, spelling of other words, or even spacing of the letters and words. As time went on, Laura's sentences got shorter and shorter. After several months, the teacher was compelled to add more instructions to the assignments. "Each sentence must contain at least six words and must also contain at least one adjective." Interestingly, Laura's initial sentences went far beyond even these criteria.

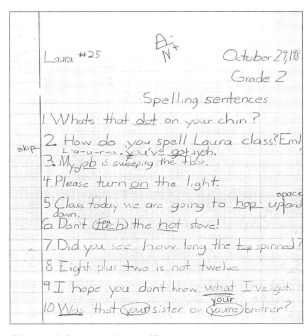

Figure 4:3 Laura's spelling sentences.

A university professor had been teaching reading in a second-grade classroom. At the end of the lesson, the teacher asked the professor if he would like to conduct some reading conferences with students. He readily agreed. The first little girl came for her conference. He chatted briefly with her about her reading and the kinds of books she liked. She then read several pages in the book she was reading at the time. After finishing, the professor and the students discussed the story. The professor then thanked the girl for reading with him and complimented her on the way she read with expression. As she got up to return to her seat, she asked, "What grade did I get?" The professor was surprised by this question and said, "Well, what grade do you think you earned?" The student answered, "I think I got a 'B.'" "Why?" "Because I missed one word." The student had, in fact, made a miscue on one word as she read. The professor was able to get a quick look at how miscues were being handled in that classroom.

Response

"Learners must receive feedback from exchanges with more knowledgeable others. Response must be relevant, appropriate, timely, readily available, non-threatening, with no strings attached" (Cambourne, 1988, pp. 67–68). Feedback is clearly a necessary part of the learning process. Children benefit from feedback as they learn to speak because it is given by someone engaged in the conversation, and the feedback is often done in the meaningful context of the conversation. It also seems to be given in doses that don't distract from the conversation and which support continued use of language.

Literature-response groups, in which children read and respond to books together, can offer excellent feedback. Dialog journals or letters to teachers can also provide a setting for effective feedback. Conferences provide a wonderful opportunity for teachers to give feedback to students. Teachers might benefit from thinking about the effort that students expend in completing assignments. If a simple checkmark with a comment of "good" seems to be sufficient feedback, perhaps the assignment was not authentic and could be replaced by something more meaningful. Students want, and deserve, feedback that will support and stretch if the engagement is meaningful to them.

One father reports reading his middle school daughter's language arts journal. Students were assigned to write in the journal every day. They had to write at least one page each day. The father thought this was a great assignment. As he read the journal, which had 2 or 3 months worth of entries at the time, he was shocked to find that his daughter had stopped her writing at the end of the page even if it was in the middle of the sentence. He also found that she would simply copy the words to popular songs on the radio or nursery rhymes in the middle of the page. When he asked his daughter about her work, she replied, "Oh, well, she never reads them and she never responds." Further inspection revealed checkmarks at the top of each page with no comments from the teacher.

Contrast this experience with feedback from a teacher who uses the opportunity to respond to students from the perspective of one who is also keeping a journal—one who responds by sharing her own insights, connections, and questions. This middle school student would not have wasted her time writing a page just to write a page and would have received the feedback that would have helped her grow as a writer.

Carolyn Burke's Authoring Cycle

Another view of the principles undergirding our work in supporting literacy growth comes from the Authoring Cycle (see Figure 4:4) created by Carolyn Burke and Kathy Short (Harste, Short, & Burke, 1995). They have created a view of the writing process that holds implications for what we do in our classrooms to support literacy learning. In fact, they posit that this Authoring Cycle is really a model for curriculum. While the authoring cycle seems to be directly focused to writing, the principles which allow the authoring cycle to be so powerful in supporting writing can be applied in all learning situations. These principles can help us to be very effective in supporting the diverse learners with whom we work (Harste, Short, & Burke; 1995, p. 40).

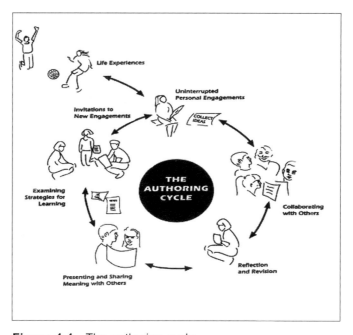

Figure 4:4   The authoring cycle.

Life Experiences

The process suggests that all writing must start with what authors know best; their own life experiences. They will write more about those things for which they "ache with passion" (Fox, 1993) and those things about which they know the most. These are typically found in their life experiences. As teachers, we must show our students that we value their life experiences and that we want them to write about those experiences. We must also help students come to value their own life experiences as well. Additionally, students must be given the time and support to connect the concepts they are learning to their own lives and what they know. This is the process that generates the questions supporting their wondering, exploring, and coming to know their world. As students know that we value their life experiences, they also come to know that we value them as individuals and that we are excited to work with them.

Often, children will say that there is nothing good to write about. What they are really saying is that, "Nothing extraordinary, nothing worthy of writing about, has ever happened in my life." We must help students know that we value who they are and what they have to say. Truly, every child has important things to say. One teacher handles the complaint that there is nothing good to write about in two ways. First, she writes about her own life—the little things that happen every day and shares those with her students. Second, she refuses to provide prompts for her students. She realizes that prompts take ownership away from her students and will, most often, result in students writing about things for which they have no "passion." She encourages her students to keep a list of potential topics about which to write. When she hears the often-used statement, "There isn't anything good to write about," she responds with a series of questions:

"What do you do at home when you go home from school?"

"Nothing."

"How do you do nothing? Do you just stand in a corner or something?"

The child laughs and says, "Well, I like to watch TV."

"What is your favorite TV show?"

"I like to watch Nick, Jr."

"Could you write about that show or something that happened on the show?"

"I don't want to write about that show."

"I didn't ask you if you wanted to write about the show, I asked if you could. Could you write about that?"

"I guess."

"Please write it on your list of topics."

"What else do you usually do at home?"

"I like to ride my bike."

"Tell me about your bike . . . could you write about it?"

"I don't want to write about my bike."

"I didn't ask you if you wanted to, I asked you if you could. Could you?"

In this conversation, the teacher is not taking ownership away from the student. She is also not letting him shirk the responsibility of all authors—to determine the topic about which they will write. She has also legitimized the small things that happen in all of our lives and possible topics for our writing. It is too easy to simply provide a prompt to our children. But, in the long run, that often makes them dependent on us, and it robs them of the opportunity to write about the things that truly matter to them. It can often rob them of the authentic reasons to write.

Uninterrupted Time

Next in the process is uninterrupted writing time. This is time set aside on a regular basis and guarded consistently, in which students can write, reflect, revise, and edit. This is their time to identify significant aspects of life about which they want to write and then explore various genres and various ways of expressing their connections. This time is vital. An extension to all learning can quickly be made. Students need time in which learning is to happen. We can't force the issue. We can't hurry through the learning process just so that we can get through the curriculum. Students might get through the required curriculum, but they will not have time to make the connections needed to sustain literacy growth and effective use. Time allows for rough draft or risk-free thinking and doing. This is the time during which students experiment and try out the concepts learned in the classroom. Students might explore the impact of writing their thoughts in a new genre or writing from a different perspective or using different words. Pacing guides can inhibit effective learning. Schedules that are too rigid and that do not allow sufficient time in which learning can take place are also counterproductive. Students need time to think and make connections, time to explore different ways of saying things, and different ways of looking at the world. They do this when the topics are meaningful, and they have the time to do it in a meaningful manner. During this time, it is essential that students save their writing in a writing folder. This sends a message that the process is valued. We don't have to complete every writing project we start. We can set it aside and come back to it later, if we feel the need or the desire.

As students come to know that they will have dedicated time in which to write and they learn the schedule of that time, they begin to think about it outside of class. They contemplate what they will write or how they might change something they have written. They puzzle over how to make it say just exactly what they want to say. Megan, a fifth-grade student, reported that she got her best ideas for writing just as she was getting into bed. She started to keep a notepad on the nightstand and would quickly jot down her ideas before falling asleep. The next morning, she would rip of the page of notes and take it to school.

A writing workshop structure is one good way to provide the time needed. Each classroom will be different, but time set aside for writing will range from 20 minutes or so in kindergarten to 60 minutes in fifth grade and up. Teachers in middle school and high school are constrained with numerous other requirements and may only be able to provide time to write every other day or two times a week. The key is consistency. During the writing time, students would be found working at writing, revising, participating in Author's Circle, editing, or publishing their work.

Author's Circle allows the writers to request and receive feedback from peers. This is the time in the process where the author shares a piece of writing and asks respected others for feedback. The feedback can highlight effective aspects of the writing, questions from the readers, and suggestions for improvement. Learning is social, and collaboration is a powerful way to support learning. This helps to facilitate a sense of community. Providing effective, supportive feedback takes time. We cannot shortchange this process. Giving meaningful, helpful feedback is more than simply assigning a grade. It is more than quickly putting a checkmark on the top of the paper and a quick "nice job" underneath it. Responding also takes time. It requires us to know our students in order to know the kind of feedback that will best help them at this specific point in time. We need to know them and know the best next steps we are striving to support. Feedback allows students to check their understanding of the world against the backdrop of significant others. It gives them a mirror through which they can gauge their own progress and see the impact their writing and thinking has on others.

Participants in an Author's Circle must work hard to listen to the piece and give meaningful feedback. Authors learn to ask for the specific feedback they are looking for. For example, "I need help with my ending. I like my story, but I can't seem to find a powerful way to end it." "Tell me what you feel as you read my poem. I want to know if you feel the way I hope my readers will feel." Students often learn to talk about what they liked best about a piece, to ask honest questions they had as a reader, and then to give suggestions that might improve the piece. Some teachers ask participants to take a notepad to the

Author's Circle in order to remember things they might wish to share with the author. One teacher continues to monitor the effectiveness of the Author's Circles in his classroom by being a participant on a regular basis but also by asking some questions as an Author's Circle is finished. He asks the author, "Did you get the help you needed?"

"Yes, they all said they like it."

"What specific comments did they make or what suggestions did they give?"

"Well, they just said they liked it."

"Okay, we need to reconvene the group." Calling those students back together, he states, "We didn't do our job. We haven't given John the feedback he deserves and needs as an author. Let's try it again."

Revision

After sharing and then receiving feedback, the author determines what, if anything, needs to be revised in the piece. This is an opportunity to rethink one's own understandings and positions on topics. Perhaps it is in the revising process that the greatest growth can be seen. This is the hard-work time, the time when students struggle with making their writing say what they want it to say. It is the time when students work hard to ensure that their writing produces the feelings they wish to evoke. It is the time when they sweat over painting the exact picture they wish to paint. It allows the learner to ground his or her thinking in the realities of a community of learners. It also allows the learner to fine-tune their thinking and to put their ideas in final form, taking what they learned from sharing their ideas with other.

One mother tells of her excitement when her fourth-grade son reported that a story he had written was going to be published in the school newsletter in the next week. The day the newsletter was to come home, she was in class at the local university. By the time she returned home, her son was already in bed. She expected to see the newsletter on the table. Not finding it there, she went to look in his room. She couldn't see it anywhere. She did notice, however, her son's pants resting on his chair. She picked them up to hang them up and found the newsletter folded up inside his pocket. She quickly read the story and was very pleased with how well he had written. In the morning, her son said nothing about the story while they were eating breakfast. Finally, the mother asked the son why he hadn't said anything about the story when he had been so excited about it the day before. She mentioned how good she thought it was. Her son's sad reply was, "But it's not my story. Ms. Barker changed it when she typed it up." We have to allow the ownership on how revisions are made to stay where it belongs—in the hands of the author.

Editing

Once the piece is ready for publication, editing allows the author to use the conventions of language to ensure that the piece is as readable as possible. It allows the author to put the writing in conventional forms in order to enhance the understanding. It is an opportunity to fine-tune our understanding and to be able to express it effectively to others. Editing provides a very effective setting in which to help students learn how to use the conventions of our language. Its place in the authoring cycle is not by chance. To deal with conventions after an author has worked with his or her piece and taken it to the point where it is doing what the author desired, helps an author keep conventions in their proper place. It avoids pitfalls of students thinking that since they made mistakes in spelling or in using commas, they aren't good writers or they have nothing of value to say.

A fifth-grade teacher was helping a student edit her piece. She had included lots of dialogue in her story but had not used quotation marks. The teacher asked an honest question. She said, "I am having a difficult time understanding who is saying what. Is there a way you can show your readers who is talking and exactly what they are saying?"

The student answered, "Oh, it's those little 'thingies,'" showing the quotation marks with her hands.

The teacher then said, "Yes. We call those things quotation marks. Let me show you how they work." A very effective learning opportunity had been taken advantage of.

Publishing

Publication allows the students to take their ideas and make them public. This facilitates the learning process as the communication process. It is different than sharing what the student knows is a rough draft. It allows them to share ideas in a format that has been finished. It builds confidence. This part of the process happens as the writers make their writing public. It is always a challenge to share with others the things that are so personal. And yet, this sharing, this collaboration, is so vital for the learning process. It allows us to enter into the thought collective of our colleagues. It invites others into the learning process. It supports the continued learning of everyone. Interestingly, if students are never able to share their work, their learning, the classroom quickly becomes a narrow two-way interaction between the teacher and individual students. This becomes limiting and stifling. It is nonmotivating. It is a way of celebrating the total process.

Celebration

Publishing is a celebration. The celebration lends support to writers and learners and sends an additional message of trust and acceptance. To be published suggests that the author's ideas and ways of presenting them are valued and accepted. It is a great way of inviting students into the learning club (Smith, 2004). Publication is also a very strong invitation to reflection about the process and more writing and learning. Celebration gives purpose for the writing and learning. The author can see how his or her ideas have added to the total group understanding and how others like their ideas and/or the ways they have said them.

Angie, a fifth grader, had written this note (see Figure 4:5) to her teacher.

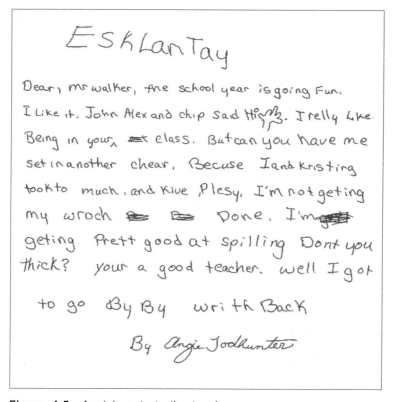

Figure 4:5   Angie's note to the teacher.

She was excited about the opportunity to write a note and express some of her thoughts. The teacher could have focused on several different areas, including several misspelled words or the need for punctuation. He chooses, however, to respond to the content of the note and sent the following note back to Angie. "Hi, Angie. Thanks for your note. Say hi to your brothers for me. You are getting better at spelling and I can see it too. Keep up the good work."

Angie was in a classroom in which the teacher tried to ensure that the above discussed principles were in place. During writing time one day in January, Angie announced to her teacher that she wanted to write a story about her grandpa. The teacher said that that sounded like an excellent idea and that he was excited to read it when she had finished. The next thing Angie did was to return to her table and begin to talk with her classmates. The teacher moved closer to the table and heard Angie ask her friends, "If you were going to interview your grandfather, what questions would you ask?" They generated an impressive list of questions, including what chores he had to do as a young boy, what punishment he received when he had done something wrong, what his hobbies were, and so forth.

The following week, Angie had apparently interviewed her grandfather and had already started her story. It began, "My grandpa is a pretty neat guy. I want to tell you about him. When he was in fifth grade, he was the best marble player in the school. If he was playing and returned home late, he would get whipped with a willow and he had to chop firewood in the dark."

About that same time, Angie checked a book out of the library. It was entitled *The Bronze Bow* by Elizabeth George Speare (1961). It is a Newbery Award book and is quite sophisticated. The fact that Angie chose this book to read is quite amazing. She was a struggling reader and writer and had been in Chapter 1/Title 1 programs for her entire school experience. The book has no pictures and is quite long. Angie's teacher wondered if he should ask Angie to put the book back and get something that was more on her level, but he decided against that. Angie later told him that it was hard reading and that she didn't understand it all but was getting the main idea.

The book begins like this:

A boy stood on the mountain path overlooking the sea. He was a tall boy, with little trace of youth in his lean, hard body. At eighteen Daniel bar Jamin was unmistakably a Galilean, with the bold features of his countrymen, the sun-browned skin, and the brilliant dark eyes that could light with fierce patriotism and blacken with swift anger.

About 1 week later, Angie came to class and said, "I have a new way to start my story."

A boy stood on the mountain path. He was tall and handsome with blonde hair and eyes as blue as the summer sky. His name was George. George Brailsford. But as a little boy, he was called Leonard. The mountain path was a special place for Leonard because it led to his Uncle Hazel's ranch up Hobble Creek canyon. On the side of the trail it had a wicked, rushing river. On the other side of the trail were big boulders. Leonard lived in Springville, in a small cabin in the east area. He thought to himself, "I'd better be getting home." He began to walk, dragging a stick behind him leaving a line in the dirt trail. He had to hurry because if he was late he would get whipped with a willow and if he played late he would have to chop firewood in the dark.

Angie continued her writing and revising for 4 months and published her story about her grandfather in May. She entitled her story, "One in a Million." The last sentence in her seven-page, single-spaced story was, "They got help from the doctor once again, and Leonard recovered and went up on the mountain path, but now he was a man."

Angie's teacher wondered what would have happened had he assigned every student in his class to write a story about his or her grandparents. He was sure that he would have received 30 half-page stories about grandparents and probably as many questions about whether this was good enough or long enough. He never heard those questions from Angie. She was writing something for which she "ached with passion." She had her own purpose and her own audience. She was writing this piece for her grandfather and for her family. The power of the principles of language learning had clearly supported Angie in making huge gains in her literacy growth.

The Authoring Cycle in Another Discipline

Another way to illustrate the power of these principles is to show how they apply to learning in all areas. Let's look at these principles as they apply to learning long division in math. For learning to be effective, we must be able to connect it to what we already know and to our past experiences (life experiences). The teacher helps students understand the usefulness of long division in solving everyday problems, such as what gas mileage their family is getting from their car or how much money they have to spend on their vacation each day. Students come to know that long division also involves subtraction and multiplication. Giving students uninterrupted time to explore the notions of long division allows them to make further connections and to identify questions they want to explore (uninterrupted time). This rough-draft time allows students to try the process and see how it works and how effective they might be in using it. This rough-draft time is risk free—there is no penalty for miscues. Students are free to look for other applications and to articulate their understanding of the process. Once this is completed, students receive input from their peers as they share what they think they have learned (Author's Circle). This allows them to gain new perspectives, and they see ways their peers have used the process as they listen to the connections that others have made. Students then need some time to attend to the differences they have noticed between their connections and understandings and those shared by peers and others (revision). This allows students time to rethink what they have learned and to attend to new questions that have been generated about the process. Next, students share what they have learned (publication). This allows students to show their understanding in a more formal way. It could be through the test or through a written description of their learning. Students celebrate their success, which is an invitation to more learning and more application of the newly obtained skills.

Establishing a Community of Learners in our Classrooms

Frank Smith's (2004) notion of a learning community gives solid understanding of the power of community in literacy learning. He reminds us that when we become a member of a club, other members quickly take us under their wings and help us "learn the ropes." They help us understand the importance of certain procedures and concepts. They show us how to problem solve, what to expect, and what we are trying to accomplish. They mentor us until we are successful members of the group. They show confidence in us and treat us as capable, competent members of the club. They interact with us in supportive ways, knowing that even though we might not possess skills at the levels of mature members when we join the club, we certainly will be able to reach those levels through our membership in the club. There is no criticizing, ridiculing, or belittling. They welcome us into the club and allow us to participate in the club as full-fledged members—participating in meaningful, significant ways. They convey this feeling by their actions and by the ways in which they interact with us. We feel comfortable in the club and enjoy club activities. Motivation is not an issue because our time in the club is fruitful, productive, and enjoyable. Simply analyzing our own classrooms against this standard would be most instructive. Do our students feel comfortable in our schools? Have we been successful in establishing a supportive learning community? Is time in our classrooms productive, fruitful, enjoyable, and exciting? In reality, literacy is all of these things. In the everyday lives of our students, literacy is always meaning-ful, productive, enjoyable, and exciting because they are using literacy to an-swer their questions and to learn about their world.

In a learning club, members feel safe. They know that when they aren't sure, there will be someone to hold their hands as they begin to take the risks neces-sary to learning. They feel safe, not threatened. They know mistakes are a natural part of learning. They see, not competition, but support and colearners around them. This sense of community—of all learners working together to support each other in their growth and learning—is comforting, powerful, and motivating.

These principles dictate everything about our classrooms, the engagements we create, the ways we interact with students, the ways we assess, and even what we call success.

Educators might benefit from reflection about elements of supportive com-munities. From day one, educators need to be about developing and building trust. It can be helpful to ensure that we don't grade everything—that we provide some safe, personal time to think and relax. Time will allow students to make the connections that are essential to learning. Communities focus on positive aspects of learners. Students are helped to see what they can do and the many ways they are being successful, not always reminded of the areas in which they fall short of expectations. Heidi Mills (1990) uses the term "three plusses and a wish" to guide our work with students (Mills & Clyde, 1990). As we work with them, we can be supportive of their work if we always identify three as-pects that are positive before inviting them to focus on an area of suggested growth. The term *wish* evokes positive attitudes and an invitation for further learning. As we allow students to engage in meaningful ways and allow them to act as if they are proficient readers and writers, we can do much to further their growth. As they use literacy in this fashion, they will come to know, as Graves (1991) suggests, what literacy can do for them. Then, supporting them be-comes a different process. Graves has also suggested that schools need to slow down so that kids can hurry up.

One teacher reports the impact of community in her classroom. Each year, students at her school were invited to submit stories and articles they had written as part of the school's young author's contest. Winners from the school were submitted to the state. The winners there were published in a book and distributed throughout the state. One girl in the class, Megan, had won the contest every year since her kindergarten year. Other fifth-grade students voiced concern over the fact that she always won and that her writing was always used as examples of excellent writing. In this fifth-grade class, however, a commu-nity of learners had been created. All students shared their writing and had their successes celebrated. The teacher made sure that each child had a chance to shine. She used the writing of all students as demonstrations of one strategy or another. As a child finished reading his or her piece, the class discussed its strengths and gave meaningful feedback. No one was singled out as the best. Rather, everyone's strengths were identified and highlighted. Often, the teacher would refer a writer to another student in the classroom. During a writing conference, she might say, "Your beginning reminds me of the story Johnny shared last week. You might want to talk with him and share notes about these kinds of beginnings."

When it came time for the young author's contest, Megan told her teacher, "I don't think I am going to win the contest this year. There are so many great writers in our classroom."

Essential/Significant Concepts of Literacy Teaching and Learning

We will be more effective in our efforts to support literacy growth if we are also cognizant of significant concepts dealing with literacy. While the purpose of this chapter is not to explain these concepts in depth, a short treatise of the concepts will help illustrate the point. We will be more effective in supporting diverse learners if we understand these concepts and understand how they impact the students with whom we work. Among those concepts are an understanding of the reading and writing processes. What happens in the minds of the reader when he or she is reading? What happens in the minds of the writer when he or she is writing? What happens in the mind of the learner when he or she is learning? What connections are being made? How are those connections being made? What questions are being asked? What is it that literacy does for us? What is it that literacy does for me that invites me to continue to engage and use it in my life?

What are the cueing systems that are involved in the process of reading, and how do proficient readers understand and use those processes? What problems must be solved in reading, and how do proficient readers solve them? What problems must be solved in writing, and how do proficient writers solve them?

What do proficient readers and writers look like? What do they do? What characteristics define them? How do they employ their craft? How do they improve their craft? What strategies do they employ? What are the component parts that make up effective readers? What does a proficient writer look like? What strategies do they employ as they write? What are the essential concepts that readers and writers must understand and be able to apply to be effective?

What is literacy within the culture of our students? What kinds of communication are valued? What conventions are used and supported? How is literacy used in the culture? How does the culture's view of literacy differ from the view of literacy in our school or classroom?

What are the essential skills and strategies of literacy and what are agreed-upon best practices in helping children learn these skills and strategies? What role does phonics play? How important is phonemic awareness? How can we best help students develop in their ability to comprehend? What skills and strategies can we use to help students with specific difficulties in literacy? How do we help students understand what literacy will do for them? How do we help them learn to ask effective questions?

Reading is so much more than decoding words and then comprehending those words. Writing is so much more than spelling, sentence structure, parts of speech, punctuation, and grammar. We will be less effective in our work with diverse learners if we use a limited view of literacy and the essential concepts contained therein. The more we try to simplify language, the more we deprive our students of using the richness of language to make it make sense.

We also need an understanding of, and an ability to effectively employ, significant ways to support learning. Regardless of our particular philosophical bent, we need to understand the strategies that best support literacy growth and the philosophical underpinnings that support those strategies or methods. We need to know what we are doing, why we are doing it, and the philosophical underpinnings that support that action. Then, when curricular and classroom decisions need to be made, we can make them, based on the significance of a set of beliefs about how we should do our work. For example, many years ago, open education was an idea that many schools dabbled with. They dabbled with it in the typical way—they sent their faculty to a day-long workshop on open education. The workshop demonstrated what open education was and what it looked like. They described what the school would look like and what classrooms would look like. They described possibilities for the daily schedule and ways in which the new structure for schooling could facilitate learning. Teachers went back to their schools enthused. Much time was spent implementing the ideas learned at the workshop. Many schools failed. In the end, they concluded that open education didn't work as well as it was purported to, and they abandoned it for something else. One major problem with the implementation was that the educators were not helped to understand the philosophical underpinnings upon which open education was built. They could copy what they had seen in the workshop and many were able to do much in difficult situations. But, when faced with a problem that was not discussed at the workshop, they were not able to implement solutions based on the philosophical underpinnings supporting open education. The educators made decisions that, eventually, worked against the success of open education. This same story is repeated numerous times throughout our educational history.

Conducting and Using Meaningful Assessment

What do I need to know about my students in order to help guide curricular decisions? How can I find out? What assessment strategies are most effective in obtaining the information needed? How do I gauge success? How do I measure success?

It is imperative that we know our students. We must come to know them as children, as learners, and as readers and writers. This includes knowing how children learn in general but also the details about our specific children in our class this year, which will allow us to tailor our engagements to fit their specific interests and needs. We will be effective in supporting our students and their growth toward literacy proficiency to the extent that we know them. We must operate from the vantage point of being able to utilize effective assessment strategies—ones that enable us to know our students as readers and to identify areas of strength from which to build. Too much of what goes on in our schools under the guise of assessment simply measures student growth against arbitrarily established standards. Or, it simply compares their performance against other children. It doesn't help us to know them as readers and writers more effectively. It doesn't help us identify best, next steps. It doesn't support our students in becoming effective self-evaluators and reflective learners. It doesn't help to empower our students. Rather, it often sends a message of inadequacy to our students, telling them that they can't do what is valued in the classroom. It doesn't help them to see their strengths and weaknesses and start to determine next steps they would like to take. Seldom do we use assessment strategies that allow us to understand our children as literacy learners and enable us to make significant curricular decisions based on that knowledge. Balanced literacy demands that all components act together in one supportive whole. The different components don't function separately. We might try to determine the curricular decisions we have made in our classrooms based on the tests that are administered. Usually, we simply get a score from the assessment measures and then worry if they are too low or celebrate when they are high. The scores do very little to help us understand our students as literate beings or give us information with which to make effective curriculum decisions. The scores might even mislead us.

A small study was conducted in a third-grade classroom in southeastern North Carolina as part of an honors thesis (Brooks, 2001). In this study, nine students were randomly selected and given a series of assessments in reading. The results of these assessments were then compared to determine if they were consistent in the picture they painted of these students as readers. The assessments used were the STAR test from Accelerated Reader (2005), an informal reading inventory, the scores from the state high-stakes accountability test

(End-of-Grade Reading Test), a story retelling, a Reading Miscue Analysis (Goodman & Burke, 1972), and an interview with the teacher. The results seemed to indicate that a false sense of security was being established. Eight of the 9 students scored at or above proficiency on the state End-of-Grade Reading Test. The informal reading inventory showed all students on or above grade level. However, the miscue analysis indicated areas of concern for 7 of the students. They were not effectively using the syntactic cueing system, their miscues did not maintain essential meaning, they did not monitor themselves while reading, and did little self-correction. Students also had difficulty retelling the story they had just read.

Interestingly, the interview with the teacher showed that she knew her students and knew their strengths and weaknesses. She knew where these students were struggling and what growth they still needed to make. Teachers are often surprised at the scores their students receive on high-stakes tests. Comments such as, "I have no idea how that student passed that test. He is still a struggling reader," have been documented. Teachers are also heard to exclaim, "I don't know how that child didn't pass. I know he is a much better reader than that." Schools, eager to show that they have met the predetermined goals of performance, quickly move to show that their scores prove they have accomplished the goals and have qualified for the awards and rewards awaiting the successful schools. These scores, however, do little to help us understand our students and know how to best support their growth. We can't allow assessment tools to reduce all we can know about our students to a set of numbers.

Essential to effective assessment is a solid understanding of what literacy is, why we want our students to succeed in becoming proficient with it, and what success in literacy entails. This allows us to know how to assess in ways that empower our students and that invite them to further use of literacy. Often, the assessment techniques we use are very distasteful to students and actually end up in what Dewey (1938) calls "noneducation," in which children might learn in an area, but they also determine not to engage in learning in that discipline again. Is it possible that the very ways we are assessing and measuring growth in literacy are actually turning our students off to literacy and what it can mean in their lives? Are our assessment and accountability procedures inviting our students to continued engagements with literacy?

Perhaps the best ways to come to know our students as learners are miscue analysis or running records, kid-watching, learning conferences, literate discussions, Author's Circles, and portfolios. Many educators look past the significance of a miscue analysis, for example, when they use it to simply count percentage of errors on a specific passage in an effort to determine the grade level of their students. When they approach assessment from this simplistic perspective, they overlook the power of the process in helping come to know our students as readers. The miscue analysis can help us see what is going on in the mind of the learner as he or she reads. Is he or she effectively using the three cueing systems? Do his or her miscues make sense? Are they self-corrected? What strategies does the reader use? The same is true for writing and other aspects of literacy. If we simply measure success by the score received on a specific writing task, we are overlooking the vast amount of knowledge we can gain from a student in a writing conference, a portfolio review, a look at a rough draft, or hearing a student discuss his or her writing.

A university student was conducting a miscue analysis on a first-grade student. The student was reading the first page of the book and stopped suddenly in the middle of the sentence. He would look at the print and then look around the room. The university student didn't know what to do. Finally, after about 5 minutes, she went to her professor. She said she was fearful that the book she had selected for the child was too difficult and that the child had just given up. The professor sat down next to the first grader and watched. The child continued to look at the text, then the pictures on the page, and then around the room. After a short while, the professor asked the student what he was thinking about. What was going on in his head? The child responded, "I'm trying to figure out this word," pointing to the word 'because.' The child continued, "I can't tell if the silent 'e' makes the 'o' or the 'u' say its own name." The story was not too difficult. The child was simply trying to apply one of the "rules" he had learned about reading. Without asking appropriate questions, without watching our students, without understanding what is going on in their heads as they read, we are left to try to help them without really knowing them as readers and writers.

Additionally, the assessments we use must be invitations to further learning and engagement. They should also be a means for supporting self-reflection and monitoring. Students shouldn't have to always wait for the teacher to tell them how they are doing. If we do our work effectively, students will know how they are progressing, will be able to monitor their own growth, and will be able to identify areas for which they would like further work. This empowers our students as lifelong, literate learners.

Developing Exciting, Inviting Learning Environments

A huge part of a balanced literacy program is an exciting, inviting learning environment. This is one in which materials for learning (books, magazines, newspapers, charts, pictures, art, music, electronic access, pencils, crayons, markers, paper, notepads, sketch pads, etc.), tools for learning (structures that facilitate sharing and working together, questioning, inquiry, ownership), and time for learning are in place and are available to the students. The students have been taught how to use the tools, materials, and time and have been given the ownership and the responsibility to use them as they best deem appropriate. This requires teachers to let go. Teachers must let go of their natural tendency to be in charge of everything and to be the decision maker. The teacher helps students learn the process, the principles, and the procedures of learning and then lets go. He or she gets out of the way. The teacher works as a colearner, as a mentor, and as a resource to helping students pursue the learning for which they have passion. A chaotic learning environment is usually not inviting, exciting, or supportive. The organization of the classroom allows for the success we are seeking. Students know where the materials are and how they are organized. They are charged with helping to keep the materials organized in order to facilitate learning. Students learn how to effectively use their time and how to make the learning decisions that they need to make in order to maximize their time and effectiveness in learning. Many of the curricular decisions must be made jointly. Gone are the days when teachers say, "This is what we are going to learn today, and this is how we are going to learn it. Ready. Set. Learn." A more empowering classroom is created as teachers and students share the decision-making responsibilities and support each other in their learning. Inviting bulletin boards, centers, please touch tables, artifacts, a variety of texts, and electronic tools for learning to work together to make this happen. Balanced education must be built upon a thorough understanding of the philosophy from which it stems. It is not a collection of activities designed to help students learn to read and write. It is what results from a solid understanding of what the reading process is, what happens as we read, and how we best learn to read. Time must be given to educators to come to grips with these far-reaching understandings. Time must also be created to allow teachers to implement the engagements that are consistent with the philosophical base. This implementation takes time.

If we look at the environment from three perspectives, perhaps we get a better understanding of how this is part of a balanced literacy perspective. While we talk about each perspective individually, it is important to remember that these three perspectives actually work together. The emotional environment is, in many ways, impacted by the ways the desks are arranged in a classroom. The instructional environment is affected by the interaction that exists between the teacher and the students.

The physical environment includes the arrangement of the items in the classroom. The ways the desks are organized and the ways students sit and gather to do their work will determine the kind of work they can do. It sends a clear message showing what is valued in the classroom. For example, it is very difficult to carry on a successful classroom discussion if all the desks are in rows and pointing to the front of the class. Likewise, it is difficult to show students that we value their input and that we encourage class discussions and questions if the teacher is always in the front of the room and all desks are pointed to that place. Can students move freely around the classroom? Does the teacher have ready access to the students or does he or she need to walk around classroom furniture to get from one student to the next? Do the students have ready access to the teacher and to other areas of the classroom? Are materials accessible to students? Are they organized in ways that foster student use? Having materials available and allowing students to get materials as needed will also support a teacher's efforts to give ownership to his or her students. Establishing procedures that foster independence and ownership will also support an environment that empowers.

Is the classroom clean, organized, and inviting? Is it safe? Is the temperature such that it doesn't distract from learning? Is it a place where children and teachers enjoy being? Is the classroom adequately lit? Is it colorful? Are there plants, displays, pets, etc., that students would find comforting, inviting, and exciting? While learning can clearly happen in any environment, it can be enhanced if attention is shown to creating an environment in which children are excited to be. Do children have space to call their own—a place to put coats, books, pencils, lunches, etc., that can be called their own? Is the environment student-friendly and easy for students to negotiate? Are learning materials, bulletin boards, charts, and graphs displayed in ways to invite and excite? Are there fun, exciting materials in the classroom? For example, a please touch table where various artifacts are displayed, with the invitation to please touch, can be an exciting invitation to explore a variety of issues centered on the artifacts. The consistency of the schedule is another aspect of the physical environment that can make a difference. It fosters a feeling of comfort and safety. Students who know what to expect each day don't have to worry about what might be coming next. They can know what will happen and can prepare for it. Graves (1991) suggests that students who know they will be able to write for an extended period of time each day, beginning at 10:00 a.m., will actually write without writing. That is his term to describe their thinking about what they will write and how they might say the things they want to express. The physical environment also includes materials and tools for learning and their being accessible for students.

The emotional environment sets the tone for what happens in the classroom. Balanced literacy calls for an environment that supports the emotional aspects of learning. It establishes trust, ensures support for risk taking, generates appropriate attitudes toward miscues, identifies what students can do—not only what they can't do—and celebrates student success.

An environment that is supportive of growth and learning generates trust among participants. The type of environment that is created determines the amount of trust that participants feel toward each other. This trust is established as children come to know that their teacher values them as a person and looks at them as someone who is capable and competent in learning. They come to know that their teacher values who they are and what they have to offer the learning experiences of all. This is further established by the ways the teacher interacts with children and the feedback that is given. If a teacher can focus on what the child is trying to say and the power of the idea, as opposed to the correctness of the conventions they are using to express their ides, this trust if fortified. The trust also provides an environment of risk taking. Students come to know how their teacher will respond, and they are more willing to take the risks that accelerate their learning.

This trust is also established by helping students come to know that their peers also value them and that they value their peers. Engagements are not organized around competition but are organized and carried out in a community of learners. Grades are determined through a process of identifying what is most important to students in their growth in literacy so that they become a motivation and invitation to engage in those experiences that will best support their growth. Structures are put in place that facilitate collaboration and working together to explore, learn, and solve problems.

Trust can also be created by giving students the answers to their homework and ask them to do a small amount, then check it, and then determine why their response wasn't right before moving on to the next set of problems. This sends a clear message that learning is what is valued, not necessarily getting the right answer. It also sends a message that the teacher trusts the students as capable, competent learners. Some educators might feel uncomfortable with this, worrying that students might cheat. Part of establishing trust is to first trust students and interact with them for who they are—able learners who want to learn and who do learn all the time.

An effective, emotional climate will help students be willing to take the risks necessary for learning to occur. Frank Smith (1997) suggests that the optimal learning situation is one in which a learner has a 50-50 chance of being right. The willingness to take risk is linked directly to the consequences of being wrong. If the consequences of being wrong are too high, students will often stop trying. If students are punished or ignored or criticized for responses that are incorrect, they will stop responding. Forcing them to respond in this environment creates stress. If students are told that their questions show a lack of thinking or are trivial in nature, they will stop asking. Often, consequences of being wrong are relayed by sighs, eyebrows, looks of disgust, or moving quickly to another student who has the right answer. The focus should be on the students and their questions and attempts to make sense of the subject being covered, not so much on the right answer.

The emotional environment also establishes an appropriate attitude toward miscues. If students see miscues as a natural part of the learning process, they are more able to learn from their mistakes as well and continue to take the risks required by learning. If teachers grade everything that students do, they soon learn to not think creatively and to not explore.

Much of what we do in school is to quantify student growth into grade levels, test scores, and grades. This might be a necessary evil in the work that we do, but teachers must also find ways to celebrate the accomplishments of students. There are so many successes along the way to proficiency or to being on grade level. Celebrating the successes as they happen and helping students to identify the successes that they are having is another important aspect of the emotional climate. Students at all levels should not have to wait for the teacher to tell them how they are doing. One elementary school teacher was amused when one of her students came up to her with a big smile on her face. In the student's hand was her report card. She said to the teacher, "Hey, I got a 'B' in reading." It was the teacher who had filled out the report card! Educators might ask for whom the students are working. If the answer is for the teacher, then, perhaps a strong, supportive, emotional climate is not in place. If students write a paper, turn it into the teacher who grades it, and then get it back, authenticity suffers. Celebrations are surface-level and less meaningful.

The instructional environment is a third component of an effective environment. It includes the many ways teachers effectively organize for, and support, learning. Balanced literacy suggests the classrooms be filled with opportunities to use literacy to learn. The classroom is filled with a variety of texts and with a variety of opportunities to use literacy skills—charts, classroom observation logs, to-do lists, summaries of learning, you gotta read this book, messages to each other, classroom libraries, including student written fiction and nonfiction, exploration plans, etc. The instructional environment also includes a place in which teachers know their students as readers, writers, learners, etc. At almost any time, they are capable of answering the question, from an administrator, parent, or other educator, "What can you tell me about Johnny as a reader (or as a writer, or as a learner, or as a speller, or as a mathematician)?" Their response is an "I'm glad you asked. Let me show you what I know about Johnny." They then proceed to outline Johnny's strengths as a reader—the strategies he uses, the ways he problem solves, the type of books he is reading, his ability to make connections and create meaning as he reads, etc. Curricular decisions are made based on the students in the classroom. Teachers know the kinds of engagements to create and the kinds of experiences to offer because they know their children, and they know the next best steps for them to take. A

minilesson on making connections to other stories we have read is not prepared because it is on the next page of the textbook, but because the teacher
knows her students and understands that they are in a position from which
they could benefit from the minilesson.

Creating an effective instructional environment also involves the effective
support of learning. Teachers are masters at learning conferences in which they
watch and listen to children. These conferences are places in which effective
instruction can be given. They understand a variety of strategies to use in
supporting learning, and they are able to match the strategies with the students and their needs. They understand the philosophical underpinnings that
support the strategies they use and are careful to ensure that the strategies they
use are consistent with their philosophical stance. Teachers also understand
curriculum and are able to skillfully match it to the needs of their students.

An effective instructional environment is established as teachers truly come
to know their students as literacy learners. They know their interests, they
know their concerns. They know their backgrounds. They know what they can
do and they understand their understanding of the literacy processes. Teachers
use this knowledge to facilitate the many curricular decisions they make, ensuring that they are meaningful and authentic. The instructional environment, about which we speak, demands that educators organize their efforts
based on the needs of their students. They do not relinquish their decision-
making responsibilities to teaching materials, programs, textbooks, or administrators and/or other educators who do not know their children. They
take the ownership that is theirs by right as professionals and eagerly answer
the accountability questions that come up asking about the effectiveness of
their work.

Effective instructional environments contain educators who are adept at
identifying and then implementing best next steps. They understand the processes involved, they understand their students, and they are effective in identifying those engagements that will best support the next growth steps of their
students. This is done against the backdrop of what proficient literacy learners
do and how they best grow.

The instructional environment is filled with authentic engagements. Teachers do not resort to activities where students must pretend they are trying to
do something. Literacy is life, and there is no end to the real reasons to use it,
whether in school or out. We don't have to have students pretend they want to
write a letter in order to learn how to write a letter. We can invite them to write
a letter to a real person for a real reason. We don't need to invite students to
learn a reading strategy and then practice it in a nonsensical context or with a
worksheet, when there are countless authentic texts that students are motivated to read to pursue their own, real questions and interests.

Accountability and a Balanced Literacy Perspective

It is essential that we not allow high-stakes accountability to push us into practices that are not supportive of children's learning or our effective teaching. In an effort to meet the demands of the various high-stakes accountability measures, we can lose sight of what we are trying to accomplish. If we are not careful, the accountability effort will become the curriculum. The tests become the focus of our work. Pressure to show good test scores and to ensure that we meet the high-stakes standards create a situation in which we begin to teach to the test and spend more time on less meaningful aspects of our work that are not tested. In many cases, we confuse standards-based work with standards-based accountability. We confuse standards created to guide our work, based on the collective knowledge and wisdom of the field, with the often arbitrary standards that are established to ensure accountability.

In a study by Jones et al. (1999), it was found that over 60% of teachers had increased the amount of time they spent in reading and math after the introduction of the high-stakes accountability movement in the state of North Carolina. This was coupled with less time in the other just-as-important-but-not-tested subjects. Additional observations identified cases where recess was at near 0% of hours per week, writing anything other than practice writing tests was at near 0 hours per week, and social studies and science teaching were diminished. In some situations, cases of science and social studies at near 0% of hours per week for low-performing students were identified. Over 55% of teachers reported that they spent at least 40% of their time practicing for the high-stakes tests. Nearly 30% of these teachers reported spending over 60% of their time preparing for the tests. Over 80% of students spent more than 1 day per week taking practice tests.

More and more time is spent on reading, writing, and math (the tested subjects) and less and less time is being spent on some of the other subjects (the nontested subjects). Furthermore, the time spent in working with reading, writing, and math seems to be very specific and focused only to the aspects tested. For example, the majority of the time spent in improving writing is focused to the specific genre expected in the end-of-year test. Rubrics used to help prepare children for the test focus on a very limited set of criteria deemed to give children an edge on passing the test. Some programs are reduced to teaching and practicing a formula in which to fit all writing because it is thought to give students an edge on passing the test. Some programs even count the numbers of specific kinds of words used as a way of evaluating good writing because use of those words is thought to produce higher scores on the test. One fourth-grade teacher was heard to ask her students, in a review of their preparation for the writing test, "Students, how many sentences does a paragraph have?" The students responded in unison, "Four!" Reading instruction is focused to the skills needed to pass the test, namely being able to read a selection and answer multiple-choice questions. The high-stakes accountability movement will limit and reduce our curriculum if we don't work to ensure that it doesn't.

The pressure to produce can also lead educators into feeling that they have no ownership in their classrooms and that they are not able to make the curricular decisions that they know are best for children. Mandates from administrators and legislators can be very controlling and limiting. Often, programs are mandated without any input from teachers. These programs offer a quick fix, and the temptation to use them to meet goals is great. One professor was in an elementary school observing interns. As he talked with teachers, he discovered that they were all complaining about a new reading program that had been mandated by their administration. None of the teachers liked the program and resented the fact that they had been forced to implement it. One teacher said, "I really don't like this program, but I can't say anything, because I think I am the only one who thinks this way." The professor responded that he had talked with most of the teachers in the building, and they had all expressed the same concerns. It is imperative that we talk with each other and work together to deal effectively with these issues.

Following is a list of do's and don'ts of dealing with accountability:

- Don't confuse high-stakes accountability based on arbitrarily established levels of achievement with standards-based accountability created by the professional organizations in our field using the combined knowledge and wisdom collected through years and years of experience and research. There is usually a big difference between the two. One will limit our work and reduce the total growth of our students. The other will support us in our work and expand the achievement of students.

- Do recognize that educators are professionals. Seize the empowerment that is the right of all professionals to make the significant curricular decisions in the classroom and to show accountability in more effective ways. Let our knowledge of our students and our balanced literacy perspectives guide the decisions we make. If working with mandated programs, modify and adapt them to ensure that our students are getting what they need. Use the programs, don't let them use us.

- Do recognize that we often have more power than we might think. Talk with other teachers, identify problems that we are facing, and create solutions to those problems. Take the solutions to administrators.

Principals and other administrators are more prone to support us when we go beyond describing programs complaining about them and bring solutions to those concerns.

- Do focus on students and the many successes that happen every day in our classrooms. Always waiting for the end-of-chapter or end-of-grade test to determine effectiveness will not be supportive of our work.

- Do maintain a focus on the big picture. Let's remember the significance of the work that we do and what we are trying to accomplish. Our work is too important to be reduced to a set of end-of-grade test scores.

- Do be accountable. Show how well we know our children in all aspects of our work. Document their growth and success in the ways that truly support their continued achievement and that are consistent with our balanced literacy perspective. Go beyond the limits of the tests. Communicate to our students what they are doing that is good—what they are doing that effective readers and writers do. Help students also begin to be accountable. They need to see the success they are achieving along the way.

- Do become a kid-watcher. Come to know our students as learners and use that knowledge with our knowledge of the literacy processes to create effective learning engagements with our students. Let it be a positive, motivating part of our work.

- Don't allow the accountability system to limit our work and reduce the engagements we create for our students.

- Do trust our own judgment. Teachers know their students better than anyone else. Use the personal wisdom gained through the years. Conduct our own research in our own schools and classrooms. Become kid-watchers and be reflective in our practice.

- Do take risks and establish support groups. It is okay to take risks in our teaching. We are more effective when we are learning and growing with our students. Establishing support groups of peers in which to learn together and discuss issues is very helpful and empowering.

The high-stakes accountability programs appear to be here to stay. However, we can rise above them and continue to do good things for our students in spite of the often unrealistic demands they place on us. A balanced literacy perspective allows us to keep focused on what is most important.

Conclusion

Empowering Our Students as Literate Learners

A balanced perspective suggests that our goal in literacy instruction is not simply to help students become readers and writers. It is not to help students read at grade level or be able to pass end-of-grade tests. It is not to help them be able to score high on comprehension tests. Our goal is not to produce writers who can score a 3 or 4 on the end-of-grade writing test, or who can write a good persuasive letter, or who know how to use conventions correctly. It must be much more than that. Our goal is to empower our students as lifelong, literate learners—students who are proficient in literacy and who choose to use literacy to enhance their understanding of the world. Our goal is to empower our students, enabling them to tap into the power that can come into their lives through literacy. Our goal is to invite them to use literacy to enable them to live a qualitatively better life.

Empowerment helps students grasp ownership of their learning and their lives. They don't need to wait for the teacher to tell them how they did. They know. They don't need to wait for the teacher to tell them the areas in which they need to improve. They monitor their progress and make determinations of aspects they want to improve before the teacher ever gets to it. Empowerment helps students see literacy as a process, a process which they control.

Every child deserves the advantage of having the gift of literacy and all it brings to our lives. This work is far too important to pass off as being done through a set of surface-level activities that cover the whole literacy area. We must approach our jobs with the passion and energy that this noble cause demands and then ensure that our efforts are part of balanced literacy. This is the way we will be able to empower our students. This is working from a balanced perspective. Our students deserve no less.

Stephen struggled a great deal in learning how to read. His parents worried about him and did every thing they knew to help him. Finally, when he was in fifth grade, they sought testing to determine if Stephen had some sort of learning disability. They requested testing through the local school system, but it seemed to be taking too long for the process to work. They asked a professor at a nearby university if she could recommend someone that could do the testing. She said that she could, but she then asked the parents what they would do when they received the results. They asked, "What do you mean?"

She replied, "Even if the results show that Stephen has some sort of learning disability, don't you want to help him learn to read?"

The parents agreed. The professor said, "Then, let's just help him learn to read and not worry about the testing." She was afraid that the results of the testing might be used as an excuse not to help. She offered to work with Stephen twice a week over the next several months. Working from a balanced perspective, this professor helped Stephen learn to read. Several years later, while attending the graduation ceremonies for his older sister, Stephen saw this professor taking part in the festivities. With excitement, he turned to his mother and father and said, "Hey, look! There is the woman who taught me how to read."

Each example of a child in this chapter is an example of a diverse learner and the challenges faced with literacy growth. Every educator can add his or her own examples of diverse learners with whom he or she has worked. It is imperative that we come to know these children as learners to the fullest extent possible and use that knowledge to create the effective, dynamic engagements needed to support their literacy growth. We need to know them, and they need to know us, as literate people. We can help them come to know what literacy will do for them, if they see what it does for us. Children do not grow in literacy at the same rate. They come to the significant connections concerning literacy at different times and in different orders. Knowing our students as learners and knowing the processes of literacy allow us to tailor the engagements needed for effective and sustained growth in literacy. As Allington and Walmsley (1995) have so skillfully written, there is "no quick fix." We can be successful in helping diverse learners be very successful in their literacy growth. It is hard, difficult work. It takes time, patience, and consistent effort.

We know how to help every child learn how to read. A balanced perspective can help us successfully bring the power of literacy to the lives of all our students.

References

Accelerated Reader. (2005). Wisconsin Rapids, WI: Renaissance Learning, Inc.

Allington, R., & Walmsley, S. (Eds.). (1995). *No quick fix: Rethinking literacy programs in America's elementary schools.* New York: Teacher's College Press.

Brooks, K. (2001). *Analysis and comparison of reading assessment strategies.* Unpublished Honors Thesis. University of North Carolina at Wilmington.

Cambourne, B. (1988). *The whole story: Natural learning and the acquisition of literacy in the classroom.* Auckland, New Zealand: Ashton Scholastic, Ltd.

DePaola, T. (1983). *The legend of the bluebonnet.* New York: G.P. Putnam's Sons.

Dewey, J. (1938). *Experience and education.* New York: Collier Books.

Durkin, D. (1987). *Teaching young children to read.* Boston: Allyn and Bacon.

Fox, M. (1993). *Radical reflections: Passionate opinions on teaching, learning, and living.* New York: Harcourt.

Goodman, Y., & Burke, C. (1972). *Reading miscue inventory: Procedure for diagnosis and evaluation.* New York: Richard C. Owens.

Graves, D. (1991). *Build a literate classroom.* Portsmouth, NH: Heinemann.

Harste, J., Short, K., & Burke, C. (1995). *Creating classrooms for authors and inquirers.* Portsmouth, NH: Heinemann.

Jones, M., Jones, G., Brett, D., Hardin, B., Chapman, L., Yarbrough, T., & Davis, M. (1999). The impact of high-stakes testing on teachers and students in North Carolina. *Phi Delta Kappan, 81*(3), 199–203.

Mills, H., & Clyde, J. A. (1990). *Portraits of whole-language classrooms: Learning for all ages.* Portsmouth, NH: Heinemann.

Pressley, M., Roehrig, A., Bogner, K., Raphael, L. M., & Dolezal, S. (2002). Balanced literacy instruction. *Focus on Exceptional Children, 34,* 1–11.

Smith, F. (1997). *Reading without nonsense.* New York: Teacher's College Press.

Smith, F. (2004). *Understanding reading: A psycholinguistic analysis of reading and learning to read.* Hillsdale, NJ: Lawrence Erlbaum.

Speare, E. G. (1961). *The bronze bow.* New York: Houghton Mifflin.

Tsuchiya, Y. (1988). *Faithful elephants.* Boston: Houghton Mifflin.

Chapter 5

The Promotion of Literacy for Minority Children in Early Childhood Classroom Settings

Hengameh Kermani

Zuri walks into Mrs. Young's classroom holding her mother's hand. Today, she will start her first day of schooling at Sunset Pre-K Center together with several other English learners. Zuri has never been to school before, and she is quite nervous because she does not know the other children, and she does not speak English. Her face registers fear and apprehension. Mrs. Young smiles and says hello. Zuri turns and hides her face in her mother's skirt. Zuri, her mother, and her younger brother, Alberto, immigrated to the United States 5 months ago from a rural area of Guerrero, Mexico, to join Zuri's father, who has been living in the United States for the past 2 years. Zuri's father is a fieldworker with no formal schooling. Zuri's family lives in a trailer park on the main street of an older downtown neighborhood among a large community of Spanish-speaking recent immigrants. Zuri's mother knows very little English to communicate with Mrs. Young. Mrs. Young invites Zuri and her mother to participate in some of the play activities she has set up for children and their parents. Zuri's mother looks a bit anxious, too! She has never had experience with people outside of her community. This is all new to her, as well, but she is determined to give Zuri the education she never received herself. With an "elemetaria" education (equivalent of sixth grade), Zuri's mother believes that education is important for her daughter and has high hopes of the school's ability to make a difference in Zuri's future. Though apprehensive, she takes Zuri by the hand and they join the other children and their parents at the table and embark on a journey new to both of them.

Introduction

Most of us now realize that children such as Zuri are frequent arrivals in our schools. The children in contemporary classrooms are more diverse than children with whom we attended school so many years ago. The children we teach today are more diverse in backgrounds, experiences, and abilities. The population in the United States has recently become more racially and ethnically diverse. Between 1970 and 1990, a period of intense immigration, there were more newcomers to the United States than almost any other time in American history (Nieto, 2002). Future projections suggest that this trend will continue at a stable rate through the year 2050 (U.S. Bureau of the Census, 2000). Children who were once considered to be the minority are now the majority in many schools. In 1994, 34.4% of the nation's public elementary and secondary students were students of color—nonwhite racial or ethnic groups (U.S. Department of Education, Office for Civil Rights, 1996). It is projected that nearly half (about 45.5%) of the nation's school-age students will be students of color by the year 2020 (Pallas, Natriello, & McDill, 1989).

The research determining that preschool programs can enhance development and school readiness has prompted a steady increase, both in the number of such programs and also in enrollment of young children. In 2003, about 5 million 3- and 4-year-old children were enrolled in some type of early childhood education and care programs, an increase from half a million in 1964 (when the data were first collected) (U.S. Census Bureau, Department of Commerce, 2003). This steady growth in preschool enrollment has brought with it a consequent increase in the preschool multiethnic student body. For example, in recent years, Head Start has witnessed increasing diversity, both within its programs and in the communities it serves. The data on Head Start racial and ethnic composition shows that 73.1% of the children enrolled in Head Start programs in 2004 were from minority backgrounds. Today, approximately 27% of the children served by Head Start speak a language other than English at home, and more than 140 languages are represented in Head Start programs nationwide (Administration for Children and Families, 2000).

Clearly, these demographic changes create new opportunities, but also challenges for U.S. educational institutions, particularly the early childhood programs that lay the foundation for children's school experience and achievement. The reality is that our classrooms are more diverse today: Early childhood educators must be aware of, and responsive to, the wide range of cultural, social, linguistic, and learning expectations of the children and families they work with. Early childhood educators bear a responsibility to learn how best to meet these children's diverse needs, especially the language and literacy needs, and how to provide effective early childhood education for *ALL*[1] children.

The preschool years, particularly formal preschool experiences, are viewed, by many, as a time to ensure that children gain the prerequisite skills that support later literacy development (e.g., Snow, Barnes, Chandler, Goodman, & Hemphill, 1991). Moreover, the literature reveals that a rich curriculum and a positive group environment support and enhance the literacy learning of young children, native- and second-language learners (Altwerger & Ivener, 1994; Guthrie & Anderson, 1999; Peregoy & Boyle, 1993), as well as those with communication disorders (Watson, Layton, Pierce, & Abraham, 1994). In light of this evidence, this chapter is designed to help caregivers, classroom teachers, literacy coaches, and curriculum designers better understand the dynamic process of literacy development in *ALL* children and provide general suggestions for classroom implementation. This chapter is grounded in current research and theory that integrates a sociocultural perspective and provides a framework that early childhood educators can use to enrich and support children's literacy learning in classroom settings. It describes the elements of emergent literacy and offers examples of specific literacy-building activities and strategies that can be used to accommodate children with developmental differences, as well as children from diverse backgrounds.

Understanding Early Literacy in Young Children

A developing body of research in the past two decades has altered how we view young children's movement into literacy (Britsch & Meier, 1999; Snow, Burns, & Griffin, 1998; Teale & Sulzby, 1986). This new knowledge of how children

---

[1] All includes all children with and without special needs and children from all diverse ethnic, socioeconomic, class, and linguistic backgrounds.

learn language, reading, and writing has resulted in a major shift in our beliefs on how to teach and assess young children's literacy development. Not too long ago, it was thought that there is a point in time when a child is ready to begin to learn to read and write. Thus, instruction in reading and writing was delayed until first grade, leaving the preschool and kindergarten to be spent in "readiness" preparation. This approach was referred to as *reading readiness* (Crawford, 1995). The reading readiness view assumes that children are ready for formal instruction at a specific age as a result of maturation. This view implies that there is a discrete time when children are not readers and an equally separate time when they are (Whitehurst & Lonigan, 2001). Recent research and firsthand observations of children engaged in the act of literacy have questioned some of the notions of reading readiness (e.g., Clay, 1966; Sulzby & Teale, 1991; Teale, 1986). The realization that signs of literate behavior can be observed at much younger ages has led to a new view of how children move toward literacy. The once-held view that reading readiness was the proper goal of any instruction received prior to first grade gave way to the view that the process of literacy emerges long before children enter formal school. Current concepts of literacy development suggest that literacy begins when a child is born and develops through the uncounted experiences of everyday life (e.g., Schickedanz, 1999). The majority of children, by virtue of being immersed in literate society, acquire literacy concepts and skills relatively effortlessly during the course of early childhood, beginning in infancy. This view of seeing children in the process of developing literacy behavior is referred to as *emergent literacy*, a term first introduced by Marie Clay (1966) and supported by many other researchers since 1966. Theories of emergent literacy assume that the child acquires some knowledge about language, reading, and writing long before entering formal school. This process of becoming literate is initiated by the child and is "... mediated by literate adults, older siblings, or events in the child's everyday life" (Teale, 1982, p. 559), thus situating emergent literacy within a social context.

Social Context of Emergent Literacy: A Conceptual Framework

The concept of emergent literacy offers a framework for thinking about enhancing children's early literacy development. On the basis of this theory, there are several factors that could influence acquisition of language and literacy development within a social context: social interaction, home culture, and language and home environment (Figure 5:1). As suggested in chapter 1, the notion of social context stems from Vygotsky's sociocultural theories, emphasizing that language and literacy development is influenced by the context and society in which the individual lives: ". . . higher mental functions are socially formed and culturally transmitted" (Vygotsky, 1978, p. 126). Vygotsky establishes that interaction with adults and peers is a vital part of the social context of learning. He argues that children's interaction with literate adults and peers

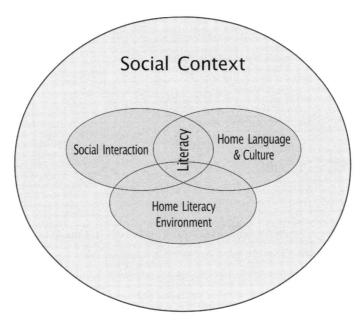

Figure 5:1 Early literacy framework.

is crucial to their cognitive and literacy development. During everyday routines and collaborative experiences with peers and adults, children build their ideas about the functions and uses of communicative symbols, such as language, and internalize many communication rules and processes. Learning language and literacy often occur in the context of everyday living. A good deal of such learning is incidental and happens in the midst of ongoing activities in which children participate with adults. For instance, by simply being around adults, talking, playing, helping, and asking questions, children learn a large amount of information relevant to their language and literacy development. Often, without intentionally trying to teach children, adults emphasize particular words and describe a setting in which they might be used. Thus, certain social settings generate particular forms of communication, which virtually shape the communicative patterns of the child. A large part of the social setting, in fact, consists of linguistic exchange. A simple exchange, such as a question, may prompt spontaneous information-extending conversations. For example, in the following dialogue, the parent uses questioning to prompt and maintain conversation with her child.

Mother:	What did you do at school today?
Child:	Play.
Mother:	Did you go on the playground?
Child:	Uh-huh.
Mother:	What did you play on?
Child:	The slide and the swing.
Mother:	Did you try the new bikes?
Child:	No.
Mother:	Why not?
Child:	Jason wouldn't share.
Mother:	Did you ask him nicely?
Child:	Uh-huh.
Mother:	And he still didn't share!
Child:	Uh-huh!
Mother:	Tomorrow, ask Ms. Young [teacher] to help you for a turn on the bike.

These conversational exchanges help to enhance the child's ability to conceptualize and provide not only general knowledge, but to a large extent, relevant social knowledge.

Young children also develop their language skills through interactions with other children. As children play with peers, they learn social, emotional, and cognitive skills. Older siblings and peers are often equally influential in socializing young children. Children practice linguistic symbols, such as words and phrases, within the context that they are used to as they play with their peers. These symbolic representations serve as a foundation for language and literacy development. In addition, as children interact with their peers, they learn to expand on their language skills by adjusting to their peers' communicative patterns. This act of adjusting to peers' communicative patterns is analogous to scaffolding strategies adults provide for children (expert–novice) in literacy activities. When children engage in instructional conversation with their peers, they participate in designating, negotiating, and coaching each other's literacy activities. Recent studies specifically highlight the unique role that may be played by older siblings and peers in linguistic-minority immigrant families where parents and other adults do not speak the dominant language of the host country (Gregory, 1998). An example is a conversation between Nancy and Ulises sitting at the table eating breakfast. Ulises speaks only a little English in class. Nancy does not speak more than one word of English at a time and speaks very little Spanish to anyone but the other Hispanic children in the class.

Ulises:	¿cómo es usted Nancy? That means 'how are you?'
Nancy:	Huh?
Ulises:	¿cómo es usted Nancy? That means 'how are you?' Say it in Inglés.
Nancy:	How are you?
Ulises:	Good Nancy! How are you? Say, I am fine.
Nancy:	I am fine. [And she giggles]

In addition to incidental social learning contexts, studies show that adults may intentionally construct activities, such as learning games, shared storybook readings, and visits to library/museums, to purposely promote emergent literacy skills. The social and cultural contexts of intentional activities help adults engage children in learning particular kinds of knowledge, including learning concepts about the functions, meaning, and forms of spoken and written language (Purcell-Gates, 1995). For example, as parents read storybooks with their young children, they can intentionally identify letter sounds or indicate names of the letters. They can also elaborate on illustrations, talk about and point to print, and ask questions to help children predict the subsequent actions in the story. In addition, through pertinent questions, the adults or parents can engage children in the events of the story and familiarize them with the kind of literary language used in books. For example, in the following dialogue between a father and his child, the father uses questioning to encourage child's participation in the story "Brown Bear, Brown Bear, What Do You See?" (Martin, 1983) and to draw his attention to print and pictures in the book. Without the use of questioning, the child's verbal participation would have been limited.

Father:	What do you see on the cover?
Child:	Uhmm, bear.
Father:	What color is the bear?
Child:	Brown.
Father:	Yes, it is a brown bear.
Father:	What do you think this says here [pointing to the title]?
Child:	Bear.
Father:	Yes, it says, 'Brown bear, brown bear, what do you see?'
Father:	What letter does the bear start with?
Child:	B.
Father:	Yeah, B. What other letters do you see?

Child:	[Pause]
Father:	This looks like [pointing to letter A] the letter in your name. What letter does your name start with?
Child:	Amir.
Father:	Yeah, your name starts with the letter A for Amir.
Father:	What other animals are we going to see in the book?
Child:	Duck, horse, . . .
Father:	Where should I begin to read?
Child:	Points to the print.
Father:	I wonder what animal is coming next! Let's read and find out.
Father:	You can help me read. "Brown bear, brown bear, . . ."

Storybook reading also gives children the opportunity to develop listening skills and to practice verbal proficiency. These varying instructional strategies provide skills and concepts children need to become conventional readers and writers within a social context. In these situations, adults serve as mediators who are in tune with the children's abilities and offer appropriate support to help the children accomplish communicative goals (Sulzby & Teale, 1991).

The concept of "scaffolding," introduced by Wood, Bruner, and Ross (1976) and discussed in chapter 1, is used to describe the supportive strategies adults employ to guide children's language and literacy learning. Rogoff and Wertsch (1984) develop this concept further in their presentation of the terms "orchestration" or "transfer" to describe the process in which the adult uses a different form of scaffolding to assist children's language development. For example, when parents or adults give young children the task of explaining the title of a story by looking at the illustrations and assisting them to read the story, they transfer the responsibility of regulating the process to children by slowly withdrawing their support as the children progress. That is, adults use a form of temporary, learner-sensitive modeling to structure, support, and guide children's emergent literacy learning, which can be de-emphasized as children's learning advances. This process lays the foundations for learning to read and write. For example, in the following dialogue, during a small-group storybook reading activity, the teacher uses questioning to elicit children's verbal responses and participation in the storybook reading. Without the use of this scaffold of questioning, the verbal participation and engagement would have been limited.

Teacher:	Today, we are going to read a story about the Gingerbread Man. Do you think the Gingerbread Man is a boy or a girl? Nino or nina?

Zuri:	Nino.
Carly:	He is a boy.
Teacher:	That's right … he is a boy. How did you know that he is a boy?
Carly:	He looks like a boy and you said man.
Teacher:	What would you say if the gingerbread person was a girl?
Carly:	You would have to say gingerbread woman. And he could wear a dress.
Teacher:	Listen to this part of the story: The Gingerbread Man ran and ran as fast as he could.
Zuri:	Él era un corredor rápido.
Teacher:	Yes, he was a fast runner!
Teacher:	Look at the fox.
Zuri:	En español usted dice zorro.
Teacher:	Thanks for telling us how to say 'fox' in Spanish. Let's all say that name together. 'Zorro.' That means fox.
Zuri:	The fox eat you if you don't run fast.
Carly:	Yeah, but he only can eat gingerbread cause it's just a story.

Through this interactive pattern of questioning, the teacher is supporting Zuri's verbal participation by recognizing her linguistic capabilities and assisting her in building a conversation. Such conversations will make children such as Zuri feel confident in using their native language, as well as practicing their English proficiency.

Home Language and Culture

Another factor within the social context of learning that influences children's language and emergent literacy development is "home language and culture." The dominant language or dialect spoken at home, and its linguistic patterns, powerfully influence the development of children's language and literacy. African-American English, for instance, has its own characteristic modes of discourse and verbal interaction (Smitherman, 1995). These linguistic modes that are part of everyday life in many African-American homes develop children's pragmatic knowledge of how language is used based on traditional African language patterns. For example, Smitherman (1995) suggests that infrequent use of possessive, singular, or plural ('s, s'), regular past tense and the use of common triple negation, and ain't for don't, haven't, hasn't, isn't, and didn't are distinct characteristics of African-American English. Furthermore, discourse modes in black English use voice rhythm and vocal inflection to convey meaning, resulting in a "phonology" (sound system) that is different from that of standard English. These variations in syntax and discourse patterns create very different verbal and nonverbal interaction between adults and children, a distinct kind of interaction in which speakers use language creatively, symbolically, and figuratively. Such discourse modes or characteristics, however, do not exist in American standard English, thus distinguishing many African-American children's communicative patterns from those of mainstream children. The following dialogue between Tynisha and her teacher demonstrates the syntactic contrast between American standard English and African-American English.

> Tynisha: Can you help me write my name?
>
> Teacher: Yes, what letter does your name start with?
>
> Tynisha: It start with a thing like this. [She draws a tall line]
>
> Teacher: Do you know what that letter is?
>
> Tynisha: It be a T.
>
> Teacher: Yes, your name does start with a T. What letter comes next? [teacher models a T]
>
> Tynisha: Uh un. My mama say it ain't like that. It's just this. That's all. [Child draws tall line again]
>
> Teacher: Okay. I see that your mom makes her Ts differently than mine. I make it like this. [Writes a T] Now, what comes next?
>
> Tynisha: I don't know. My mama ain't told me that one.
>
> Teacher: That's okay. We have all year to learn how to write it. I'll write it on this paper for you today.
>
> Tynisha: Thank you. I'll show it to my mama and see if it's right.

Children who have a first language other than English also develop distinctively different patterns of communication. Any or all of the syntactic, semantic, morphemic, phonetic, and pragmatic elements of different languages may be significantly different. Children's home language helps them build skills of processing meaning (semantics) and language structure (syntax), which may be different from the dominant language. Moreover, non-English-speaking children learn their native language by living and being socialized in particular speech communities. They develop a pragmatic awareness of what is appropriate language use in their families and communities. Thus, by the time children enter kindergarten, they have developed understanding of their native language—what that language is, what it can do, what it is for, and how to use it appropriately in their communities. Diverse children such as Zuri, however, will soon find themselves in settings where the language of common use is distinctively different.

The ways in which adults interact with children is always determined by cultural traditions, which vary significantly among cultures. Through everyday interaction with those around them, all children learn, and are socialized to learn, the cultural and linguistic knowledge necessary to participate in everyday social activities and interactions. Cultural learning (through interaction with adults) begins at birth and affects every aspect of a child's life, from ordinary daily activities, which include feeding, dressing, sleeping routines, interaction with family and friends, conforming to gender roles, gender-specific activities, to specific norms of communications, including oral and written language.

Different cultural groups have different ways of socializing children's language and literacy processes. Some cultures may see children as unique individuals, thus emphasizing independence of both thought and action in their children. They may put a high value on self and encourage children to assert themselves and express their feelings. Members of these cultures, who are typically part of the mainstream European American middle class, are very vocal and use verbal language as the main mode of communication. In mainstream cultures, children are considered as conversational partners with adults at a very young age and are allowed to participate in adults' conversations and to question their parents' intentions and actions. This early emphasis on verbalization makes a difference in school performance later: Children with good verbal skills do better academically (Gonzalez-Mena, 2006). On the other hand, some cultures may put more emphasis on the self as a member of a group, expecting individuals to blend in. In such cultures, with a collective orientation where conformity and group harmony are valued, caregivers de-emphasize individuality and self-expression and convey a significant amount of information through nonverbal forms of communication, including silence, facial expressions, eye contact, body movements and gestures, and posture and positioning. For example, Latino parents are more likely to use modeling and demonstration as a teaching strategy instead of specific verbal explanations that are typical of mainstream families. In many cultures, children are expected to listen while adults or older siblings speak and do not need to initiate communication to make their wants and needs known because these are anticipated by adults. In some cultures, self-dependence is either not encouraged or encouraged in somewhat different ways. For instance, Latino families encourage physical independence, while African-American families are particularly concerned to avoid overindulgence of children so that they do not become "spoiled" (Field & Widmayer, 1981). Similarly, in many Asian cultures, because of the importance of obedience and respect for rank, there is very little interactive communication between adults and children (Klein & Chen, 2001). Generally, in many Asian families, adults speak and children listen. These differences in cultural patterns of adult–child interactions have consequences in how children use and practice language at home and school.

Home Literacy Environment

The third factor within the social context of learning that influences how children's language and emergent literacy develop is the "home literacy environment." The importance of the home literacy environment stems from the fact that the home uniformly serves as the social setting in which early language and literacy is first encountered (Strickland & Taylor, 1989; Wells, 1985). A number of variables, such as literacy-related activities/materials, socioeconomic status (SES) and parents' educational level, have been shown to exert a powerful influence over how children develop language and literacy. Examples of literacy activities and materials include shared book reading, regular oral home conversation, reading materials and resources, academic guidance, and cultural activities. The range of activities that takes place within homes gives children many models of how language is used and literacy is practiced. As participants in literacy events, children come to learn a great deal about both oral and written language.

Research (e.g., Anderson, Hiebert, Scott, & Wilkinson, 1985) has shown that there is a positive relationship between the type and number of literacy activities, social class, and education of parents. Predictably, more books, magazines, and educational literacy materials are often found in the homes of higher-income families and families of children who perform well in school. For example, in research conducted with young children, Whitehurst and Lonigan (1998) reported that children from low-income homes had less experience with books, writing, rhymes, and other school-based, literacy-promoting activities than did children from higher-income homes. In addition, low-income parents model less book and magazine reading and tend to take children to libraries less than do higher-income parents (Fitzgerald, Spiegel, & Cunningham, 1991; Baker, Sonnenschein, Serpell, Fernandez-Fein, & Scher, 1994). Taylor (1995) also found that there is a significant correlation between mothers' education and family literacy activities, such as the type and frequency of reading and family literacy interactions.

A large number of studies have also pointed to differences between the social classes in the way the parents/adults interact or talk with children. Conclusions drawn from these studies assert a consistent difference in the way parents from low-income households use language with their children as compared to parents from middle-class households. The amount and frequency of parents' verbal communication with children in low SES families are often less than the amount and frequency of verbal communication in middle-class SES families. In addition, parents of low SES families are less likely to respond to their children's utterances: When verbal interaction does occur, it is more likely to take the form of directives than to take a form (such as inquiries) that maintains the conversation.

Parents' education is also an important factor in shaping the home literacy of young children (Storch & Whithurst, 2001). Research shows that children from homes whose parents are not highly educated may not experience language or literacy experiences that are commensurate with the expectations of mainstream schools. Because parents or caregivers are trying to survive and provide the basics of life, such as food and shelter, oral and written language stimulation often does not receive priority, since parents have not learned its value from their own education. Limited funds also means that families may not place priority on taking their children to many places and expose them to experiences, such as zoos or museums, that many mainstream educators take for granted. Lack of literacy transmission and specific environmental experiences often means that children from low-educated families are at a disadvantage with regard to language and literacy development.

Meeting the Needs of Children with Language and Literacy Differences

Research indicates that the types and forms of literacy practiced in some families, especially low-income, ethnic, cultural-minority, and immigrant families, are frequently incongruent with, and are mismatched with, the types of literacy practices promoted in the mainstream schools (Heath, 1983; Taylor & Dorsey-Gaines, 1988). Such mismatches mean that some children have greater difficulty understanding and meeting both the school's and their teachers' demands (Dickinson & McCabe, 1991; Heath, 1983; Michaels, 1981). Many researchers have suggested that mismatches between the nature and use of literacy at home and at school may be a primary cause of children's difficulties with literacy in early schooling (e.g., Barton, 1994; Heath, 1983). Some have argued that when schools actively attempt to match children's home and school literacies, children's literacy development is facilitated (e.g., Moll & González, 1994; Neuman & Roskos, 1992). When school curriculum does not match home literacy, children may experience difficulty in transferring their literacy knowledge and dispositions across settings (Duke, 2003).

What to Do When There Is a Mismatch between What Children Bring to School and What the School Expects of Them

As described in the conceptual framework, young children's language and literacy learning are socialized in ways that may not necessarily match the skills promoted in mainstream schools. This mismatch may create some difficulties for young children in order to function successfully within the classroom setting. So what could early childhood educators do in order to be able to meet the challenge of making the school educational experience as compatible as possible for young children such as Zuri? The first step in this process is for early childhood educators to identify and recognize *ALL* families as literate in ways defined by their culture and communities. This could be done by accepting the legitimacy of children's home language and showing respect for their home culture. It is important that educators make every effort to create a connection between each child's home and school literacy experiences. In the following section, using the above conceptual framework, I will recommend some specific strategies using Zuri's case. These strategies can be used by early childhood educators to enrich and support children's literacy learning in classroom settings.

Provide a Welcoming Classroom Climate that Values Culturally and Linguistically Diverse Children

First, create a warm and welcoming classroom environment where children feel safe to use their dialect or native language. Coming to a new school in a new country can be frightening for non-English-speaking children such as Zuri. These children may experience anxiety and fear beyond that of other children because they lack the language skills to communicate their needs. Not only are they faced with a new language, they have to figure out appropriate ways for interacting socially and understand new ways of learning, too (i.e., playing with other children, sharing possibly unfamiliar toys and materials with other children). Having adults and peers who can explain classroom tasks to Zuri in her native language can be comforting and make the changes less frightening. When the teacher, other adults, and children speak the children's language (even just a few words) and show positive regard for the home culture, children are more likely to acquire a sense of belonging in the school.

Create a Language-Rich Environment that Offers Children Opportunities to Engage in Meaningful Activities

Evaluate your classroom environment to make certain that literacy materials (books, newsletters, signs, environmental prints, etc.) meet both children's developmental needs as well as convey a positive message about diversity. Recognize the value of home languages that are different from English and promote their use by children and their parents. Research indicates that children's first language is a strong support for learning English. Thus, the classroom should contain a variety of literacy materials (e.g., oral, visuals, and texts) in native languages of non-English speakers. For example, if you have a child such as Zuri with Spanish as her first language, you can read books and sing songs in Spanish. If you don't speak Spanish, invite a speaker from Zuri's family, or maybe community or a nearby college. Introduce books with excellent language usage. For instance, high-interest picture books and books with predictable patterns are particularly useful for Zuri's language and literacy development. Offer a variety of books, songs, and poems, both in English and Spanish. Offer multicultural literature that constitutes accurate portrayals of Zuri's culture with rich detail. Consequently, a culturally responsive classroom environment facilitates children's language and literacy development in an authentic and meaningful way. Stories about children's heritage and community/home activities can provide excellent links between home and school and can stimulate good discussions. For example, for Zuri, books written in two languages, such as *My Day/Mi Dia* (Emberley, 1994), *In My Family/En Mi Familia* (Garza, 1996), *The Woman who Outshone the Sun/La Mujer que Brillaba aun Mas que el Sol* (Martinez, 1991), and *Abuela* (Dorros, 1991), offer support and model her language in authentic and interesting ways. Provide abundant and diverse opportunities for children to practice speaking and listening.

Children's oral language competencies develop both in receptive (listening) and expressive (speaking) modes. Classrooms that promote conversations and discussions are critical to the language growth of English language learners. Teachers should understand that every child's language or dialect is worthy of respect as a valid system for communication. It reflects the identities and values of the child's family and community. It is also important for teachers to treat children as conversationalists, even if they are not yet talking. However, when conversing with non-English-speaking children, teachers need to provide contextual and linguistic support for their spoken language in the form of gestures, acting out, facial expressions, and use of visual aids. Read-aloud experiences (storybook readings), sharing talk, language play (sharing of rhymes, songs, riddle, games), and storytelling are ideal contexts for promoting attentive listening and oral discussion skills. As mentioned in the previous chapter, books chosen for read-alouds should contain high-quality stories that are relevant to children's home culture. For many non-English-speaking children who come from cultures with rich oral stories and storytelling traditions, the activity of storytelling, respectfully compatible with the traditions of their cultures, is of great importance.

Model Use of Written Language for Children

Children acquire concepts about written language when their classrooms are filled with print and when teachers model how to use that print in play. Just as children learn oral language by being surrounded by people talking, they learn about literacy by being surrounded by people who use written language. Modeling use of written language is especially important for children such as Zuri, who may not have had many opportunities observing their parents engaging in literate tasks. As described in chapter 6, teachers can model writing for children by shared writing. When teachers write stories with children, they have the opportunity to develop a deeper understanding of the writing process as they watch an adult model. Teachers can also model journal writing with specific messages, such as, "I'm very excited today. I am getting a new puppy today." If given explicit examples, children can generate ideas about different kinds of entries that are appropriate. Various writing materials, such as markers, pencils, crayons, and papers, should also be incorporated at every center. The accessibility of these materials not only encourages children's writing, but also extends their knowledge of the reading and writing process.

Integrate Literacy into Children's Play Activities

To promote children's knowledge of the functions and uses of literacy, real-life situations can be especially helpful. For example, the teacher might set up the dramatic play area of the classroom as a Mexican restaurant. Included in such a setting could be a great deal of print—menus (both in Spanish and English), cash register, order pads, "open" and "closed" signs, coupons, and write-on boards on which to write the day's "special." Of course, writing materials would be present so that children could write orders. Also, in the dramatic play area, plastic foods that are culturally appropriate for a Mexican restaurant, such as tortillas and refried beans, can be available for children. Playing in the Mexican restaurant provides a familiar setting for Zuri and children such as her to play in. As Zuri engages in such culturally familiar restaurant play, she explores the functions of the environmental print by having access to examples such as foods, menus, signs, and coupons. In addition, the opportunity to play with other children within the restaurant-theme play activity extends the social and linguistic skills of Zuri and starts her off to figure out appropriate ways for interacting socially with other children.

Conclusion

As today's schools include more diverse groups of children and a greater number of English Language Learners with different family cultures and circumstances, instructional practices must increasingly be considered in the context of cultural and linguistic diversity. As presented in the conceptual framework, the cultural influence of adult–child interactions and home language and literacy experiences influence a child's development and readiness for school. Educators who work with young children need to be aware of, and sensitive to, social, cultural, and linguistic differences and use these as opportunities to enrich literacy learning in the classroom. It is important to remember that there is no single approach to literacy learning; no set of activities will guarantee to present all concepts and skills necessary for getting children "ready" for reading and writing. What does help is a literate classroom environment where educators accept the legitimacy of children's home language, show respect for, and value, the home culture, demonstrate the value of literacy, and manifest a commitment to the idea that young children enter school already engaged in literacy explorations. Ideal early childhood classrooms are places where children's emergent language and literacy is fostered and allowed to grow.

References

Altwerger, B., & Ivener, B. L. (1994). Self-esteem: Access to literacy in multicultural and multilingual classrooms. In K. Spanenberg-Urbschat & R. Pritchard (Eds.), *Kids come in all languages: Reading instruction for ESL students* (pp. 65–81). Newark, DE: International Reading Association.

Administration for Children and Families. (2000). Head Start Program Information Report, 2000–2001. Washington, DC: U.S. Department of Health and Human Services.

Anderson, R. C., Hiebert, E. H., Scott, J. A., & Wilkinson, I. (1985). *Becoming a nation of readers: The report of the Commission on Reading*. Washington, DC: The National Institute of Education.

Baker, L., Sonnenschein, S., Serpell, R., Fernandez-Fein, S., & Scher, D. (1994). *Contexts of emergent literacy: Everyday home experiences of urban prekindergarten children*. [research report] Athens, GA: National Reading Research Center, University of Georgia and University of Maryland.

Barton, D. (1994). *Literacy: An introduction to the ecology of written language.* Oxford, England: Blackwell.

Britsch, S., & Meier, D. (1999). Building a literacy community: The role of literacy and social practice in early childhood programs. *Early Childhood Education Journal, 26*(4), 209–215.

Clay, M. (1966). *Emergent reading behaviour.* Unpublished doctoral dissertation. University of Auckland Library.

Crawford, P. A. (1995). Early Literacy: Emerging perspectives. *Journal of Research in Childhood, 10*(1), 71–85.

Dickinson, D. K., & McCabe, A. (1991). A social interactionist account of language and literacy development. In J. F. Kavanagh (Ed.), *The language continuum* (pp. 1–40). Parkton, MD: York Press.

Dorros, A. (1991). *Abuela.* New York: Scholastic.

Duke, N. K. (2003). Genres at home and at school: Bridging the known to the new. *The Reading Teacher, 57*(1), 30–37.

Emberley, R. (1994). *My day/Mi dia.* New York: Little Brown.

Field, T., & Widmayer, S. M. (1981). Mother–infant interactions among lower SES Black, Cuban, Puerto Rican, and South American immigrants. In T. M. Field, A. M. Sosteck, P. Vietze, & P. H. Leiderman (Eds.), *Culture and early interactions.* Hillsdale, NJ: Lawrence Erlbaum.

Fitzgerald, J., Spiegel, D. L., & Cunningham, J. W. (1991). The relationship between parental literacy level and perceptions of emergent literacy. *Journal of Reading Behavior, 13*(2), 191–212.

Garza, C. L. (1996). *In my family/En mi familia.* San Francisco: Children's Book Press.

Gonzalez-Mena, J. (2006). *The young child in the family and the community* (4th ed.). Columbus, OH: Merill Prentice Hall.

Gregory, E. (1998). Siblings as mediators of literacy in linguistic minority communities. *Language and Education, 12*(1), 33–54.

Guthrie, J., & Anderson, E. (1999). Engagement in reading: Processes of motivated, strategic, knowledgeable, social readers. In J. Guthrie & D. Alvermann (Eds.), *Engaged reading: Processes, practices, and policy implications,* pp. 17–46. New York: Teachers College Press.

Heath, S. B. (1983). *Ways with words.* New York: Cambridge University Press.

Klein, M. D., & Chen, D. (2001). *Working with children from culturally diverse backgrounds.*

Martin, B. (1983). *Brown bear, brown bear, what do you see?* NY: Holt, Rinehart, Winston.

Martinez, A. C. (1991). *The woman who outshone the sun/lamujer que brillaba aun mas que el sol.* San Francisco: Children's Book Press.

Michaels, S. (1981). "Sharing Time": Children's narrative styles and differential access to literacy. *Language in Society, 10,* 423–442.

Moll, L. C. & González, N. (1994). Lessons from research with language-minority children. *Journal of Reading Behavior, 26,* 439–456.

Nieto, S. (2002). *Language, culture, and teaching: Critical perspective for a new century.* Hillsdale, NJ: Lawrence Erlbaum.

Neuman, S. B., & Roskos, K. (1992). Literacy objects as cultural tools: Effects on children's literacy conversations in play. *Reading Research Quarterly*, 27, 202–225.

Pallas, A. M., Natriello, G., & McDill, E. L. (1989). The changing nature of the disadvantaged population: Current dimensions and future trends. *Educational Researcher, 18,* 16–22.

Peregoy, S., & Boyle, O. (1993). *Reading, writing, and learning in ESL: A resource book for K–8.* New York: Longman.

Purcell-Gates, V. (1995). *Other people's words: The cycle of low literacy.* Cambridge, MA: Harvard University Press.

Rogoff, B., & Wertsch, J. (1984). Editor's note. In B. Rogoff & J. Wertsch (Eds.), *Children's learning in the "zone of proximal development": New directions for child development* (No. 23). San Francisco: Jossey-Bass.

Schickedanz, J. (1999). *Much more than ABCs: The early stages of reading and writing.* Washington, DC: NAEYC.

Strickland, D. S., & Taylor, D. (1989). Family storybook reading: Implications for children, families, and curriculum. In D. S. Strickland & L. M. Morrow (Eds.), *Emerging literacy: Young children learn to read and write* (pp. 27–34). Newark, DE: International Reading Association.

Smitherman, G. (1995). The forms of things unknown: Black modes of discourse. In Durkin, D. (Ed.), *Language issues: Readings for teachers* (pp. 314–330). White Plains, NY: Longman.

Snow, C. E., Barnes, M. S., Chandler, J., Goodman, I. F., & Hamphill, L. (1991). *Unfulfilled expectations: Home and school influences on literacy.* Cambridge, MA: Harvard University Press.

Snow, C., Burns, M. S., & Griffin, P. (Eds.). (1998). *Preventing reading difficulties in young children.* Washington, DC: National Academy Press.

Storch, S. A., & Whithurst, G. (2001). The role of family and home in the literacy development of children from low-income backgrounds. In R. R. Bitto & J. Brooks-Gunn (Eds.), *The role of family literacy environments in promoting young children's emergent literacy skills* (pp. 53–72). San Francisco: Josey-Bass

Sulzby, E., & Teale, W. (1991). Emergent literacy. In R. Barr, M. Kamil, P. Mosenthal, & P. D. Peterson (Eds.), *Handbook of reading research*, (Vol. 2, pp. 727–757). New York: Longman.

Taylor, R. L. (1995). Functional uses of reading and shared literacy activities in Icelandic homes: A monograph in family literacy. *Reading Research Quarterly, 30*(2), 194–219.

Taylor, D., & Dorsey-Gains, C. (1988). *Growing literate: Learning from inner-city families.* Portsmouth, NH: Heinemann.

Teale, W. H. (1982). Toward a theory of how children learn to read and write naturally. *Language Arts, 59,* 555–570.

Teale, W. H. (1986). The beginning of reading and writing: Written language development during the preschool and kindergarten years. In M. Sampson (Ed.), *The pursuit of literacy: Early reading and writing.* Dubuque, IA: Kednall/Hunt.

Teale, W. H., & Sulzby, E. (1986). Home background and young children's literacy development. In *Emergent literacy: Writing and reading* (pp. 173–206). Norwood, NJ: ABLEX.

U.S. Department of Education, Office for Civil Rights. (1996). State summaries of elementary and secondary school civil rights survey; and National Center for Education Statistics, common core of data survey. Washington, DC: U.S. Government Printing Office.

U.S. Census Bureau, Department of Commerce. (2003). School enrollment–Social and economic characteristics of students. Online document at: http://www.census.gov/population/www/socdemo/school.html

U.S. Bureau of the Census. (2000). *Statistical Abstract of the United States.*

Vygotsky, L. S. (1978). *Mind in society: The development of higher psychological processes* (pp. 79–91). Cambridge. MA: Harvard University Press.

Watson, L. R., Layton, T. L., Pierce, P. L., & Abraham, L. M. (1994). Enhancing emergent literacy in a language preschool. *Language, Speech, and Hearing Services in Schools, 25,* 136–145.

Wells, G. (1985). *Language development in the preschool years.* New York: Cambridge University Press.

Whitehurst, C., & Lonigan, C. J. (2001). Emergent literacy: Development from prereaders to readers. In S. B. Newman & D. K. Dickinson (Eds.), *Handbook of early literacy research* (pp. 11–28). New York: Guildford Press.

Wood, D., Bruner, L. S., & Ross, G. (1976). The role of tutoring in problem solving. *Journal of Child Psychology and Psychiatry, 17,* 89–100.

Chapter 6

Understanding the Interface between Home- and School-Based Literacy

Melissa M. Schulz

Andrew caught my attention on the first day of the new school year in my second-grade classroom. Andrew's first-grade teacher had considered him to be a behavior problem, and he was enrolled in the school's reading intervention program. Andrew tried very hard to fit in with the other students. During the first weeks of school, Andrew had difficulty staying on-task during independent reading and independent writing workshop time. I soon noticed that Andrew struggled with reading and writing and "acted out" to avoid engaging in the tasks. I decided to call Andrew's parents to invite them to school to learn more about Andrew and his life at home. I gained valuable information from numerous meetings and phone calls with Nilesh Nguyen (Andrew's father). This was the beginning of a strong, parent–teacher collaboration with the Nguyen family.

One year later, Andrew was in the third grade; I was no longer his teacher, but he and his family were participants in my research study. I made weekly 2-hour visits to the Nguyen's home and gained even more valuable information about the nuances of the Nguyen family's literacy and cultural practices, many of which related back to their original home in North Vietnam. Andrew wants to like school and wants to be successful. Andrew's parents, Nilesh and Lee Nguyen, also share this dream for Andrew. This chapter is the story of Andrew's struggle with literacy learning and his parents' struggle to build a relationship with the school.

When Rachel arrived in my second-grade classroom on the first day of the same new school year, I could not help but compare her to her older sister, Allison, whom I had taught 2 years earlier as a second grader. I had a strong parent–teacher relationship with Mrs. Smith that had continued over the years through phone calls. Mrs. Smith was a consistent volunteer in the classroom and in the school. Rachel wants to be successful in school. Rachel's parents, Mary and Rick, also share this dream for Rachel.

One year later, when Rachel was in third grade and no longer my student, I began my weekly 2-hour visits to the Smith's home, as they were also participants in my research. I gained valuable insight into Rachel's journey from home to school and the cultural and family literacy values that are woven into the intricate fabric of the Smith family life. This chapter is also the story of Rachel's literacy learning and her parents' relationship with the school.

Introduction

Importance of the Study

It is very challenging to meet the needs of students from diverse backgrounds. Teachers are expected to support students who speak a nonalphabetic language, such as Japanese, or students from another country with no previous exposure to English. Some students who are new to American schools may be chronologically placed in the right grade, but the curriculum is above their English-speaking competence. Students who are developmentally delayed may be chronologically placed in the right grade, but the curriculum is above their ability level.

Recent *No Child Left Behind* (summarized in U.S. Department of Education, 2001) legislation, with its mandated achievement benchmarks for various minority populations of students, has refocused teachers and administrators on the critical need to address discrepancies in student performance. Teachers are responsible for teaching and supporting *all* students who enter their classroom door.

In this chapter, I provide teachers with recommendations for working with children and families from diverse backgrounds. I chose the word "working" because I recommend that teachers begin to develop a relationship with diverse children and families. Over the course of the school year, I hope teachers can develop a partnership with diverse children and families. Academic and personal successes are more likely if teachers, administrators, parents, and children work together in partnership with each other.

In the first section of this chapter, I provide recommendations for working with families. I include a sample questionnaire that will be useful for teachers to gain information about the children and family's cultural background and their reading and writing practices inside and outside of school. This section will be useful for teachers who want to build more meaningful relationships with children and families from diverse backgrounds. This section will provide teachers with practical strategies, so families can learn to negotiate schools effectively.

In the second section, I discuss how teachers might work with children to construct learning opportunities around children's individual reading and writing needs. This section will be useful for teachers who are uncertain of how they can meet the academic needs of their diverse students who may be chronologically placed in the right grade, but the reading and writing curriculum is above their English-speaking competence. This section also provides suggestions to teachers who are working with children from diverse backgrounds who are in mainstream classrooms, and the reading and writing curriculum may be above their ability level.

Background of Homestead Study

Student's earliest learning experiences occur in the context of their home language and culture. Building from the work of Moll, Amanti, Neff, and Gonzales (1992), culturally responsive teachers recognize, learn about, and draw from the many people who are part of a child's world outside of school. I wanted to learn more about teaching students who are learning English as a second language and their relationship with the school community. In this chapter, I take an in-depth look at Andrew's literacy learning journey. This case study was part of a year-long study that included a total of four case studies of families who live in a Midwest suburb I call "Homestead." According to Homestead City School District historical information, in 1991–1992, there were 7,255 students enrolled in the entire (K–12) school district, and in 2005–2006, there were 14,779 enrolled students. Along with the rapid increase in enrollment has been a rapid increase in diversity. In fact, as reported in the 2005 general enrollment profile for one elementary school in Homestead City School District, 12 native languages were spoken across the student's homes. It must be recognized that diversity in Homestead is relatively new, and the school practices have not been transformed to meet that diversity. For example, it is uncommon for teachers and principals to have classroom or school newsletters translated into the many native languages that the students and their families speak at home. This raises many problems with communication between the school and student's homes. If parents are not able to read information from the school, how can they be expected to keep updated and stay as informed as parents who speak English fluently? This is a common problem for schools throughout this Midwestern city, where language and cultural diversity has rapidly intensified for the past 5–10 years. New immigrant groups from Somalia, Sudan, the Middle East, Latino countries, and the former Soviet Union have changed the complexion of the student body and family community of Homestead.

Learning about School

Parents learn about the value of education and beliefs about how schooling should take place, based on their personal experiences in American schools (Hicks, 2002). Based on informal conversations with Rachel's parents, it is obvious that Mary and Rick feel very comfortable with the school community. In contrast, based on conversations with Andrew's father, Nilesh Nguyen, it is obvious that he feels like an "outsider" and is uncomfortable with the school community.

The Smith Family

Rachel's parents (Mary and Rick) both grew up in a small rural town in the Midwest. Mary's father was a principal, and Mary's mom worked at home rearing the children. During the study, I asked Mary about her parent's (Rachel's grandparents) influence on her education, and she discussed them below:

Melissa: What was your parent's role in school?

Mary: That is funny about today and then, they had a small student-to-teacher ratio. So they didn't need moms to come into the school to help. My mom did all of the [Parent and Teacher Association] PTA meetings and whatever the school or church offered because there were lots of books and things like that

that they (parents) could help with. They [parents] never came into the classrooms. We had nuns and strict and orderly classrooms and nothing to distract the class, I don't even recall parents coming in to observe. Even talking to my mom now and I tell her I am going to the school to volunteer she says, "Oh my gosh!" They [her parents] just don't understand that. Plus, I think back then that we had only one vehicle, so she couldn't have gotten to school, anyway.

Melissa: So what was your Dad's role in your schoolwork?

Mary: He did flashcards or math. My mom did a lot of reading with us. But as far as homework, it was my father.

In Mary's retelling of her family life, she conserves the basic value of parent participation but "transforms" (Taylor, 1983) her role from the PTA support of the previous generation to a more hands-on, classroom-based participation (i.e., volunteer support to the teacher). Through her volunteer work in her children's classroom and her easy communication with the teacher, Mary has learned a lot about how reading and writing are taught at her children's school. At Homestead, writing is an emphasized aspect of the literacy program, where writing journals store ideas for stories that are then composed on the computer and assessed though writer's workshop routines. Guided reading, independent reading and writing, interactive writing (Fountas & Pinnell, 1996), and word study are the main strategies used in a balanced literacy approach. Books are carefully chosen at the student's reading level, and writing is an embedded and natural part of all aspects of daily life and across the curriculum.

Mary's ideas about supporting her children's reading and writing at home are informal. Mary encourages her children to keep story journals, travel journals on family trips, she encourages them to write and send e-mails to family and friends, she encourages reading out loud together, and she checks out videos from the library to support story comprehension of assigned books, for example, *Little House on the Prairie* (Wilder, 1935), and reading the newspaper together each morning. These family literacy practices seem very congruent with those of the Homestead City School District.

The Nguyen Family

In contrast, Nilesh had his first parent–teacher conversation about book selection when Andrew was in second grade. Nilesh came to the United States as an adult refugee (in his forties) from Vietnam. His greatest dream is for Andrew to become successful at school and to have a "good" life. He expressed that he learned to value literacy from his own father (Andrew's grandfather), who valued writing. Nilesh's mother (Andrew's grandmother) did not have the opportunity to go to school in Vietnam. Nilesh explains:

Melissa: Did your parents read and write?

Nilesh: Yes, mostly my Dad. My Mom, just a little bit, women in my country (Vietnam) don't have a chance to go to school if they were born before 1950. But now, girls can go to school equal to boys but not in my Mom and Dad's time.

Melissa: Did you have reading materials around your house? Did you see your parents doing much reading and writing at home?

Nilesh: It depends on what type, my Dad liked poems. He would write about poems and stories. He learned a lot about oral traditions of my country (Vietnam), he liked to learn about old people.

Typical of the immigrant families described by Puchner and Hardman (1996), Nilesh focuses on organizational routines to help Andrew since, in his view, his limited English skills prevent him from helping with homework. Organizing routines around homework, monitoring homework, and offering incentives for good grades are strategies that have been noted by others (Puchner & Hardman, 1996). This is certainly true for Nilesh Nguyen, who establishes highly structured and very organized routines for Andrew's out-of-school time. Andrew's father, Nilesh, talked about his values around academics and morality and his belief that it is his job as a parent to teach Andrew these values. He also feels that Andrew will maximize his success if he adheres to a set homework routine each day. Nilesh has established a daily reading and writing routine in their home. Andrew has a snack after school and watches television until 5:00 p.m. each day. But, at 5:00 p.m., Andrew sits at the quiet dining-room table to complete all of the homework assigned by his classroom teacher. After Andrew completes his school homework, Nilesh gives him additional work. The daily reading work that Nilesh assigns is for Andrew to read one chapter from a book he selects for himself, for example, *Goosebumps: Horror and Camp Jellyjam* (Stine, 1995). These books are not always at Andrew's independent reading level, but after Andrew reads the chapter, he is expected to copy the entire chapter verbatim in his writing journal, a composition notebook. Twelve to 15 of these composition notebooks filled with his transcribed books were stored on a shelf in Andrew's bedroom. When I asked Nilesh about the purpose of the writing journal assignment, he explained that this was the way he was taught to read and write in Vietnam. Andrew has been doing his reading and writing routine for 3 years, since first grade. Andrew explained to me how he became interested in reading and writing:

Melissa:	When did you become interested in reading and writing?
Andrew:	It all started in second grade. In first grade, [Mrs. Hartley] gave me a book, so I read it.
Melissa:	How about writing, when did you start writing in these notebooks with your Dad?
Andrew:	It was when I was 7, when I was in first grade.
Melissa:	Do you think that writing in these notebooks is helping you become a better reader?
Andrew:	Yes, it helps and sometimes I read the writing to my Dad. If I don't know a word, I say it back to him about five times, and I remember it.

Nilesh finds additional work for Andrew on a specific fee-based Web site that has grade-specific educational worksheets for children. Nilesh listens to Andrew read every night. Since English is a second language for Nilesh, occasionally, he is unable to read some of Andrew's words in his books and, therefore, is unable to help him. However, if Andrew comes to a word that he cannot read, Nilesh asks Andrew to attempt to read the word several times to commit it to his memory. Nilesh explained that he learned this way in Vietnam.

Nilesh wants Andrew to learn English at school because he knows, from his own personal experience as an immigrant, that English is essential for work and daily living. Nilesh explains:

Nilesh:	I do think it is necessary to teach him [Andrew] reading at home, but I am not able to do it well because I don't think my English is good enough.
Melissa:	What kinds of things have you done with Andrew at home to help him with reading?
Nilesh:	We go to the library and I let him read every night. It is all I can do, but I don't know if I pronounce good enough or not. I don't know the American sayings, only the Vietnamese sayings, so I listen to him read the whole book or half of the book. I want him to read hard books.
Melissa:	Who picks out the books, when you go to the library?
Nilesh:	I take him, but he chooses the books.

In his telling of his life as Andrew's father, Nilesh reveals his reliance upon his personal family and schooling history in Vietnam and upon his own literacy background as his frame of reference to support Andrew at home with school-related work. What he reveals (choosing hard books and copying verbatim from them) is that he is not connected to the teaching practices of the school—instead, he "conserves" the traditions of his family and culture with Andrew (Taylor, 1983).

In short, even though the Nguyen family has high aspirations and encourages Andrew to be successful in school, neither of Andrew's parents attended American schools, so they do not understand the expectations of the school. During the study, I asked Nilesh about his school participation in first grade, and he shared the following story:

Melissa: Did you participate in school-related activities in kindergarten and first grade, such as parent–teacher conferences, curriculum night, and attend school plays?

Nilesh: Yes, I attend all parent–teacher conferences and curriculum nights; whatever the teacher asked me to do, I did to help Andrew. I did not go into the school for Andrew's musical, but I took him to the school and I waited in the car for him.

What Nilesh does not share in this story is that while he waited in his car at the curb, all of the other parents were inside in the auditorium. Based on informal conversations with Rachel's parents, it is obvious that Mary and Rick feel very comfortable with school. The metaphor of Nilesh waiting in the car for his son, Andrew, who is performing in a school musical, illustrates how he is a parent on the "outside" because he is a "diverse" parent who is learning English as a second language. Nilesh either doesn't feel welcome in the school or simply feels too much like an outsider within the school community to join the other parents in the school auditorium. Nilesh, and many parents like him, need an "ambassador" who understands the new, and sometimes strange, institutional world called "school."

Connecting with Students and Families

Teachers can be an "ambassador" for diverse families who are trying to navigate through the school community. Communication between teachers and families ideally allow parents to become more knowledgeable about the events that take place in school, and teachers become more knowledgeable about the events that take place in the lives of children outside of school.

Teachers can begin to honor a child's world outside of school. First, teachers can collect cultural information from all of the students' families. If teachers collect the information formally in a questionnaire format, it must be collected equally from *all* children in a classroom. It is important for teachers and administrators to not make any assumptions about student's cultural or linguistic background without obtaining further information. It is very challenging to meet the needs of students from diverse backgrounds, but there are resources for teachers and administrators that can help facilitate communication.

After teachers develop a questionnaire, the second step is to carefully decide the most effective way to communicate with parents using their home language. If you do not speak the language of your students, it is important to ask the school to provide you with an aide or interpreter who speaks the students' mother tongue. If this is not a possibility, you may need to elicit assistance from a parent liaison or volunteer in the community who are speakers of the language to come to the classroom to provide assistance. If a school does not have access to parent liaisons, it will be necessary to establish relationships with community members who can act in that capacity. Of course, to learn from parents and students, a questionnaire needs to be as user-friendly as possible and made available in the different languages of parents or caregivers.

It is important to determine the type of information that will be useful for the teacher when creating a questionnaire (see Figure 6:1). Some of the categories of information may include (1) student and family background, (2) student and family cultural background, and (3) reading and writing practices inside and outside of the home.

Parent Questionnaire

Directions: Please answer each question by checking the appropriate box. Return the questionnaire in the envelope provided.

1. What language did your child speak when he or she first talked?

    O English

    O Spanish

    O Other

2. What language does your child use most often at home?

    O English

    O Spanish

    O Other

3. What language do you use most often at home?

    O English

    O Spanish

    O Other

(Continued on next page)

4.   What language do you use most often when you talk to your child?

 O English

 O Spanish

 O Other

5.   What language do adults use most often in your home?

 O English

 O Spanish

 O Other

6.   How often do you attend your child's school to meet with the teacher during the school year?

 O 0 times

 O 1–3 times

 O 3 or more times

7.   How long has your child attended school in the United States?

 O 1–5 months

 O 6 months to 1 year

 O Over 1 year

8.   Do you feel comfortable attending your child's school to meet with the teacher or to attend a school event or play?

 O Yes

 O No

9.   If you want to find out how your child is doing in school, how will you get in touch with the teacher?

 O Phone

 O Go to school

 O Letter or e-mail

10. Is it important to talk to your child's teacher about how you can help your child at home?

 O Yes

 O No

(Continued on next page)

11.   How often do you read with your child?

      O Every day

      O Twice a week

      O Never

12.   How often do you write with your child?

      O Every day

      O Twice a week

      O Never

13.   In what language do you read with your children?

      O English

      O Spanish

      O Other

14.   What educational materials do you have in your home?

      O Library card

      O Access to Internet

      O Calculators

      O Dictionary

15.   How often do you use a bilingual dictionary?

      O Never

      O 1–3 times a week

      O 3 or more times a week

16.   If the school offered an English-language learning class for any adult in your family, would you or someone in your family attend?

      O Yes

      O No

Figure 6:1   Parent questionnaire.

Teachers can use the information they gain from the questionnaires to improve their work with parents and children from diverse backgrounds in the following ways: (1) including parents in the classroom, (2) conducting parent–teacher conferences, (3) involving parents and families, and (4) sharing a skill or talent with the classroom or school community. Becoming an "ambassador" for diverse families may require teachers to engage in some additional work that they may not have been required to do in the past. The potential benefit for families from diverse backgrounds and to the teacher will be worth it, because they will be more willing to work with the teacher and school when they have a better understanding of the school's expectations.

Including Parents in the Classroom

Many teachers invite parents into their classroom to help as volunteers. In fact, Mary Smith, as previously described, learns valuable information about what goes on in her children's classroom as a classroom volunteer. Mary learned how her children's teachers taught reading and writing, and she was able to implement some of the strategies at home. As a former second- and third-grade teacher, I would sometimes ask parent volunteers to read and write with children one-on-one. Parents of second-language–learning children may not feel comfortable meeting with students, especially struggling students, and helping them with reading or writing. Parents of second-language–learning children can be invited to visit the classroom just to spend time in the class-room and learn more about what goes on in the classroom. Later, parents of second-language–learning children can be encouraged to help out with a variety of tasks, such as working in the art area or helping with a hands-on science or math activity. While visiting the classroom, parents can get a firsthand glance at what happens in the classroom and may begin to feel more comfortable with the classroom and, possibly, with the larger school community.

Parent–Teacher Conferences

Most teachers are required to provide parent–teacher conferences at least twice per school year. Most parents want to know how their child is settling into a classroom and how he or she is learning the curriculum. Parent–teacher conferences are prearranged times when parents and teachers get together to discuss a student's social and academic progress. One relatively simple way for teachers to transform school practice to meet diverse students and families needs is to have information about school open houses, curriculum night, parent–teacher conferences, and classroom newsletters translated into the different languages that the students and their families speak at home. If parents are not able to read information sent home from the school, how can parents be expected to stay informed or attend school-based events? It is also important for teachers to hold parent–teacher conferences at various times during the day to accommodate parents' work schedules. Offering conferences before school, during the day, and in the evening will give parents multiple opportunities to meet with you.

Involving Parents and Families

Many teachers and administrators invite parents to the school periodically for "Meet the Teacher Night," or similar evening events, so parents, students, and teachers can get to know each other before the school year begins. Later in the fall, teachers may hold another evening event called "Curriculum Night" to help parents become familiarized with their child's grade-level curriculum. All of the teachers at a specific grade level may coordinate the curriculum night together, or individual teachers may prepare their own specific agenda for parents and hold the curriculum night within their own classrooms.

For example, as a second-grade teacher, my colleagues and I met and prepared a second-grade Curriculum Night in the auditorium. We each were responsible for a certain aspect of the presentation to all of the second-grade parents. Afterward, we met with parents in our own classrooms and talked more informally about the curriculum or just engaged in casual conversation.

Sharing a Skill or Talent

Teachers who have passed out a questionnaire (see Figure 6:1) to better understand and honor a child's world outside of school will have information about their students' and families' cultural background and their reading and writing practices outside of school. Many teachers consider parents to be valuable resources to be tapped that will enrich the classroom curriculum. In the questionnaire, teachers may ask parents what type of activities they like to share with children. If a teacher asks a parent to conduct an in-class presentation, it is important to make sure that the parent presentation fits in with the context of the overall classroom curriculum. Parent presentations can be very meaningful in introducing children to a variety of cultural experiences. For example, in my third-grade classroom, we were studying "Winter Holidays around the World" as one of our third-grade social studies themes. Ashraf was a student in my classroom, and both of his parents were from the Middle East. Ashraf's mother, Rundsara, was a parent volunteer in my classroom, and I knew their family celebrated Ramadan. I asked Rundsara to come to our class as a guest speaker and share with the students how her family celebrates the Ramadan holiday. If cultural activities are presented with a tone of acceptance and appreciation, they can enhance students' cultural understanding and help *all* children feel more comfortable. If cultural activities are presented so that they seem odd and unusual, this may, in fact, heighten students' feelings of difference and a sense of commonality or cultural understanding will not occur. In the next section of this chapter, I will address how teachers can work with children to construct learning opportunities around children's individual and diverse needs as beginning readers and writers. I begin the second section of the chapter with a description of Anka, a former student in my second-grade classroom.

Anka caught my attention on the first day of the new school year in my second-grade classroom. Anka was very shy and spoke only when I asked her specific questions such as, "Are you buying or packing your lunch today?" Her body language and quiet voice let me know that she was uncomfortable speaking up in front of the class. When Anka's first-grade teacher, Mrs. Sanders, discovered that Anka was in my class, she wanted to share how she came into her first-grade classroom in March of the previous school year, and while she struggled with reading and writing, she was eager to learn and was very well behaved. Mrs. Sanders, like myself, sees students as individuals. Mrs. Sanders and I work hard to develop our personal relationships with students and determine their academic strengths and weaknesses. Differences are appreciated in both of our classrooms. Anka and her family are from Russia. Anka spoke very little English, and when I assessed her using Clay's (2002) *Observation Survey*, Anka recognized eight letters. This was my first time teaching an English as a second language (ESL) student with such limited concepts of print (letter knowledge, reading, and writing practices). I welcomed this opportunity for my students and for myself.

Recommendations for Working with Diverse Families

Teachers gain valuable information from parent questionnaires that will enhance their teaching. Teachers, who take the time to create, distribute, and collect a questionnaire from parents and caregivers, will be more equipped to support diverse learners who have been a concern for educators and administrators for many years. Over the previous decade, the number of African-American people living in America has increased by 22%, while the number of Hispanic/Latino people has increased by 58% (U.S. Bureau of the Census, 2000). These increases affect schools throughout the country and have brought issues of equity and achievement to the forefront for pre- and in-service teachers, administrators, and literacy coordinators (coaches) who are working with students and families from diverse backgrounds.

Recently, as an elementary school teacher, I welcomed the cultural diversity that so many students brought to my classroom. I made a concerted effort to recognize their individual strengths and needs as learners. I made an effort to not only recognize, but appreciate, each student's diverse needs. All students have rich stories and diverse lives outside of school. Teachers can capitalize on a student's background by letting students take ownership in the writing process. If you ask students to write about picking a pumpkin and this is an experience that a diverse student has not participated in before, this will be a challenging writing activity. All students need to be provided with the opportunity to select writing topics that are interesting and related to their personal experiences. In the next section, I will discuss how I made an attempt to meet Anka's literacy needs as an English language learner.

Conversation Supports Reading and Writing

I was not quite ready to meet Anka's needs when she entered my second-grade classroom. As I reflect on the year that Anka was in my second-grade classroom, I realize that working with Anka was a gift because it provided me with the opportunity to better understand my pedagogy (teaching philosophy) in action. I believe that students learn while engaged in conversation with other students and/or the teacher. I also believe that students learn through listening to classroom conversation between other students and/or the teacher. As Judith Lindfors (1999) says in her book about children's language development:

> "In conversations between two individuals, partners are speakers; both are listeners; both are responders. And in dialogic events involving more than two individuals (class discussions, church services, dinner conversations), listeners may participate fully even if they do not speak at all, vicariously 'speaking,' interpreting, raising objections, agreeing, disagreeing, and so on" (1999, p. 142).

In short, Lindfors is saying that children learn about language when engaged in conversation, and they also learn about language simply by listening to others who are in a conversation. Many children from diverse backgrounds spend a significant amount of instructional time listening to others (teacher and students) engaged in conversation. Diverse learners may feel like "outsiders" in a classroom and may feel uncomfortable speaking to the teacher or to another child because their English-speaking skills may be inferior to their grade-level classmates. A diverse learner may also feel inferior because their academic ability may be less advanced than their classmates, so they try to go unnoticed by the teacher. The child might think, If the teacher does not notice me, he or she will not know that I am struggling with reading or writing. As a teacher, I have often wondered how much English language learners actually learn when they are immersed in an English-speaking classroom with other children whose native English-speaking competence is far different than their own. I have learned through firsthand teaching experience, and through

Lindfor's (1999) research, the most effective way to support all learners, especially English language learners, is through genuine and authentic conversation. Genuine conversation between teachers and their students is critical for supporting young children's reading and writing efforts. If teachers are working with students on reading and writing one-on-one or in a small group, a conversation about a book or about a personal experience can provide the motivation for reading and writing. For instance, I was working with Anka, a second-grade English language learner. Anka just finished reading *Oh No!* by Scharlaine Cairns (1987). Anka and I talked about a ketchup spot that she had on her shirt from lunch. I intentionally used the book she had just read as a springboard for a conversation with Anka.

Anka:	I have a spot on my shirt just like the story!
Melissa:	Yes! You do have a spot on your white sweater, how did it get there?
Anka:	At lunch.
Melissa:	What is the spot from?
Anka:	Ketchup from my hot dog.
Melissa:	Maybe you would like to write about your ketchup spot today? What could you say?
Anka:	There is a spot on my sweater from ketchup. Oh no!
Melissa:	I like that!

I could have extended our conversation even more by asking Anka more questions about items she has spilled and so forth. The point is that teachers can use genuine conversations about events in a book or pictures in a book, or draw on children's experiences to engage and support children's reading and writing efforts. Marie Clay (1991) discusses the importance of oral language development: "We have known for a long time that conversation with an adult was the best tutorial situation in which to raise the child's functioning to a high level" (1991, p. 70).

In the example with Anka, it is apparent that Anka heard the new language structure "Oh no!" on each page of the patterned book, and she assimilated this new language structure into her expanding English-language system. Anka needs to expand her oral language, reading, and writing vocabulary to reach an academic competence similar to her peers. Similar to many English language learners, she was placed in a grade level in school based on her chronological age. At the beginning of second grade, Anka knew eight letters, and she could not recognize any high-frequency words in isolation on the "Ohio Word Test." Anka could write her name and *I* and *no*.

Anka is acquiring a new language, which is no small task. Anka is like scores of English language learners who receive small-group support for 30 minutes a day with other English language learners. Then, for the rest of day, Anka is immersed in a general first-grade classroom with classmates whose reading and writing capabilities are much more advanced than her own. Many of the native English language learners found in primary (kindergarten through third grade) classrooms have had experiences at home that are more closely aligned with the school-based practices (the kinds of reading and writing done at school). In other words, there are many students in American schools today who are like Rachel Smith, who I described previously. Rachel is a student who, like many middle-class, European-American students, reads at home, engages in writing on the computer, and has parents whose work schedules allow them to volunteer in her classroom to gain knowledge about school-based practices. Schools throughout the United States are rapidly changing and are growing more diverse every day. Current U.S. demographics show that 9.9 million children, or 22% of the school-age population, reside in homes where a language other than English is spoken (Anstron, 1996; Crawford; 1997). Teachers need to be prepared to support diverse learners in all academic areas. This book focuses primarily on reading and writing. Teachers are given the charge to educate *all* students who enter their classroom door, so understanding how to support a diverse student population is critical for teachers in classrooms today. In the next section, I will describe some ways teachers can differentiate instruction to meet the needs of *all* students.

Differentiated Instruction

In classrooms today, students have a wide range of academic abilities and are from unique and diverse backgrounds. Teachers are expected to meet the needs of each and every learner within their classroom. In this section, I will first address how reading and writing are reciprocal processes that contribute to each other when taught simultaneously. Second, I will address how teachers can explicitly model reading and writing as a method of support for diverse literacy learners. Then, I will discuss how guided reading and interactive writing are methods that incorporate the joint construction of both reading and writing processes to effectively meet the needs of diverse learners in our current classrooms. First, I will discuss how reading and writing are complex processes and are related to each other. Teachers who integrate reading and writing instruction will further diversify learner's reading and writing development.

Reading and Writing Are Interrelated

Marie Clay (2001) describes a model of reading acquisition as connected to continuous text. As she explains, reading words in isolation is not the goal of reading and reading, is a far more complex process that involves much more than reading words. This complex model of reading "acknowledges writers have to know how to do certain things with language which overlaps with the things that readers have to know or do" (Clay, 2001, p. 12). As children read books and engage in writing, they access and use many sources of information in complex ways. Children who are engaged in reading and writing are learning about the printer's code (letter and word knowledge) each and every time they read and write.

One of Marie Clay's most significant contributions to the field of literacy is communicating to the educational community that reciprocity exists between reading and writing. Since her very first observations of children, Clay has attended to the relationship between reading and writing, and it has been central to her work. In 1991, Clay explained in detail "how writing contributes to early reading progress" (1991, p. 108). She noted that "what the child writes is a rough indicator of what he is attending to in print, and demonstrates the programmes of action he is using for word production" (Clay, 1991, p. 109). Clay notes that writing forces children to slow down and attend to the details of print that can be easily ignored in reading. For example, a child may read the word "crocodile" because there is a picture in the book that resembles a crocodile when, actually, the word in the book is "alligator." This same child may less likely make this type of miscue in writing, because the child is forced to focus on letter formation and how letters work within words and so forth. Writing the word "crocodile" requires the writer to use different letters in a different order than the word "alligator." In writing, children are working on several levels of language at the same time. First, they have to place the letters in the word, words within phrases, phrases within sentences, and sentences within longer text. When children are writing, they need to consider the meaning behind their intended message and use the precise language to convey their intended meaning. Young children who are first learning to write need to not only attend to certain words, they also simultaneously have to focus on sounds in words, parts of words, and letters. In order to illustrate my point, I will share an example of a conversation I had with Jose, who is an English language learner from Mexico. Jose was in my second-grade classroom, and while he chronologically should have been placed in second grade, he was academically performing at a preschool or early kindergarten level of development. I usually met with Jose one-on-one for reading and writing during our literacy block. I tried to link reading and writing for Jose to build on the reciprocity between the two interrelated processes, because I knew this would be helpful and more meaningful for Jose. One day, Jose had just finished reading the patterned book *My Bike* in the Ready to Read Series. I selected this book because it was at his reading level, and I knew he owned a bike and he enjoyed riding it. After he finished reading the book to me, I wanted Jose to write about his bike and I wanted to use the book as a springboard for his writing. Even though I worked really hard to develop a sense of community in our classroom, Jose, like many English language learners, was shy and reluctant to read and write because he felt "different" in comparison to his classmates. In the following transcript, you will notice how I have to initiate conversation and ask Jose multiple questions to invite him to talk. I am trying to encourage Jose to elaborate and extend his oral language and to come up with a longer, more extensive sentence to write about his bike.

Melissa:	What color is your bike?
Jose:	Red.
Melissa:	Where do you ride?
Jose:	At home.
Melissa:	Do you ride on a hill or on a sidewalk?
Jose:	Sidewalk.
Melissa:	Do you ride in the street?
Jose:	[Shakes his head side to side, indicating no]
Melissa:	Is your bike like this one? [I point to the cover of the book]
Jose:	[Shakes his head up and down, indicating yes]
Melissa:	Could you tell me a story about your bike? Can we write about your bike?
Jose:	[Says nothing]
Melissa:	You want to tell me where you have your bike at home?
Jose:	I put my bike at home.
Melissa:	Where do you put it at home? Where do you keep your bike at home?
Jose:	[Smiling, no response]
Melissa:	Do you put your bike in the basement or in your room?
Jose:	In my room.
Melissa:	I put my bike at home in my room.

Jose:	[He writes the word "I" independently on the paper. He is thinking about how to write the word "put."]
Melissa:	Are you thinking about "put"?
Jose:	[He shakes his head up and down, indicating yes]
Melissa:	Write it up here. [pointing to a piece of practice writing paper]
Jose:	[He writes the letter "P" and waits]
Melissa:	Say it slowly and see what you hear?
Jose:	No response. [He writes the letter "T" and waits]
Melissa:	Here, move these pennies up and say p-u-t as you move them.
Jose:	P-u-t.
Melissa:	What letter goes in the middle?
Jose:	O.
Melissa:	It is the letter "U." Now write p-u-t in your story.

In this teaching and learning example, it is apparent that while Jose is a reluctant writer, with tailored support at his level of development, he can independently write about a topic that is important to him. Jose learned new things about print each and every time we wrote together. In the previous example, Jose learned how to pay attention to the sounds he hears in words, such as "put." I tried to support Jose by getting him to use movement, visual, and auditory information while focusing on the written construction of the word "put." According to Carol Lyons (2003), "Children must be taught how to look, what to look at, and what to look for. The most difficult-to-teach children have difficulty acquiring visual and auditory perception skills" (p. 97). In the previous example, I tried to build Jose's understanding of the connection between reading and writing, so I intentionally taught them side-by-side.

In her later work, Marie Clay (2002) describes how engaging children in authentic reading and writing tasks provides opportunities for children to discover new things about print. She explains that reading and writing should be taught side-by-side so that knowledge from one activity can inform the other. Specifically, Clay (2002, p. 20) maintains that writing influences reading by:

- moving in a left-to-right direction (for English) and controlling serial order
- drawing on the language information stored in memory

- making and recognizing visual symbols
- using visual and sound information together
- holding the message so far in mind
- drawing on the known words and structures of language
- searching, checking, and correcting

Reading and writing are interrelated, reciprocal processes. The reciprocity between reading and writing can positively impact our teaching if we actively strive to make the connection between reading and writing explicit in our demonstrations with children. I will describe, in the next section, how teachers can use techniques, such as read aloud, shared reading, guided reading, and interactive writing, to make the connection between reading and writing apparent for children through explicit teaching points.

Modeling Reading and Writing

Young children who are just learning to read and write need to have reading and writing modeled by a more experienced teacher. This is especially important for learners who are learning English as a second language or for children who have a limited background with literacy experiences, such as read alouds or shared writing. Whole-group demonstrations, such as read alouds, allow children to see how a complex process such as reading occurs without the pressure of actually engaging in reading independently.

Shared Writing

It is critical for teachers to differentiate instruction for learners from diverse backgrounds. Shared writing is a method of whole-group instruction that provides children with the chance to see how a complex process such as writing occurs without the responsibility of having to write independently. Shared writing is very useful for beginning readers and writers, especially children who are just learning English as a second language or children who have limited literacy experiences. During shared writing, the teacher and children compose a text together. For example, maybe a class went on a field trip to the zoo, so the teacher and children may recount the events of the trip. During shared writing, the teacher writes on a large piece of chart paper in front of the children and the children, will tell the teacher what to write and together the children and teacher will work out conventions of print, spelling, and grammar. At the end of the shared writing session, the teacher can highlight the skill or strategy that he or she wants the children to learn and address the skill or strategy using the shared writing that was just completed.

Guided Reading

Young children, who are just learning how to read and write, benefit from instruction that gives them the opportunity to read and write with the teacher—especially diverse learners who are learning English as a second language or children who are chronologically placed in the right grade level but whose academic ability is delayed. As previously described in this chapter, reading and writing are complex processes and teachers must find a way to support children who are just learning these processes. Guided reading is an effective teaching approach to provide children in kindergarten through third grade with support while they are engaged in the act of reading. Specifically, Fountas and Pinnell (1996, pp. 1–2) maintain that: "Guided reading leads to independent reading that builds on the process; it is the heart of a balanced literacy program:

- It gives children the opportunity to develop as individual readers while participating in a socially supported activity.
- It gives teachers the opportunity to observe individuals as they process new texts.
- It gives individual readers the opportunity to develop reading strategies so that they can read increasingly difficult texts independently.
- It gives children enjoyable, successful experiences in reading for meaning.
- It develops the abilities needed for independent reading.
- It helps children learn how to introduce text to themselves."

In guided reading, the teacher works with children who are reading books that are at similar text levels and who are using similar reading processes. The teacher introduces the book to the group, and the children independently read the book. During a guided reading group, the teacher may work briefly with individual children, specifically teaching them about the reading process. During guided reading, teachers are making teaching points about reading "on the run." As Fountas and Pinnell explain: "The ultimate goal in guided reading is to help children learn how to use independent reading strategies successfully" (1996, p. 2). As a former classroom teacher and a Reading Recovery teacher, guided reading provides teachers with the opportunity to pinpoint reading instruction to meet each child's specific reading needs. In the general classroom (kindergarten through third grade), teachers are working with so many young children who are just learning how to read and who each have unique needs. In guided reading, teachers are encouraged to place students into flexible reading groups, based on each student's individual reading needs. The teacher moves students into different groups, based on each student's individual reading progress. For example, as a second-grade teacher, I often had as many as five different guided reading groups. For instance, one guided reading group was composed of children who were able to use essential reading skills, such as monitoring, searching, and self-correcting, independently while engaged in reading. The children in this group were reading beginning chapter books while another reading group was composed of children who were just beginning to monitor their reading, and sometimes they noticed discrepancies when they made a mistake or miscue while reading. In this group, the children were reading books that contained a patterned text with two or three sentences per page. This type of text supported their current reading capabilities. Yet, another, smaller reading group, with only 3 children, was reading very simple books that contained one sentence per page, and the sentence contained a patterned text. Anka, who I described previously, was in this reading group. When Anka started second grade, I assessed her reading and writing by administering Marie Clay's (2002) *Observation Survey*. Anka could write her name and the words "no" and "I." She knew five uppercase letters and three lowercase letters in the alphabet. She understood some concepts of print, such as where to begin to read a book, one-to-one correspondence, she could recognize the first and last part of a sentence, and she knew to read the left page before the right page. It is a tremendous challenge for teachers to meet the variety of reading needs within the general classroom without grouping the students according to similar abilities. Guided reading allows teachers to attend to diverse learner needs more directly, and the teacher can individualize and personalize instruction more easily using a small-group reading approach.

Interactive Writing

As previously noted, writing is a complex process for young children to understand. It is even more challenging if you are simultaneously learning to write in a second language or if you can only independently write 15 words and you are in second grade. Specifically, McCarrier, Pinnell, and Fountas (2000) maintain that interactive writing is an effective instructional method that is "a dynamic, collaborative literacy event in which children actively compose together, considering appropriate words, phrases, organization of text, and layout" (p. xv). During interactive writing, the teacher will carefully select specific teaching points to address with children when they are engaged in the act of writing together. Interactive writing is different than shared writing, because the children take part in the writing process and "share the pen" with the teacher. In shared writing, the teacher acts as a scribe for a group of children. The teacher may focus the children's attention toward spelling or word patterns, which will ultimately help them gain a better understanding of how words "work." Interactive writing provides beginning writers with the opportunity to move from approximation to actual development in writing, and this technique allows teachers to provide specific support at just the right time. For example, a first-grade classroom is learning about plant growth in science. The children have each planted a seed and they are watching it sprout. Every other day, the children are expected to observe their plant and write about it in their plant journal. Before the children write independently in their journals, the teacher decides to conduct an interactive writing lesson with the children. The teacher and children write a journal entry together about plant growth. In an interactive writing lesson, such as the lesson just described, the teacher carefully plans teaching points that are directly related to certain writing conventions that the children need to learn or that can be reinforced.

Interactive writing is an effective teaching tool for young children, especially diverse learners; after all, writing on your own may be overwhelming for a child with a limited writing vocabulary. During interactive writing, a child can observe how more academically advanced classmates and the teacher construct words from phonemes and clusters, attend to certain spelling patterns, and discuss ideas for writing. While listening to an interactive writing conversation between classmates and the teacher who are cocreating a piece of writing, a diverse learner can learn more about the act of writing that he or she may use later in his or her own writing.

Conclusion

In this chapter, I offered teachers recommendations for working with children and families from diverse backgrounds. I suggested that teachers look beyond their classroom and into the homes of children from diverse backgrounds. First, teachers can prepare a questionnaire for all children and have it translated into the languages being spoken in your children's homes. The questionnaire will provide teachers with more in-depth knowledge about the reading, writing, and cultural practices of the children and families whom they are working with. Second, teachers can act as an ambassador for children and families from diverse backgrounds and try to support them as they learn more about "American" schools that may be foreign and dislocating for them. Teachers can invite parents into the classroom to participate in meaningful ways, which will allow the parents to observe firsthand the events of the classroom. Teachers can customize instruction to meet each child's diverse needs more effectively through small-group instruction. In this chapter, I discussed how read alouds, shared writing, guided reading, and interactive writing are beneficial literacy approaches for meeting the range of learners who are in today's classrooms.

References

Anstron, K. (1996). Defining the limited-English-proficient population. *Directions in Language and Education, 1*(9). Washington, DC: National Clearinghouse for Bilingual Education.

Cairns, S. (1987). *Oh No!* Crystal Lake, IL: Rigby Education.

Clay, M. M. (1991). *Becoming literate: The construction of inner control.* Portsmouth, NH: Heinemann.

Clay, M. M. (2001). *Change over time: In children's literacy development.* Portsmouth, NH: Heinemann.

Clay, M. M. (2002). *An observation survey of early literacy achievement.* Portsmouth, NH: Heinemann.

Crawford, J. (1997). *Best evidence: Research foundations of the Bilingual Education Act.* Washington, DC: National Clearinghouse for Bilingual Education.

Fountas, I. C., & Pinnell, G. S. (1996). *Guided reading: Good first teaching for all children.* Portsmouth, NH: Heinemann.

Hicks, D. (2002). *Reading lives: Working class children and literacy learning.* New York: Cambridge University Press.

Lindfors, J. W. (1999). *Children's inquiry: Using language to make sense of the world.* New York: Teacher's College Press.

Lyons, C. (2003). *Teaching struggling readers: How to use brain-based research to maximize learning.* Portsmouth, NH: Heineman.

Martin, C. (1997). *My bike.* Huntington Beach, CA: Pacific Learning.

McCarrier, A., Pinnell, G. S., & Fountas, I. C. (2000). *Interactive writing: How language and literacy come together, K–2.* Portsmouth, NH: Heinemann.

Moll, L. C., Amanti, C., Neff, D., & Gonzales, N. (1992). Funds of knowledge for teaching: Using a qualitative approach to connect homes and classrooms. *Theory Into Practice, XXXI*(2), 132–141.

Puchner, L. D., & Hardman, J. (1996). Family literacy in a cultural context: Southeast Asian immigrants in the United States. *NCAL connections* (pp. 1–3). Philadelphia: National Center on Adult Literacy, University of Pennsylvania.

Stine, R. L. (1995). *Goosebumps: Horror at camp jellyjam.* New York: Scholastic.

Tabors, P. O. (1997). *One child, two languages: A guide for preschool educators learning English as a second language.* Baltimore: Paul H. Brookes.

Taylor, D. (1983). *Family literacy: Young children learning to read and write.* Portsmouth, NH: Heinemann.

U.S. Bureau of the Census. (2000). Statistical Abstract of the United States.

U.S. Census Bureau. (2000). Population change and distribution. Online: www.census.gov/prod/2001pubs/p.1-7.pdf

U.S. Department of Education. (2001). Executive Summary of the No Child Left Behind Act of 2001. Online: www.ed.gov/nclb/overview/intro/execusumm.html/ p.1-4.pdf

Wilder, L. (1935). *Little house on the prairie.* New York: Harper Collins.

Chapter 7

Why First-Language Literacy Is Important for Second-Language Learners

Vickie Ellison

Edgardo is 8 years old, and he is in the second grade. His family came from Mexico 2 months before he started school. He was placed in second grade based on his chronological age. Edgardo is fluent in Spanish and did well in school in Mexico. Unfortunately, Edgardo is struggling in second grade because of his limited knowledge of English and limited ability to read and write in English. Most of his classmates and his teacher read and write English easily, so he feels like an "outsider." Edgardo can write 18 letters of the alphabet. He can write eight English words independently. Edgardo is trying to "fit in" and he wants to do well in school. His parents also share the same dream for Edgardo; they want him to be successful.

Introduction

"Institutionalized bilingualism shuts doors. It nourishes self-ghettoization, and ghettoization nourishes racial antagonism...Using some language other than English dooms people to second-class citizenship in American society ... Monolingual education opens doors to the larger world" (Schlesinger, Jr., 1998, pp. 113–114).

Teachers have a very important role to play in the development of literacy of their students. They must recognize that students do not come into the classrooms as empty vessels waiting to be filled with knowledge. Students come into the classroom with experiences and their life histories; the culturally relevant teacher will use these experiences and life histories to assist the child in achieving academic success.

What can the classroom teacher do to assist a second-language learner of English in his or her classroom? First, the teacher must learn about the student's culture and understand, as well as appreciate, that culture. This is more than sympathy for the children and their culture—nor should teachers feel these children need to be rescued. If someone is familiar with a topic, then they have a better understanding of it. The same is true with people and culture. The more knowledge teachers have of their students' culture, the more effective they will be at addressing their specific needs. Ladson-Billings (1995) advocates to use the cultural background of the students as a vehicle of learning— to deny who they are is to demean or belittle them, and they will shut down and turn away from learning.

Equally important is to know you. A teacher must know his or her own weaknesses, strengths, and prejudices. Ladson-Billings (1994) states that one element of culturally relevant teaching is the teachers' perceptions of themselves as well as others. She further maintains that culturally relevant teachers see themselves as professionals and strongly identify with teaching. Be willing to learn from the students as well and take what they bring with them to the classroom and use it to help them learn.

There are crucial issues about language and identity that need to be understood by anyone who is teaching a person of a different ethnic/cultural background. It simply is not a matter of assimilation into a new culture, such as pouring chocolate syrup over ice cream and mixing it up. Simply learning to speak English does not automatically mean that the child will be treated just like any white middle-class American child. The intersection of language and identity are going to be discussed in the next section.

Language, Identity, and Culture

Culture is becoming a very important issue not only in educational setting, but in the political arena as well. The last presidential election was, in part, a cultural war about values and beliefs. Culture, according to Kalantzig et al. (1989), is a whole way of life, not just aspects of high culture or folk culture:

"Language is the key to a person's identity because it is so often taken as a biological inheritance that its association with ethnic paternity is both frequent and powerful. It is 'acquired with the mother's milk.' It is not only shaped by the inherited organism of speech, but it, in turn, shapes the mind and the mental process" (Giles, 1977, p. 26).

Giles (1977) states that language is saturated with the tears and joys of the ancestors. It is loved with all one's being:

"Language is commonly among the conscious 'do' and 'don'ts' as well as the unconscious ones: That is, it is among the evaluated dimensions of ethnicity membership (whether consciously or not). It is particularly touched by the sanctity of verbal rituals, and by the specialness of written ones, and, quite naturally, comes to be classed with the sanctities of which they are part and which depend upon them. Language is not only code, but Code. For the ethnicity experience; language is much more than 'merely communication'; just as ethnicity is much more than 'mere life'" (Giles, 1977, p. 28).

Students have been punished for speaking their first language (L1) and have been made to feel ashamed of their own language and cultural background, because many in education feel that bilingualism is a disease that needs to be eradicated in order for these students to become good Americans. Trueba (1993) states language is one of the most powerful human resources needed to maintain a sense of self-identity and self-fulfillment. Without a full command of one's own language, ethnic identity, the sharing of fundamental common cultural values and norms, the social context of interpersonal communication that guides interactional understandings, and the feeling of belonging within a group are not possible. Trueba (1993) further states that without language and a strong self-identity, the ability to learn other languages and understand other cultures is impaired.

Trueba (1993) strongly advocates the importance of understanding the inseparability of language and culture in the process of learning and the role of schools in facilitating the learning of minority students. It is his belief, and that of many others, that teachers must make serious attempts at using cultural and linguistic knowledge to advance teaching and learning and the quality of life for immigrant and minority groups in Western societies.

Many students of color, such as Edgardo, enter schools and are told, or it is understood from nonverbal communication by their teachers, that their language is bad or substandard or that their native language should not be spoken. In order to succeed, they must speak and act in a specific, prescribed way, and this way is the only way. According to Delpit (1997), to tell a child who comes to school with a language that is intimately connected with loved ones, community, and personal identity that this language is wrong or ignorant and that something is wrong with the student and his or her family, in essence, to denigrate their language has dire consequences for that child. She goes on to say that teachers must know how to effectively teach to students whose culture and language differ from that of the school and must understand how and why students decide to add another language form to their repertoire. Thus, students' cultures, languages, and identities cannot be dismissed and should not be belittled.

According to Peale (1991), two presidential reports describe students' native language competency as untapped resources, and by being brought into the mainstream of educational and employment opportunities, "they can build on their existing linguistic resources so that they may contribute more to American education, diplomacy, and international business" (p. 447). It seems apparent from the research that home/first-language maintenance would strengthen the United States and benefit international politics and commerce.

In a world that is becoming more and more global each day, the United States would benefit by having more citizens who are proficient in more than just one language. It is clear that many misunderstandings between nations are the result of not only a failure to understand each other's language, but also there is a critical misunderstanding of each other's cultures as well.

In an educational setting, such as the classroom, for second-language learners to be successful in school, it would be beneficial for teachers to have a thorough understanding and knowledge of the cultural backgrounds of their students.

Cultural Awareness Knowledge

Cultural understanding is often a neglected notion in teacher training institutions. As a result of a lack of cultural understanding of students, some teachers blame the students as a reason for the students' underachievement. Gay (2002) states: "Too many teachers are inadequately prepared to teach ethnically diverse students" (p. 106). Gay (2002) further maintains that teachers need to have knowledge about cultural diversity that goes beyond mere awareness of, respect for, and general recognition of the fact that ethnic groups have different values or express similar values in various ways" (p. 107).

Barnes (1991) states that teachers must also have a deep understanding of the experience and cultural backgrounds that their students bring to the school setting. Teachers must be able to work with all students, not just students who look the same and come from the same culture as that of the teacher. They must also be able to teach children of color, children with different cultural backgrounds, and children with special needs. Teachers need to have an action plan for meeting the diverse needs of students such as Edgardo. For example, in Mexico, students do not call their teachers by their names, such as Mrs. Jones or Mr. Smith, but rather call them Teacher, and this is considered respectful. Also, when a teacher is talking to a student in Mexico, it would be rude or disrespectful for the student to look at the teacher; however, in the United States, it would be disrespectful for the student not to look at the teacher. Teachers who have students from a different culture need to be aware of these cultural differences that may cause major misunderstandings in the classroom between the student and teacher.

The attitudes and beliefs teachers have about these students are crucial. Grossman, Wilson, and Shulman (1989) have investigated teacher beliefs and the effect those beliefs have on teaching knowledge. They state that teachers frequently treat their beliefs as knowledge and that teachers' beliefs about subject matter powerfully affect their teaching in the same way as the relationship between subject-matter knowledge and pedagogy. Many current theories of learning view learners as active constructors of knowledge who make sense of the world and learn by interpreting events through their existing knowledge and beliefs (Putnam & Borko, 1997).

Putnam and Borko (1997) also state that teachers interpret experiences through the filters of their existing knowledge and beliefs. Furthermore, teachers' knowledge and beliefs about learning, teaching, and subject matter are critically important determinants of how those teachers teach. Teachers' conceptions of students' abilities and expectations for students from different backgrounds lead to differential treatment of students in classrooms. Those knowledge and beliefs determine what and how the teacher learns from experiences in the classroom or from various professional-development experiences. Teachers can make sense of new instructional practices or ideas only through the lenses of what they already know and believe (Putnam & Borko, 1997).

Teachers should have knowledge of the culture of their students just as they are expected to have subject-matter knowledge of the language. García-Moya (1981) states:

"Teachers must be aware of the many social functions of language in order to convey to their students the wonder and greatness of this uniquely human phenomenon. One's needs, aspirations, and sentiments—indeed, one's culture—are expressed by language in many different ways" (p. 60).

Additionally, García-Moya (1981) maintains that the teacher's attitudes toward language is essential to the success of any language program.

Ladson-Billings (1995) states: "Culturally relevant teachers utilize students' culture as a vehicle for learning" (p. 161). Ladson-Billings (1994) also maintains: "Culturally relevant pedagogy rests on three criteria or propositions:

(1) Students must experience academic success;

(2) Students must develop and/or maintain cultural competence; and

(3) Students must develop a critical consciousness through which they challenge the status quo of the current social order" (p. 160).

Ladson-Billings (1995) goes on to state that culturally relevant teaching requires that teachers attend to students' academic needs, not simply make them feel good. The goal of culturally relevant teaching is to get students to select academic excellence.

In order to utilize culturally relevant teaching and learning, the teacher must first know and understand the culture as well as the students. This knowledge involves a certain degree of caring, not just well wishing, or sympathy, or even merely an interest in what happens to another person. As Mayeroff (1971) states:

> "To care for someone, I must know many things. I must know, for example, how the other is, what his powers and limitations are, what his needs are, and what is conducive to his growth; I must know how to respond to his needs, and what my own powers and limitations are" (p. 13).

Furthermore, a belief that all students can learn is essential. This is the third tenet of Ladson-Billings' (1995) culturally relevant pedagogy. She advocates providing many opportunities for students to learn in the classroom, as well as presenting clear expectations.

Be an advocate for the students in your classroom. If there are no heritage/first-language or English as a second language (ESL) classes, provide evidence to the school administrators, principal, school board members, and parents as to why there should be and how such classes would benefit second-language learners.

Help parents of English language learners understand the policies and procedures at your school. Many parents of ESL students are not involved as actively in the schools as their U.S. counterparts because they do not know the language, they are at work during the time of school functions, and they feel that the teachers and the school officials know what is best and should not be questioned.

An effort should be made by schools to provide limited English-speaking parents with information about the school in their native language, if possible, to foster a working relationship between parents and the schools. When parents know that there is someone at the school who speaks their language, they may be more inclined to get involved with their children's education, as well as becoming more actively involved in the school. School officials, teachers, and administrators should also be flexible in setting up open houses and other meetings so that parents who work during hours other than nine to five can be accommodated and be made to feel welcome in the school.

Parents should not be told to speak English to their children. Forcing parents to speak English to their children, when the parents themselves speak little English or none at all, harms the relationship between parents and their children. For example, parents can no longer communicate with their children, because the children speak more English than they do (Marujo, 1993; García, Wilkinson, & Ortiz, 1995; Rodriguez, 1982). Children, often times, must serve as translators and interpreters for their parents, putting extreme pressure on the children to perform skills in which they have not been trained. De Houwer (1999) states that: "The abrupt end of the use of the home language by a child's parents may lead to great emotional and psychological difficulties, both for the parents and for the child" (p. 7).

In the classroom, if you have a student whose first language is not English, it is important to draw on that student's prior knowledge and background knowledge to help him or her learn the content. Prior knowledge is existing knowledge of a topic that a student can recall. For example, baking a cake; anyone who has baked a cake before can tell another person what is involved in baking a cake. Asking students if they have heard of something and asking them to describe what they know can easily access prior knowledge. Background knowledge is information needed for the student to understand new information. Before a student can use multiplication, they must first know how to use addition. Thus, it is important that you, as the teacher, scaffold the content for the English language learner. For example, before reading a short story or novel, you might do a series of prereading activities to get the students ready for what they are about to read. Such strategies are not only beneficial for the second-language learner, but are also beneficial for the native English speaker.

If you do not speak the language of the student, ask the school to provide you with an aide or interpreter who speaks the students' mother tongue. If this is not possible, elicit assistance from the community by asking for volunteers who are speakers of the language to come to the classroom and assist the students to learn the content.

Contact the national Teaching English to Speakers of Other Languages (TESOL) organization for assistance in finding a local chapter and also to learn about up-to-date methods and strategies for teaching ESL students. There are many ways in which you can help your students learn and, moreover, you do not need to reinvent the wheel to do so. Connect with other teachers in your school who have the same students and share your concerns for the students. If there is no one at the school who works with ESL students, then connect with teachers at other schools in nearby school districts who have ESL programs or offer sheltered English programs to find the support and assistance you need. Sheltered English programs, according to Curtain and Dahlberg (2004, p. 250), are designed to teach English and subject content to English language learners using specially adapted (but not watered-down) curriculum and materials. In essence, according to Curtain and Dahlberg (2004), language is a tool through which subject content is learned and not primarily the object of instruction.

There are many ways to help English language learners in the classroom. Teachers must also be aware that there is no added time or cost to providing children with instruction in their native language, and doing so is not only beneficial for the child, but beneficial for society as well. One such way is by asking parents or other members of the community to volunteer in the classroom to assist second-language learners. Teachers can also write to the embassy where their students are from and ask for resources that will benefit their students.

A brief discussion of how first- and second-languages are acquired may be beneficial in facilitating the understanding of how mother-tongue maintenance can be very beneficial in the learning of a second language. The differences in learning a foreign language versus acquiring a language from birth are related to how language is acquired. Although there are some similarities in the first- and second-language acquisition process, there are also differences. In terms of the similarities, both are complex processes, and both involve imitation, repetition, and practice, to some degree (Titone & Danesi, 1985). A major difference is the age of acquiring the language; usually, a native language is acquired through a natural process from birth (e.g., in a family).

First- and Second-Language Acquisition

Foreign/Second languages (L2) are generally learned later in life, as a teenager or an adult. Neurological aspects are also different, such as the role the speech muscles play in articulation. Along with neurological aspects, psychological aspects must also be considered; for example, the phonological and syntactical contrast between the two languages.

Another major difference between first and second acquisition is the context of learning. First-language (L1) acquisition, generally, occurs in a home environment without formal pedagogical instruction. Second-language learning normally occurs in a classroom environment and is typically under the control of a teacher (Titone & Danesi, 1985).

Literacy in the first language occurs over a period of time. For example, by the age of 18 months, children have a vocabulary of approximately 40 or 50 words. They combine single-word utterances with gestures and context to communicate a great deal. Mastery of one's first language comes from being part of a language community, not from direct instruction (Williams & Capizzi Snipper, 1990). Language is acquired rather than learned, because acquisition is related to unconscious knowledge of language and learning is related to conscious knowledge about language that comes when children are older, through formal instruction (Williams & Capizzi Snipper, 1990).

In reference to second-language acquisition and learning, a distinction must be made between young children, teenagers, and adults. Children taught a second language at a very early age acquire the second language in much the same way as their first language. Leopold (Williams & Capizzi Snipper, 1990) maintains that children who have more than one label with which to identify an object soon realize that language is an abstraction of reality than can be subjective and malleable. He also states that rather than being confusing, two labels enhance flexibility and creativity.

Older learners face different issues in learning a second language: motivation, social factors, L1 literacy, and cognitive ability, just to name a few. However, one cannot simply say that younger children are better at learning languages than adults. Krashen (1987) makes a distinction between learning a language and acquiring a language. He is a strong advocate of adults acquiring a second language, provided that comprehensible input is provided. Comprehensible input is defined as providing language that contains linguistic items that are slightly beyond the learner's present linguistic ability (Richards, Platt, & Platt, 1992). Motivation, self-confidence, and anxiety are factors that relate to success in learning a second language. According to Krashen (1987), children are better language learners over time because they have a longer time in which to acquire the language than do adults.

Thus, learning a language is a very complex process that involves a number of different variables that affect the degree to which a person is successful at learning a second language.

Language Literacy

From the discussion of first- and second-language acquisition comes the issue of literacy and how literacy is learned. Literacy, very simply defined, is the ability to read and write in a language. It is important to note that children learn to speak a language before they learn to read and write in a language. Edgardo is beginning to learn English, and he can be understood quite well by his teacher and classmates. However, when it comes to independent reading and writing, Edgardo is struggling and is far behind his fellow classmates.

Literacy has also been defined as having two discourses or uses. Primary discourse or informal spoken language serves for communication with family, friend, and neighbors, and secondary discourse or formal language is used in institutions, such as schools, stores, workplaces, government offices, churches, and businesses (Brisk & Harrington, 2000, p. 2). According to Brisk and Harrington (2000, p. 3) literacy is developmental, that is, that children get better at it with time and experience. Thus, that this formal language may start at home and then at school is a continuation and enhancement of efforts started at home. It is very important for teachers to carve out time in their daily schedules for students to talk to each other. Children who are learning English as a second language and children who are native English learners but speak with a dialect need opportunities to engage in conversation at school to further develop their oral language communication skills.

Generally speaking, when students in the United States have the opportunity to learn a foreign/second language, they are literate in their first. Thus, they can use the skills they acquired in their first language to learn the second. Nouns, verbs, adverbs, adjectives, etc., are the same concept in any language. This prior language knowledge that second-language learners already have about learning language can assist them in learning a second or third language. There is considerable evidence, according to Cummins (2000), of interdependence of literacy-related or academic skills across languages, such that the better developed children's L1 conceptual foundation, the more likely they are to develop similarly high levels of conceptual abilities in their L2.

Lingering Misconceptions

In a literature review, Cummins (1983, 2000) documents some 30 studies of heritage language and bilingual education in Canada, the United States, Europe, and South Africa. Cummins (1983) found the following: "The findings for each study are virtually identical in that minority students enrolled in heritage language bilingual programs progress academically at least as well as equivalent students enrolled in the regular school program" (p. 51). In the many recent studies of students enrolled in heritage language bilingual programs, bilingual students' academic performance was better than their monolingual counterparts. Heritage languages are languages spoken by people in an ethnic or linguistic community in a country, whereas the dominant members of society speak the national or prestige language. Monolingual refers to a person who speaks one language—which is usually the national or prestige language.

Cummins discusses the misconceptions educators and ethnic parents had in regard to such programs. There is a fear among parents that focusing on the native language would hinder their children from learning the dominant language. Some teachers believe that teaching students in their native language is too time-consuming and disruptive. There are many people in our current society who perceive heritage language teaching as socially divisive, excessively costly, as well as detrimental in the minority students' need to learn the dominant language. Cummins (2000) maintains that parental and community involvement may be crucial in the academic success of students or lack thereof. In nearly all of the studies, the studies show substantial evidence that these concerns are baseless. He also addresses the concern about ghettoization, in a report in Sweden, that this problem can be avoided by offering heritage language classes in schools were there are other classes offered so that the students would be able to join in using common resources available, as well as joining in other activities together with other children.

Cummins (1983, 2000) also proposes an interdependence hypothesis that might account for academic achievement of bilingual students. For example, when a student is learning reading skills in his or her native language, he or she is not just learning skills that are specific only to that native language; rather, that student is learning deeper conceptual and linguistic proficiency, which is strongly related to the development of literacy in the second language and general academic skills. Cummins purports that there is an underlying cognitive/academic proficiency, which is common across languages, and that this common proficiency makes possible the transfer of cognitive/academic or literacy-related skills across languages.

The same misconceptions are still very much in the forefront as the U.S. society enters into the 21st century. Tse (2001) makes the same claim now as Cummins did in 1983. Tse (2001) discusses the parental and school misconceptions of language learning. Once again, parents want to make certain that all their child's energy is focused on learning English. There is a fear in the community that maintaining one's heritage/first language will prohibit children from becoming "fully" American. Tse addresses the issue of language ghettos, just as Cummins did. She calls the notion a myth due to the fact that in the United States, the pattern of migration makes it virtually impossible that successive generations would live in the same enclave community, thus creating a language ghetto. Tse believes that this myth came about because such enclaves continually house new immigrant families, creating the illusion that there are language ghettos all over the United States. She states that the children and grandchildren of immigrants usually move out of the enclave and are replaced by new immigrant families.

Tse (2001) also discusses the benefits of bilingualism for the society as well as the individual. The economy is now more global than it has ever been; thus, there is a need to have government officials, business people, and others who can communicate with their global neighbors, as well as have the cultural awareness and understanding to do so effectively. Tse highlights the difficulty of finding "true bilinguals" to work in fields such as foreign trade, tourism, and international banking in such a commonly taught language as Spanish. She cites a senior vice president of Visa's Latin American operations as saying that it was difficult to find true bilinguals and that more are mediocre.

Tse (2001, p. 45) also illustrates how having prior experience and knowledge helps a student to learn another language with relative ease. She gives an example of Rita, a native English speaker wanting to learn French. Rita's neighbor, Jane, is a French speaker who keeps up on current events. When the two women get together, Jane speaks in simplified French, and Rita is able to understand because she has already read the paper they are discussing in English. Therefore, in this example, Rita is using her prior knowledge and her background knowledge to assist her in understanding the French she hears from Jane. This explanation is useful in understanding why first-language acquisition is important to anyone who must, or wants to, learn a second language, unless as Cummins (1979) states, if the two languages are very dissimilar. At this point, it is necessary to discuss Cummins' notion of academic language proficiency and basic interpersonal communicative skills.

Knowing a Language for Interpersonal Communication

Cummins (1981, 2000) defines basic interpersonal communicative skills (BICS) as basic vocabulary and grammar that are manifested in everyday interpersonal communicative situations (1981, p. 17). He maintains that in a monolingual context, everyone acquires BICS, except for the severely retarded and autistic. Cognitive/Academic Language Proficiency (CALP) are cognitive abilities associated with language that includes academic aspects of language learning.

There is a distinct difference between knowing a language in a general sense and knowing a language to the degree that one can discuss or understand higher order concepts. To illustrate my point, I will share the following vignette of my former student, Omar. Omar is a junior in a high school. His family came from Mexico 7 years ago. Omar took ESL classes in middle school. His grades were average, and it took him a long time to do his homework. When he entered high school, a counselor determined that his English was good and he did not need further ESL support and should be mainstreamed into regular classes.

Omar's grades began to slip in high school, and homework was increasingly more difficult and time-consuming. For his junior year, Omar signed up to take my Spanish Language Arts (SLA) class. On occasion, Omar would bring in his assignments from English for help. I would remind him of what we did in SLA that was similar to what he was being asked to do in his English class. Subsequently, his grades improved and he became more confident in his English-only classes. In my SLA class, Omar was one of my best students. Omar was placed in English-only classes based on his oral skills, or as Cummins maintains, his basic interpersonal communicative skills. What the counselor failed to realize was that it takes a second-language learner more time to obtain CALP in the second language.

It is this very concept that confuses many monolingual speakers when they hear a second-language learner of English speak; they may automatically assume that that person is capable of processing language academically. Thus, because a person speaks well, it is assumed that they have the language skills necessary to do academic work as well. If this were the case, then a native English speaker should be able to talk about the underlying themes in Cervantes' (1997) *El ingenioso Don Quijote de la Mancha* after only a year or two of taking Spanish as a foreign language. The idea would be ludicrous to teachers who teach beginning and beginning intermediate Spanish courses. Unfortunately, this very notion is what is expected of children learning English as a second language. In many transitional and bilingual programs, students are mainstreamed into regular classes and it is expected that they be able to work at the same academic level as native English speakers.

Knowing a Language for Academic Purposes

Cummins (1981, 2000) maintains that it may take from 5 to 7 years, on average, for a second-language learner to learn CALP. Maintaining the heritage/first language could be very beneficial in assisting a second-language learner to develop the needed academic proficiency in the target language. Therefore, a child who is literate in his or her first language can draw on new knowledge and prior knowledge from learning the first language to assist them in learning a second language. Returning to Tse's (2001, p. 45) example of Rita, the native

English speaker, it is possible to consider how Rita uses English to help her with French. Rita has read many newspapers, and English and French newspapers are generally written in the same style. Therefore, Rita can look at a French newspaper and she can identify the title of a story, the table of contents, as well as the different sections of the paper, that is, the opinion page, the arts and theater section, and the home and gardening section. Rita can use her knowledge of reading newspapers in English to assist her in acquiring new labels in French. That is, because she is already familiar with reading newspapers, she does not need to be taught how to read a newspaper in French and learn the French terminology for reading newspapers.

Utilizing Background Knowledge in the First Language to Learn a Second Language

The same would be true for second-language learners of English. If a student such as Edgardo comes to a classroom with very limited knowledge or no knowledge of English, but is literate in Spanish, that student will learn English much more rapidly than a student who is not literate in Spanish. In the case of the literate student, it is only a matter of learning the new labels for the same information. Another example is Consuelo, a literate Spanish-speaking student who is in an ESL class reading a short story. The teacher wants to know who the main character is and explains the concept of a main character to the class. Consuelo recognizes that this description fits the same definition as the "personaje" principal in Spanish and raises her hand to offer the name of the main character. She now knows that main character and "personaje" principal are the same concept. Consuelo does not need to be taught the word main character, as well as the concept of what a main character is, because she already knows that information. She only needed to learn the new label in English. In the case of the illiterate student, it would mean that the student had to learn the content, as well as learning the labels of the content.

The situation would be different for Paco, who is also in an ESL class; however, he stopped attending school after the third grade and is a freshman in high school. Paco would need to be taught the concept of a main character of a story, as well as the vocabulary work "main character" because his literacy level is very low for his native language—Spanish. Therefore, it would take Paco longer to learn about main characters in a story because he would have to learn the concept associated with the term. He may have to read several short stories before he is able to understand the concept of the main character and be able to identify the main character in a story. He will need exposure to short stories, whereas Consuelo is already familiar with what a short story is, as well as a main character.

Some opponents of heritage/first language education may say that since the student doesn't know their first language, then they may as well just learn English. Unfortunately, this is very much like building a house on a weak foundation or building a house with no foundation at all. What may happen is that the student will learn English poorly because of the double work he or she must do to learn the language. There is also the issue of time second-language learners of English are quickly transitioned out of many bilingual programs and put into mainstream classrooms, where they are expected to have the necessary academic language skills to succeed and do not have the support they need to succeed in that classroom.

This is a critical issue facing many ESL teachers and administrators who complain that their students are having to take proficiency tests after being enrolled in an ESL class for less than a year. The only assistance students are able to receive is the use of a dictionary and perhaps an interpreter. However, a dictionary or an interpreter will do little to assist a student who has no concept of what is meant by the "time capsule" in English. The benefit of an interpreter is that he or she can interpret into the student's native language but cannot explain any terminology. A dictionary is equally inadequate, especially if the students have not used a dictionary or have not been trained to use a dictionary effectively.

What opponents of heritage/first language development and bilingual education fail to realize is that a person who is literate in their first language will learn a second language faster than a person who is not literate in their mother tongue. Thus, the amount of time spent in an ESL classroom may be reduced by as much as half, that is, rather than taking 5–7 years to develop CALPs, the same results could be achieved in 3–4 years with developing the heritage/first language along with ESL instruction.

Teachers, administrators, and other school personnel need to recognize that although a student may appear to speak good English, that does not necessarily mean that that student can do academic grade-level school work without some form of assistance. As I stated earlier, basic interpersonal communicative skills are learned rather quickly; however, it takes more time, 5–7 years, on average, to obtain CALP. If the second-language learner is given support, that time could be reduced to 3–5 years. There are many ways in which a teacher can assist second-language learners to be successful in the classroom. The following sections are recommendations that teachers can implement quickly in their lessons.

Recommendations for Teachers

Mrs. Smith told her third graders to get out a pencil and a piece of paper and begin copying the letters on the board. Courtney raised her hand and said, "I ain't got any pencil." Mrs. Smith responded, "I don't have a pencil. You don't have a pencil. She doesn't have a pencil. He doesn't have a pencil." Courtney looked at the teacher and asked, "Ain't nobody here got any pencil?"

The above vignette demonstrates the need for teachers to address student needs and to treat students as individuals. The following recommendations are useful for second-language learners and native English-speakers whose primary dialect is not standard English.

Prepare Students for Major Activities

Utilize prereading activities to help students navigate the text, such as a prediction activity, where new words are presented, and in groups, students predict what the meaning of the words are and then go over the words with the students. Utilize prewriting activities to help students learn to write and realize that writing is a process. For example, have students brainstorm ideas, then write down more information about their brainstormed ideas.

Reduce the Cognitive Load of Your Lessons

Keep in mind that some immigrant students may not have much schooling prior to coming to the United States, or their educational experience was very different than what is the norm for the United States. For example, as stated above, in Mexico, it is considered polite and a sign of respect for students to address their teacher as "Teacher" rather than Mrs. Marks or Mr. North. It is also disrespectful for a student to look directly at the teacher when he or she is talking to the student. Explain the rules of the American classroom to your second-language students and let them know about your expectations of them. Also, choose activities and assignments that allow students to draw on their prior knowledge and life experiences (Miller & Endo, 2004).

Reduce the Language Load of Your Lessons

That is, be aware of how much language you use in your lessons. Use gestures to help students understand the meaning of important vocabulary. Write directions on the board as well as saying them orally. For example, while telling students to turn to a particular page in the book, you can also write the page number on the blackboard. Purposefully select words and sentence structure that will help students learn, rather than hinder their success in the classroom. This does not mean to oversimplify vocabulary, but rather to model academic language, surrounding it with appropriate context clues and other information that will help English language learners to understand and learn these words (Miller & Endo, 2004, p. 790).

Build Relationships with Students

Learn about your students' lives beyond the classroom. This inquiry can be formal or informal. For example, walk around the neighborhood, paying attention to the types of public messages (business signs to graffiti), the language utilized, and the purposes of text. Walking around students' homes or other impromptu acts offer insights into children's lives beyond the school (MacGillivray & Rueda, 2003).

Narrative Strategies

Use literature-based activities to initiate dialogue and provide a meaningful context for conversations. For example, reading patterned and predictable books can assist ESL learners familiar with narrative mode of communication, understand the structure of English language, and learn about the syntax, rhythm, and pacing of the English language. After story reading, the students can be invited to improvise dialogue or to retell the story, in which they are able to draw on their personal experiences to elaborate the characters' conversations (Smith, 2003).

Create Environments for Discovery and Learning

Link reading with writing, listening, and speaking, so that students of diverse backgrounds can use their strengths in all language processes when learning to read.

Provide students of diverse backgrounds with motivating, purposeful literacy activities that will promote their ownership of literacy. Give students many opportunities for wide independent reading and help them develop their own tastes and interests as readers. Have high expectations for literacy achievement of students of diverse backgrounds while realizing that instruction to help students meet these expectations may need to be responsive to their cultural values. Center reading instruction on literature, drawing from our knowledge of students' backgrounds, to help them make personal connections to literature and encouraging them to share their thoughts about literature in writing and discussions with peers. Utilize approaches that emphasize higher level thinking with text, promote student risk taking as literacy learners, and encourage students' active involvement in developing their own understandings of reading and writing (Yaden & Tardibuono, 2004, pp. 53–54).

Continuing Education

Many universities and community colleges offer courses on ESL instruction (see Appendix 7:1). You can also attend a TESOL, ACTFL (American Council on the Teaching of Foreign Languages), or regional language organization, such as OFLA (Ohio Foreign Language Association) and CSC (Central States Conference). These organizations have annual conferences, where you can learn more about second-language learners.

Conclusion

Institutional bilingualism does not shut doors, as Schlesinger, Jr. (1998), claims, but rather, opens door for the second-language learner of English. The notion of self-ghettoization does not exist, as has been documented by decades of research (see Cummins, 1979, 1981, 1983, 2001; Tse, 2001; Brisk & Harrington, 2000; Williams & Capizzi Snipper, 1990). Using a language other than English does not doom people to second-class citizenship in American society; instead, it opens the door to possibilities to maintain one's identity, one's sense of worth and value, as well as becoming a productive member of American society. Bilingualism, not monolingualism, opens doors to the larger, *global* world.

It is time now to put such misconceptions about language learning to rest. It is sad that they have persisted in the United States for such a long time. I have heard many people say, "My grandmother/grandfather came to this country and didn't know English and was put in class where only English was spoken and did just fine." I would rather hear from that grandmother or grandfather how they felt about being in an environment where they understand very little or anything at all that was going on around them, and how they were made to feel by other students because they did not speak the language. I am quite certain that the memories evoked may not be pleasant ones.

It is critical, as the world population increases, that countries begin to work on a global level to celebrate the diversity that exists among each other, rather than viewing diversity as a threat or a disease to be eradicated. Anyone who learns a language at a young age begins to see that there are people who are different than they are—be it by language or culture. As that person continues to learn that language, he or she also begins to learn more about the culture of the people who speak that language. It is only through this kind of acceptance that people can begin to realize that they have much more in common as they start to look past color, religion, and ethnicity and begin to see people as individuals. If recent *No Child Left Behind* (2001) legislation, with its mandated achievement benchmarks for various minority populations of students, is to really mean something, then it must begin by the elimination of the belief that children of color and children whose first language is not English are genetically inferior and, therefore, nothing can be done for them. It would mean that children who speak another language other than English and have a different culture have something valuable to bring to the table. They have knowledge and expertise that is greatly needed in this country today—the ability to understand and relate to global communities. The more countries are able to understand and appreciate other's culture and language, the less of a chance of misunderstanding between those countries.

Suppose every country believed that everyone should speak only the language of that country, as Schlesinger, Jr. (1998), suggests. There would be no global economy, no trade between countries, and no exchange of ideas—that would be an example of self-ghettoization.

Europe, Africa, and Asia have established multilingual societies where they are learning English, but they are also maintaining their mother tongues, and they are doing quite well. There exists no tower of Babel on these continents. It is time for the United States to follow the lead of many other countries and to embrace diversity. It is only through understanding differences will we be able to find common ground and acceptance of who we are.

References

Barnes, H. (1991). Reconceptualizing the knowledge base for teacher education. In M. Pugach, H. Barnes, L. Beckum (Eds.), *Changing the practice of teacher education.* Washington, DC: American Association of Colleges for Teacher Education.

Brisk, M., & Harrington, M. (2000). *Literacy and bilingualism: A handbook for all teachers.* Mahwah, NJ: Lawrence Erlbaum.

Cervantes, M. S. (1997). *El ingenioso hidalgo don Quijote de la Mancha.* Newark: DE: Juan de la Cuesta.

Cummins, J. (1979). *Cognitive/academic language proficiency, linguistic interdependence, the optimum age question, and some other matters.* Working Papers on Bilingualism, No. 19.

Cummins, J. (1981). Empirical and theoretical underpinnings of bilingual education. *Journal of Education, 163*(1), 16–29.

Cummins, J. (1983). *Heritage language education: A literature review.* Toronto, Ontario, Canada: The Minister of Education, Ontario, Canada.

Cummins, J. (2000). *Language, power, and pedagogy.* Clevedon, England: Multilingual Matters Ltd.

Cummins, J. (2001). Instructional conditions for trilingual development. *International Journal of Bilingual Education and Bilingualism, 4*(1), 61–75.

Curtain, H., & Dahlberg, C. (2004). *Languages and children: Making the match.* Boston: Pearson Education.

De Houwer, A. (1999). Two or more languages in early childhood. *ERIC Digest.* Washington, DC: Center for Applied Linguistics (EDO-FL-99-03).

Delpit, L. (1997). What should teacher do? Ebonics and culturally responsive instruction. *Rethinking Schools: An Urban Educational Journal, 12*(1), 6–7.

García, S., Wilkinson, C., & Ortiz, A. (1995). Enhancing achievement for language-minority students: Classroom, school, and family contexts. *Education and Urban Society, 27*(4), 441–462.

García-Moya, R. (1981). Teaching Spanish to Spanish speakers: Some considerations for the preparation of teachers. In G. Valdés, A. Lozano, R. García-Moya (Eds.), *Teaching Spanish to the Hispanic bilingual: Issues, aims, and methods.* New York: Teachers College Columbia University Press.

Gay, G. (2002). Preparing for culturally responsive teaching. *Journal of Teacher Education, 53*(2), 106–116.

Giles, H. (Ed). (1977). *Language and ethnicity in intergroup relations* (pp. 83–98). New York: Academic Press.

Grossman, P., Wilson, S., & Shulman, L. S. (1989). Teachers of substance: Subject matter knowledge for teaching. In M. Reynolds (Ed.), *Knowledge for the beginning teacher* (pp. 23–36). New York: Pergamon.

Kalantzig, M., et al. (1989). *Minority languages and dominate culture.* Washington, DC: The Falmer Press.

Krashen, S. (1987). *Principles and practice in second-language acquisition.* New York: Prentice-Hall International.

Ladson-Billings, G. (1994). *The dream keepers: Successful teachers of African-American children.* San Francisco: Jossey-Bass.

Ladson-Billings, G. (1995). But that's just good teaching! The case for culturally relevant pedagogy. *Theory into Practice, 34*(3), 159–165.

MacGillivray, L., & Rueda, R. (2003). Listening to inner-city teachers of English language learners: Differentiating literacy instruction. Washington, DC: Office of Educational Research and Improvement (ED 479984).

Marujo, M. (1993). Narrative and voice: Marginalized perspectives in teacher education. Heritage Language Teachers in Ontario Schools (ERIC Document Reproduction Service No. ED362477).

Mayeroff, M. (1971). *On caring.* New York: Harper and Row.

Miller, P. C., & Endo, H. (2004). Understanding and meeting the need of ESL students. *Phi Delta Kappan, 85*(10), 786–791.

Peale, C. G. (1991). Spanish for Spanish speakers (and other "native languages") in California's Schools: A Rationale Statement. *Hispania, 74,* 446–451.

Putnam, R., & Borko, H. (1997). Teacher learning implications of new views of cognition. In B. Biddle & T. Good, (Eds.), *International handbook of teachers and teaching.* (Vol. 3, Part II). Dordrecht, Netherlands: Kluwer Academic.

Richards, J., Platt, J., & Platt, H. (1992*). Dictionary of language teaching & applied linguistics.* Essex, England: Longman Group UK.

Rodriguez, R. (1982). *Hunger of memory: The education of Richard Rodriguez: An autobiography.* Boston: D.R. Godine.

Schlesinger, Jr., A. (1998). *The disuniting of America: Reflections on a multicultural society.* New York: W.W. Norton & Company.

Smith, C. (2003). Oral language and the second-language learner. Bloomington, IN: Eric Clearinghouse on Reading, English, and Communication. (ED 482403).

Titone, R., & Danesi, M. (1985). *Applied psycholinguistics: An introduction to the psychology of language learning and teaching* (pp. 83–90). Toronto, Canada: University of Toronto Press.

Trueba, H. (1993). The relevance of theory on language and culture with pedagogical practices. In B. Merino, H. Trueba, & F. Samaniego (Eds.), *Language and Culture in Learning* (pp. 259–267). Washington, DC: The Falmer Press.

Tse, L. (2001). *Why don't they learn English: Separating fact from fallacy in the U.S. language debate.* New York: Teachers College Press.

Yaden, D., & Tardibuono, J. (2004). The emergent writing development of urban Latino preschoolers: Developmental perspectives and instructional environments for second-language learners. *Reading & Writing Quarterly, 20*(1), 29–61.

Williams, J., & Capizzi Snipper, G. (1990). *Literacy and bilingualism.* White Plains, NY: Longman.

Appendix 7:1

Electronic Resources

Center for Applied Linguistics (CAL):
    http://www.cal.org/admin/about.html

Dr. Cummins' ESL and Second-Language Learning Web:
    http://www.iteachilearn.com/cummins

National Clearinghouse for English Language Acquisition (NCELA) and Language Instructional Educational Programs:
    http://www.ncela.gwu.edu

National Council of Teachers of English (NCTE) Hot Topics on Bilingual/ELL: http://www.ncte.org/elem/topics/109336.htm

TESOL: http://www.tesol.org

Translation and Interpretation Services

You read the work of a translator. You hear the work of an interpreter. To find a translator or interpreter, or to find a company that offers translation or interpretation services, contact the American Translators Association at: (703) 683-6100, or online at: http://www.atanet.org

Chapter 8

Writing As a Vital Way in to Literacy

Denise N. Morgan

It is November of Misa's first year in an American classroom, having moved to the United States from Japan. Misa's teacher passes out a single sheet of paper to each student. On the paper is a broad outline of a turkey with lines for writing within the body. "Okay class, today I want you to write about your Thanksgiving traditions." Misa looks confused and raises her hand. "Yes, Misa?" the teacher asks. "What is Thanksgiving?" Misa inquires. "It is a time we celebrate and give thanks for what we have. We get together with family and friends and usually eat turkey," the teacher supplies. Misa still looks confused. "Just do the best you can, Misa," the teacher adds. Misa asks her neighbor, "What's turkey?" Misa sits still while the other students write. "Just do the best you can," the teacher tells her again. Slowly, Misa picks up her pencil and writes: I like Thanksgiving. I eat turkey.

Introduction

Misa completed the assignment, but does her writing come from a place of knowing? Does her writing represent who she is and her experiences throughout her 8-year-old life? Does Misa's writing provide the teacher with a window into Misa's strengths and accomplishments as a writer? I believe many would agree that this piece does not demonstrate Misa's potential, nor does it provide the teacher with any real direction as to how to help Misa grow as a writer. Yet, the writing of many diverse learners takes on this stilted quality as they try earnestly to complete writing assignments they don't understand or have the background knowledge to attempt. But it doesn't have to be that way for Misa or for any other culturally or ethnically diverse student when they write. There are other options.

Within each child is a writer waiting to emerge. The degree to which each writer develops in a classroom is a direct result of the kinds of experiences and explicit instruction teachers provide their students. There is much to be gained by having students "dance with the pen" (New Zealand Ministry of Education, 1995) or write daily. But first, students need teachers who hold important beliefs about them as learners and how writing should be taught. Namely, teachers must believe that all students, especially diverse students, are capable of learning to write and have interesting things to say. Diverse and struggling students do not need different experiences than their classmates; rather, they need more of the same authentic reading and writing experiences with a strong, knowledgeable teacher to guide them and monitor their progress. In a review of the research, August and Hakuta (1997) concluded it is not necessarily the language of instruction that makes a difference for English language learners as much as the quality and methods of instruction. Other known effective practices for English language learners are the importance of teacher's high student expectations (August & Hakuta, 1997), acknowledgement and inclusion of home culture (August & Hakuta, 1997), and student engagement in authentic literacy tasks (Au, 2003).

In today's classrooms, there are students with a wide range of abilities from diverse backgrounds. How does a teacher meet the needs of varying students in something as specific as writing? Teachers face many challenges as they encounter students who speak nonalphabetic languages, such as Japanese or Farsi, or students from another country with no previous exposure to English. There are also students who have been in the United States for several years who, chronologically, are in the right grade, but the coursework at that level is beyond their English-speaking ability. Teachers face students whose home literacies (the kinds of reading and writing done in their home) differ from school literacies (those reading and writing acts expected in school) and, therefore, these students experience difficulty doing "school." It is hard work to meet the writing needs of students from diverse backgrounds. But research has demonstrated the powerful effects writing has on children's literacy development (e.g., National Writing Project & Nagin, 2003) and, therefore, it cannot be neglected. In the remainder of this chapter, I will address the numerous advantages writing offers students, how it helps foster their sense of self, and then discuss the kinds of conditions that nurture and support these writers.

Reading-Writing Benefits

Writing helps children fully develop as literate individuals, as reading and writing share common ground (Clay, 2001). There is reciprocity (Dyson, 1984, 1985; Tierney and Pearson, 1985) between reading and writing, a sort of "two for one" bargain (Clay, 2001). And although reading and writing are not "mirror images," they "mutually reinforce each other in the process of literacy development" (Teale & Martinez, 1989, p. 184). There is a "synergistic relationship between learning to write and learning to read" (Pearson, 2003, p. 33). Simply put, writing helps children develop as readers, and reading helps children develop as writers. Reading and writing are "intertwined and inseparable language tools" (Langer & Flihan, 2000, p. 127). A review of 50 years of reading and writing relationship correlation and experimental studies found that:

- Better writers tend to be better readers (of their own writing as well as of other reading material).
- Better writers tend to read more than poorer writers.
- Better readers tend to produce more syntactically mature writing than poorer readers (Stotsky, as cited in National Writing Project & Nagin, 2003, p. 31).

So, at any grade level, limiting or neglecting writing instruction inhibits children's growth as writers and readers.

In children's unique path of becoming literate (a never-ending process, even for adults), many children walk first through the writing door and apply what they understand about writing to their reading. "Writing can contribute to building almost every kind of inner control of literacy learning that is needed by the successful reader" (Clay, 2001. p. 12). Clay (1975, 1987) has shown how writing helps children pay attention to the details of print they encounter in reading, and this attention helps them organize their reading behaviors. Writing is a slow process, one that allows the learner to examine language in a way that is not visible while speaking (Clay, 1998; Pearson, 2003). Clay (1998) shares that "the act of writing provides one with the means of making one's own language somewhat opaque, revealing things about oral language to young writers" (p. 137). It may be through writing that children discover that *onceuponatime* is really four different words, *once upon a time*. Children who understand that they write from left to right can also utilize that knowledge while reading. Writing helps children pay attention to details as children produce letter forms and sequences, which allow them time to observe things about visual language not previously noted (Clay, 1998).

Children, who need to write a word they cannot automatically spell, learn to break the word into parts and then write the letters they hear to record the first part, the second part, and so on, going from sound to letter, developing their knowledge of phonics. Children can also use that ability to break words apart while reading, this time going from letter to sound, again strengthening their phonics knowledge. Writing engages children at multiple levels in the language hierarchy at once (Clay, 1998). Clay (1998) explains that the writer must first compose a message, think of the first word to write, and then begin with the first letter of that word. The writer writes letter by letter to build up words, then words turn into phrases, phrases into sentences, paragraphs, stories, or informational writing. The child is discovering many things simultaneously while writing. Lastly:

"Reading and writing draw on the same sources of knowledge about letters, sounds, chunks, clusters, words, syntax (or grammar and sentence construction), the rules of discourse, and narrative structures and genre differences; gains in reading may enrich writing and vice versa; and dipping into a large pool of both reading and writing knowledge will help those with limited knowledge of the language" (Clay, 1998, p. 139).

Writing offers other benefits. Writing allows children to make greater use of their oral vocabulary. There are many words students might not recognize while reading, but they can use that word in their writing because the desire or need for that word is coming from within the realm of their lived experience. They then apply their knowledge of sound-letter correspondence to write the word. Students have a more sophisticated oral vocabulary than they do a reading vocabulary. By writing, they can expand their reading vocabulary. In addition, students are allowed greater approximations in writing than in reading. Reading calls for precise action on the part of the student; you must read what is on the page, and a misspoken word may not convey meaning. On the other hand, in writing, students can make their best attempt at spelling a word and still successfully convey the meaning of the piece to the reader. In this way, writing can offer students more ways to successfully complete the task. The benefits of helping children develop as readers and writers simultaneously are limitless. Everything children learn about writing can be applied to their reading and vice versa. Writing can, and should, become an equal partner in children's paths to literacy.

Identity Development

When a child is struggling in school, put a pencil, crayon, or marker in the child's hand. For students, writing is an opportunity to express themselves by capturing their ideas and sharing those ideas with others (Dyson, 1999). When children self-select a topic, they can draw upon their own personal "funds of knowledge," a rich bank of experiences from their home and school lives from which to write (Moll & Greenberg, 1992). When a child writes, he or she constructs meaning from his or her personal experiences and social interaction with others. Dyson (1999) explains, "Given that it is social intention and participation that energizes and organizes the complex writing act, children must figure out not only *how* to write but *what* and *why*, given their present lives as children" (p. 129). This act of writing serves as an act of "discovery, self-expression, and communication" (Freedman & Daiute, as cited in National Writing Project & Nagin, 2003). We know from the work of Anne Haas Dyson (1999) that children often "lift" ideas from popular media, music, and film to put in their writing, and this gives students a sense of "belonging, competence, and fun" (p. 144). Students do complex work as they take the lifted text forms and recreate those forms for themselves. They are playing with text forms and language. Dyson (1999) reminds us that we must look closely at these texts because, at first glance or hearing, we might overlook children's creative use of text. And since with everything children write, they are leaving a little bit of themselves on the page, we will want to take notice of what they are doing and who they are becoming.

We need to think deeply about the teaching of writing in the classroom. It goes beyond helping children read. Writing helps children discover their voice and their place in the world. It allows them to grapple with tough issues and capture special moments in time. In short, writing helps students understand what it means to write and understand the kinds of work writing can accomplish in the classroom and real world.

Again, The Important Teacher Beliefs

Teachers must find a way to instruct all learners within a supportive environment, one that is manageable, but allow students flexibility to progress at their own pace. For diverse students to be successful or, for that matter, any student to be successful, teachers must be willing to accept students' approximations in their learning journey. As presented in detail in chapter 4, approximations represent students' attempts to try the task at hand (Cambourne, 1998). All learners do what they know how to do until someone teaches them or through repeated experience they learn how to do it better. Each child's starting point as a writer needs to be celebrated and accepted. To expect struggling students to be at the same point as their age-equivalent peers is to set these students up for failure by viewing some students through a deficit model, a lens that focuses on what students are not doing rather than what they can do. It is impossible or unrealistic to ask students to be anywhere else than where they currently are. By appreciating what is, we can focus our attention and energy on what could be, given in a supportive environment and thoughtful teaching. Teaching is taking children where they are and moving them forward in their development (Vygotsky, 1978). Accepting children's current abilities help children's growth as writers.

Real-World Writing

Children should be able to confidently make their mark, on the page and on their audience. In order for children to become writers, they need to see themselves as writers, doing the kinds of writing work (Ray & Cleveland, 2004) that real writers do daily. The writing needed in the real world goes beyond stories and reports. We make lists, write poems, conduct and complete surveys, take notes, send notes, capture observations, etc. By expanding our notion of the kinds of writing children can do in the classroom, we open a world of possibilities for the students to complete their writing work. Students may have an experience they want to share and now must find a way to capture that on paper or they have a real purpose to make a sign or note. Students may want to label the art project they made or write a "letter" to a classmate. They may want to conduct a survey for science. Their writing is going somewhere or serving a personal purpose. Children, just like adults, need authentic reasons to write. Not only that, their writing needs to be seen, not tucked away between the covers of a journal, never shared with each other or worked on for a second day. Children's writing must breathe in the classroom, be shared and seen by others, because if not, what is the point of writing, if it no longer serves a purpose once the pencil or marker it put down.

Encouraging various kinds of writing offers students more opportunities for writing success, as each kind of writing requires different decisions by the writer. Sometimes, the ability to create shorter text is initially easier for the diverse student and might not seem as overwhelming as an expectation to fill a blank notebook page or multiple pages. For instance, students could create a menu listing their favorite dishes with a simple picture and/or description. In this case, students write about something they know, and most likely, something they care for deeply (good food!). When finished, they could share their menus with the class, allowing for the larger class to get to know that child better. Prior to doing this kind of writing, the child should have access to many menus, including those that offer pictures, so they can study the menu format, look at multiple examples, and decide how they will organize their menu. Making something that seems as simple as a menu requires many decisions; students must decide the way the menu will be read (thus, the need for different kinds of paper), the placement of picture, the type of description, and so on. The child is writing but under supportive conditions. This act of reading and studying the kinds of texts they are to eventually write is especially important for students. It gives them a vision and encourages them to think, "I can write something like that" (Ray & Cleveland, 2004).

In order to write "something like that," students need the proper environment and other conditions in place to support their work as writers. Teachers need to consider aspects such as providing ample time, encouraging students to write a lot, establishing a predictable routine, choosing topics of personal significance, encouraging talking and drawing before or as a part of writing, and developing writing mentors. In addition, the teacher must think about supporting his or her own growth as a writer and providing ample writing demonstrations to the students to support their growth as writers. These pieces weave together to form an environment where young writers thrive. In the remaining section, I further discuss these topics along with providing suggestions for ideas to consider and writing opportunities you can try with all students but ones that are especially supportive for students from diverse backgrounds.

Time and Volume

Children need time to write daily, and they need to write a lot in order to consistently get better at writing. Daily attention and work results in improvement and reaps benefits. The same is true with writing. Professional writers get better at writing because they do it more often, and as Donald Murray (1996) says, "The rear end is the writing muscle that makes the difference between the writers who want to write and don't, and those writers who want to write and do" (p. 22). Writing every day matters.

Writing daily allows children to develop the habit of writing. Each day, the students know they will write. It is not a question of if there will be time for writing but, rather, a question of what they will write and how they will add to or revise what they have already written. A year of daily writing means that at the end of the year, students will have produced a lot of writing, trying their hand at different genres.

Making writing a part of the daily instruction sends several messages to the students. It tells students that writing matters. It tells students that writing is something they can do. It lets students learn that they have something to say and provides them with choice and ownership in how they share that information. It also gives students the opportunity to take control of their learning. They can experiment by trying a technique a favorite author used or by following a familiar format to share their writing. Writing is also an act of discovery; it helps children learn what it is they want to say and gets them to think about events and experiences in a different way. Many times writers do not know what they want to say until they begin writing. A writer may begin with one angle or topic and find that the topic blossoms into something else or takes another direction. Writing helps you think and helps the writer uncover what he or she really wants to say and share with the world.

Students need sufficient time to get "writing work" done. It takes time to "get ready to write." Think about your own personal habits before you write something such as a paper for class, newsletter, report cards, or a family update to friends. Rarely, as writers, do we just jump in and begin writing. Rather, we need to get ready for the task. We gather materials, think about what we want to say, get a drink of water, call a friend, and finally, we start and stop for various reasons. In essence, we need warm-up time to get started. We must allow students the same considerations we give ourselves. We need time to write. So this means that 10 minutes of writing time daily will not help us progress as writers. That simply is not enough time to get started and get any real amount of writing completed. Children need large blocks of time to write. It takes a while to get in a "writing groove" and that is rarely accomplished in a few minutes. In addition, children have to build up stamina for writing. They must learn how to stay with ideas and write for longer periods of time. In the beginning of the year, the amount of time devoted to writing should be short as students get into the daily habit of writing. As the year progresses, however, the time for writing should increase.

Ideas to Consider Regarding Time and Volume:

- It would be difficult for a child to sustain writing for long periods of time in a language he does not yet know. In the beginning, this time could be divided into some reading and writing time. If the child reads simple books with predictable patterns, he or she could then use that pattern while writing her- or himself. For instance, the child could create his or her own "I like" book or my family book with a page for each family member using the book he or she read as a model.

- Have already stapled books ready so the children can "make stuff" (Ray & Cleveland, 2004). The simple act of handing a child a multipage book helps the child write longer text than simply giving the child a simple piece of paper.

- Students could listen to books on tape during this time, allowing them to build up their knowledge of story and English language structure. English language learners often use text they read to develop their understanding of the English language (Franklin, as cited in Garcia & Bauer, 2004).

The Importance of Routine

Writing time should have a predictable structure. This predictable structure lets students know what to expect during writing time, allowing students to focus on what they will say rather than wondering if they will get to write today. This predictability allows students to devote energy to developing their piece. It is common for writing time to begin with a brief 10–15 minute minilesson, followed by a large block of time for writing, and ending with a time for sharing and problem solving with classmates at the end of the workshop time (Calkins, 1994; Fletcher & Portalupi, 2001; Hindely, 1996; Ray & Laminack, 2001). So a predictable time and daily format help children know what to expect and gives them the opportunity to focus on their writing. This is similar to what children do at recess. They anticipate recess time and often make plans for what they will do that day. Recess is predictable; it happens daily at the same time, and, therefore, students devote their thinking to what they will do at recess so they are ready to play when recess begins. The same can be true of writing; when it is predictable and happens daily, children plan for what they will write next.

Ideas to Consider Regarding Routine

- Routine can be especially important for the students new to the language. They often do not understand what you are saying but understand that during this time certain things happen; for instance, they go to the carpet for a story and then some teaching time, and then they go back to their seats and work on their writing. This predictability can offer much comfort for a student who, initially, does not understand what is happening in the classroom. As adults, we seek out this security. When we are faced with an unfamiliar situation in which we must act, we often look to others who are doing it with ease or who go before us so we understand what we are supposed to do. Sometimes, we are anxious when we must drive someplace new because we do not know the route or the area, but the remaining trips are more comfortable since we have a sense of what to expect. Routine provides that safety net for students.

- After the minilesson, the teacher could talk briefly with students to help them with their "writing plan" for the day. This way, those students in need of extra support can begin their writing time with a focused plan of what they will do.

Writing from a Place of Knowing

When children draw upon their lives, they have rich stories to tell classmates, teachers, and caregivers. They live diverse lives outside of school, and these lives are full of anecdotes, experiences, and stories ripe for sharing. As mentioned by Fox in chapter 9, children bring with them "funds of knowledge" (Moll & Greenberg, 1990), those outside family and community learning experiences that have contributed, shaped, and enriched his or her growth as a person. This knowledge can be overlooked in schools or it can be tapped and fostered so it blossoms. This, however, requires a specific mindset on the part of the teacher. This mindset is one of "I believe there is much to be gained from the lives that children lead outside of school." In this way, the diversity of experiences and cultures in a classroom becomes an asset rather than a deficit.

Children write more freely and expressively about a topic that they know, love, or live than a topic that is removed from their personal experiences. This is true even for adults. If you were asked to write about Australia's foreign trade policy, would you be able to fill your page with all the things you know? What you write would directly depend on your knowledge or connection to Australia. Maybe you are an Australian citizen living in the United States, and you keep abreast of what is happening in your home country, or maybe you developed a product you would like to introduce to the market in Australia. If so, you would likely know the rules and regulations. What you can write depends on your past experiences. Too often, children are asked to write about topics far removed from their experiences. Students who have never seen or tasted pumpkin would have a hard time imagining they were pumpkins and writing about their adventures. Children, such as Misa, who have never experienced Thanksgiving or do not celebrate Thanksgiving, would not be able to write convincingly about their Thanksgiving traditions. Just imagine, as an adult, if you were assigned to write about your snow-skiing adventures and told to "just try," even if you have never seen snow or been skiing. It would be difficult for you to write about a topic for which you have no knowledge or experience, nor would it probably be an enjoyable experience. We appreciate choice in life and feel restricted or resentful when we do not have choice in matters. Children often feel the same way.

In order to contain the chaos of students writing all different kinds of pieces at once, it is possible to give the entire class a broad topic, such as a special family tradition, and allow each child to tell his or her story. Because children are writing from a place of knowing, their voices will be strong and their details more vivid. To fully develop as writers, children need opportunities to write about topics that matter to them. They become invested in the topic, and that investment usually results in greater commitment to a finished product.

Many children bring with them skills, knowledge, experience, and wisdom not generally acknowledged as relevant to school practices. When we allow children to share their social and cultural histories in class and through their writing, we celebrate and embrace each child. In the end, the whole class benefits when space is made for students to share the important stories in their lives.

Ideas to Consider Regarding a Place of Knowing

- There are now many books that are published in both English and Spanish. Using that as a model, students could write their story in both languages. The act of writing something in their native language allows students to fully engage in the development of the piece without having to filter their story first through English. Then, they can go back and write the English translation by themselves or with help. We want to celebrate the act of writing, knowing that allowing students to utilize their native language is beneficial to students' growth in their second language (Garcia & Bauer, 2004).

- When selecting a broad topic for the entire class, make sure to propose a universal theme. Writing about a favorite memory is more accessible to all students then writing about Valentine's Day. It will be important to read many books that also highlight a favorite memory, so children can hear different ways to approach their writing and understand that the memory can be a very small thing (such as the time you found a rock rather than your 2-week trip to Disneyworld).

- Create individual "you" maps with your students. On a piece of chart paper or on an overhead, begin naming those important events in your life while drawing a symbolic representation on paper. For example, I was born in Hawaii and could draw a pineapple to represent that fact. I would draw a moving truck to represent all the times I have moved in my life. The students work on their own map, so it becomes a treasure chest of possible writing topics. Students can return to their "you" maps and select a topic that comes from a "place of knowing" when in need of a new topic.

Talk and Drawing

Talking and drawing are two ways to quickly improve the quality of writing by students. Drawing should be viewed not as an avoidance of writing, but as a way for children to work out the story in their minds before they write. Drawing is a rehearsal of what they want to write. It is a way to "frame thinking before writing," (Ray & Cleveland, 2004, p. 129). For younger children and struggling writers, allowing drawing first often allows better writing to emerge. For the struggling writer, the picture provides the teacher with insight into the child's sense of story even though the writing might not be a direct match. Drawing can be a stepping stone for the concept of adding more details, at first to their pictures and eventually to their story. Children often describe their pictures beyond what is actually represented on the page in their drawings or writing. When they do that, students can be asked to add those details and then write down some of those details so they will remember the story behind the picture. Drawing can be seen as a first draft of a story for the child, serving the same kind of function that list making does for many adults. The list provides a focus of what's important, a reminder of what needs to get done or purchased. Drawing helps students focus their writing, as their drawing represents what it is important to the writer. Student writing can be more elaborate and more complete if they have a drawing to bolster their ideas. It is important to remember, however, that students' drawings are often more complete than their writing. It is possible that there will be more detail in the drawings than in writing. And that is okay.

Talk, this is the one thing we must simply increase the amount of in school. Children learn from and with each other. Learning is social, and it is through our talk and interactions with others that we learn (Vygotsky, 1978; Wood, 1988). Children must have ample opportunities to talk with their classmates about their writing. In this sense, talking serves, like drawings, as a rehearsal of what you want to write. You tell someone your idea, and they naturally respond with interest, excitement, or confusion about what you shared. Talk is critical, as what we share gets an advanced reaction. (Did people find my story funny like I thought they would? Were they shocked at the ending? Did it make sense? Did they laugh? Is this a story worth writing down?) Talking with another about our writing helps us answer these questions and shape or reshape our writing accordingly. The act of writing is primarily an individual task; you are alone with your thoughts as you put words down on paper. Talking helps make the writing easier for students because they have shared once what they wanted to say, and this helps warm up writers for writing. To prevent children from talking about their writing is like preventing them from fully thinking.

Ideas to Consider Regarding Talk and Drawing

- There simply cannot be enough talk for diverse students. It helps children practice what they want to say before they write. By doing this, they form a plan before they even see the white page. The listener may use words in responding to the speaker that the speaker can use to enrich the writing.

- Make sure you demonstrate the importance of drawing as a way to tell your story. On an overhead or chart paper, you can tell your story by drawing pictures along the way. The very act of you doing this allows students to do this same thing. Through drawing, the students are visually representing a story while talking through the storyline or account. This develops children's sense of story while allowing them immediately to be successful because drawing is a universal language.

- Students can interview each other through drawings. This can be a great getting-to-know-you activity. Demonstrate this by interviewing a student or another teacher asking questions and taking notes by drawing a symbol to help you remember information about that person. If, for instance, the person I interviewed said she had a little dog, drawing a small dog would allow me to remember that fact. In their interview, Manuel told Tatini he liked Sprite. She simply drew a can with an "S" on it to serve as a reminder. Once finished, students can share this information with the class, talking off of the picture or using the information to write or dictate a paragraph. Drawing creates something concrete from which to strengthen oral and written experiences.

- Teachers and schools can support writing development, if they are social places (Dyson & Freedman, 2003). Children talking with other children is critical to their learning.

- In addition to drawing, students can write labels for their visual representations. Labels are a meaningful way to encourage children's use of print. They learn about matching pictures with labels and find that these labels serve a purpose. Then, students can move to labeling items in the room, again matching label to object and serving a larger purpose of naming items in the room, providing a visual reminder of that object and serving as a "living classroom dictionary" to the young writers.

Developing Writing Mentors

Writers benefit from reading and studying the work of writers they admire. Students should develop their own writing mentors. If students develop an affinity for an author, they can "stand on the shoulders" of that author when they write and "write under the influence" of that writer (Ray & Cleveland, 2004). Closely studying, naming, and trying techniques used by authors provides multiple possibilities for students' own work. A child whose favorite book is *Tough Boris* (Fox, 1998) can "borrow" the technique of using the see-saw refrain as Fox did in her book ("Tough Boris was massive. All pirates were massive") in his or her own writing ("Tulips are pretty. All flowers are pretty."). Writing mentors can serve as coteachers in your class. If students decide to write a book in a similar vein as one they love, then they have access to an established structure. For the struggling student, it is often a challenge to manage both the content and the underlying structure of the piece. If students follow a familiar structure, as one found in a book they like, they are better able to focus on the content of their piece. Therefore, their energy is focused on what they want to say instead of torn between what they want to say and how can they say it in a way that will make sense for the reader. Finding a writing mentor allows students to write books in the tradition of books they love, a practice writers have done for years. Student may choose not to follow a certain structure but choose instead to use a certain technique or play with language like an author does.

Ideas to Consider Regarding Writing Mentors

- Play with a technique orally, an "oral try-it." Notice what an author does, name it with your children, and then try it out using your writing topic. You orally rehearse what you try in your writing, inviting children to do some "oral writing" also.

- You can start by helping children know one or two really good authors well as writers. Pick an author you love, and read those books repeatedly, noticing with students what that author does, the decision that author makes, and patterns across books. Then, try writing in the style of that author with your students in a shared writing experience. Your students can also find authors they love and look for those same moves or decisions in their books.

Knowledgeable Teachers

While the factors mentioned above support a writer's growth, what makes the biggest difference in students' writing is teacher knowledge. The more the teacher knows about writing, the better able he or she is to move students forward as writers. As teachers, we must become knowledgeable about what good writers do when they write, just as we understand what good readers do when they read and use that information to guide our reading instruction. Too often, teachers categorize themselves as either good or poor writers. Yet, professional writers say they get better at writing because they write daily (Lamott, 1994; Murray, 1996). Knowledge of the writing craft and what real writers do should influence what and how we teach our students. Writing needs to be taught now; no one should hold back from teaching writing until they know or learn "it all." Knowing it all is a mythical point that will never be reached. There is always more to learn. As teachers, we must move past any personal fears about writing and decide that good writing is something we want to investigate. Writing is something you can learn alongside your students. By example, you show what it means to be a lifelong learner.

There are many ways to deepen your knowledge about writing with your students. Begin with the books you read aloud to the class. Talk, not only about the story, but also about the writing. Were there words that the students loved, phrases that tingled their ears, or a part of the story that delighted their imagination? Talking about these things is a way to help students notice, and use, writer's techniques while developing a collective knowledge base, creating meaningful labels for these writing moves you notice. You can talk about good writing without knowing technical terms. There may or may not be a technical term for this "thing" that the class noticed, but the most important point is that the label should make sense to the class. For example, Jeff Williams and his second-grade class studied the way the fiction books they were reading were structured. They noticed that the main character and setting were almost always introduced immediately, followed quickly by a problem for the character, and in the end, the character response to that problem that often resulted in a change in the character. Jeff drew a gradual incline and decline to show visually what was happening in the books they were reading. His students named this visual the "fiction hill," and they used this term for the rest of the year to describe this pattern they noticed in their reading or in their writing.

Good teachers of writing write themselves. They write so they can share firsthand the writing decisions they make and share sticky situations they encounter along the way. Instead of telling the students about writing, they write alongside their students, again showing what it means to be a lifelong learner. When you write, and especially when you share what you write, are vulnerable. This reminds us of how vulnerable children may feel when writing and sharing their work with the class. This helps us, as teachers, create a safe space for children to share their own work. Writing with the students also sends the message that writing is something we all work on in this room. You only have to write a little bit better than your students in order to teach them something about writing, and as teachers of our youngest writers, even the most reluctant teacher will easily meet that basic requirement.

Writing Demonstrations

In addition to studying the work of authors, demonstrations are an opportunity for teachers to show students exactly what they can do when writing. Demonstrations are where rigorous, thoughtful, explicit teaching occurs and where writing techniques, "all the things writers know how to do with both text and illustrations (word choice, sentence structure, punctuation, paragraphs, text structures, genre specifics, etc.) to make writing good" are shared (Ray & Cleveland, 2004, p. 86). During these demonstrations, students see ideas they might try in their writing and learn ways they can go about their writing work (Ray & Cleveland, 2004).

Active teaching is at the heart of all demonstrations (Cambourne, 1988). These demonstrations often occur during minilessons when the teacher often writes in front of the students, thinking aloud about the writing decisions made along the way. The possibilities for demonstrations are endless, with the most powerful demonstrations coming from what the students need to know next. If students struggle with transitions, then demonstrating how to think through transitions (highlighting the decisions about when to make a transition and what language signals the reader that a transition will occur) will provide the student with a possible path. If students need guidance on staying on topic, then the demonstration can highlight the questions writers ask themselves to determine if they have stayed on topic or presented information in a logical order. If you are unsure how to start your new piece of writing, you could think aloud for the students as you conduct the internal debate orally about how to begin. "Okay, let's see, I could start by writing 'Once I got lost' or I could start by doing something the author Denise Flemming (1991) does in her book *In the Tall, Tall Grass* and write, 'In the hot, hot summer, I got lost.' Which one do you like as a reader?" Sometimes, we can get inspiration from other writers. We can go to books we love and see how the author began the book and decide to try it that way ourselves. To the students, we might say, "Find a favorite book and see how the author wrote that first line. Why don't you try writing like this author and see how you like it? Then, decide if you want to use that new sentence or the one you first had." With the demonstration, we often ask the child to try something out, to see how it feels, and consider using it in their piece, with the understanding that the author makes the final decision.

These demonstrations take time and should not be rushed as the teacher goes through the process of thinking, writing, rereading, and decision making in front of the students. The power of demonstrations comes from slowing down and actually sharing your thinking. Demonstrations are like coaching when the coach, instead of telling, actually takes the bat or the ball and does the very thing he or she wants the player to think about and try. Demonstrations show one way something can be done, allowing for flexibility and new interpretations, rather than a strict adherence to a "single right way." Demonstrations show possibilities.

Writing as Power

In this world, we are shaped by what we read. We read newspapers, magazines, online articles, commentaries, and editorials written by authors with the purpose of sharing information and challenging, shaping, or pushing our thoughts. Those authors behind the pen (or computer) have power, through their choice and arrangement of words, to influence the readers to think and to consider new ideas or alternative viewpoints. With the written word comes power. When real action must be taken, writing is involved. If your phone calls or in-person complaints do not produce the desired result, you often put your complaints in writing. We share concerns about issues with our neighbors and friends, but a letter to the editor of a newspaper or magazine extends the audience who comes across our ideas and concerns. In order to do the work of this world, children need to fully understand how writing works and what writing can do for them. Children must learn words have power, but many times, *written* words have more power. To not prepare students to use the power of writing to get things done in the world does not leave them fully equipped to work within that world. Therefore, we must do everything possible to help students see themselves as confident and powerful writers.

Conclusion

Children are writers. They are capable of writing wonderful stories and accounts of their lives and dreams. As teachers, our decision to have students write daily fosters, honors, and respects their lives and dreams. To deny students the opportunity to refine their writing ability is to silence their voices. By making time, space, choice, and rigorous teaching daily ingredients in the classroom, children begin to realize their potential as writers. As teachers, a willingness to learn from professional writers can help students on their journey of living a life as writers, as people who observe closely and capture sights and sounds in a memorable way. By doing this, teachers empower writers who understand that their words have impact and make a difference on their readers. They learn that their words and, more importantly, they matter.

References

Au, K. (2003). Literacy research and students of diverse backgrounds: What does it take to improve achievement? In C. M. Fairbanks, J. Worthy, B. Maloch, J. V. Hoffman, & D. L. Schallert (Eds.), *52nd yearbook of the National Reading Conference* (pp. 85–91). Oak Creek, WI: National Reading Conference.

August, D., & Hakuta, K. (1997). *Improving schooling for language-minority children: A research agenda.* Washington, DC: National Academy Press.

Calkins, L. M. (1994). *The art of teaching writing* (2nd ed.). Portsmouth, NH: Heinemann.

Cambourne, B. (1988). *The whole story: Natural learning and the acquisition of literacy in the classroom.* Auckland, New Zealand: Scholastic.

Clay, M. M. (1975). *What did I write? Beginning writing behavior.* Portsmouth, NH: Heinemann.

Clay, M. M. (1987). *Writing begins at home: Preparing children for writing before they go to school.* Portsmouth, NH: Heinemann.

Clay, M. M. (1998). *By different paths to common outcomes.* Portsmouth, NH: Heinemann.

Clay, M. M. (2001). *Change over time.* Portsmouth, NH: Heinemann.

Dyson, A. H. (1984). Emerging alphabetic literacy in school contexts. *Written Communication, 1,* 5–55.

Dyson, A. H. (1985). Individual differences in emerging writing. In M. Farr (Ed.), *Advances in writing research: Vol. 1: Children's early writing development* (pp. 59–125). Norwood, NJ: Ablex.

Dyson, A. H. (1999). Writing (Dallas) Cowboys: A dialogic perspective on the "What did I write?" Question. In J. S. Gaffney & B. J. Askew (Eds.), *Stirring the waters: The influence of Marie Clay* (pp. 127–148). Portsmouth, NH: Heinemann.

Dyson, A. H., & Freedman, S. W. (2003). Writing. In J. Flood, D. Lapp, J. Squire, & J. Jenson (Eds.), *Handbook of research on teaching the English language arts* (2nd ed.) (pp. 967–992). Mahwah, NJ: Lawrence Erlbaum.

Fletcher, R. J., & Portalupi, J. (2001). *Writing workshop: The essential guide.* Portsmouth, NH: Heinemann.

Flemming, D. (1991). *In the tall, tall grass.* New York: Henry Holt and Company.

Fox, M. (1998). *Tough Boris.* New York: Harcourt.

Garcia, G. E., & Bauer, E. B. (2004). The selection and use of English texts with young language learners. In J. V. Hoffman & D. L. Schallert (Eds.), *The texts in elementary classroom* (pp. 177–193). Mahwah, NJ: Lawrence Erlbaum.

Hindley, J. (1996). *In the company of children.* Portland, ME: Stenhouse.

Lamott, A. (1994). *Bird by bird: Some instructions on writing and life.* New York: Anchor Books.

Langer, J., & Flihan, S. (2000). Writing and reading relationships: Constructive tasks. In R. Indrisano & J. R. Squire (Eds.), *Perspectives on writing: Research, theory, and practice.* Newark, DE.: International Reading Association.

Moll, L., & Greenberg, J. B. (1990). Creating zones of possibilities: Combining social contexts for instruction in L. C. Moll (Ed.), *Vygotsky and education: Instructional implications and applications of sociohistorical pyschology.* Cambridge, England: Cambridge University Press.

Murray, D. (1996). *Crafting a life in essay, story, poem.* Portsmouth, NH: Heinemann.

National Writing Project, & Nagin, C. (2003). *Because writing matters: Improving student writing in our schools.* San Francisco: Jossey-Bass.

New Zealand Ministry of Education. (1995). *Dancing with the pen: The learner as a writer.* Wellington, New Zealand: Learning Media Limited.

Pearson, D. P. (2003). The synergies of writing and reading in young children. In National Writing Project, & C. Nagin (Eds.), *Because writing matters: Improving student writing in our schools.* San Francisco: Jossey-Bass.

Ray, K. W., & Cleveland, L. B. (2004). *About the authors: Writing workshop with our youngest writers.* Portsmouth, NH: Heinemann.

Ray, K. W., & Laminack, L. L. (2001). *The writing workshop: Working through the hard parts (and they're all hard parts).* Urbana, IL: National Council of Teachers of English.

Teale, W. H., & Martinez, M. G. (1989). Connecting writing: Fostering emergent literacy in kindergarten children. In J. M. Mason (Ed.), *Reading and writing connections* (pp. 177–199). Boston: Allyn and Bacon.

Tierney, R., & Pearson, P. D. (1985). Towards a composing model or reading: Writing, reading, and learning. In C. Headley & A. Baratta (Eds.), *Contexts of reading* (pp. 63–78). Norwood, NJ: Ablex.

Vygotsky, L. V. (1978). *Mind in society.* Cambridge, MA: Harvard University Press.

Wood, D. (1988). *How children think and learn.* Oxford, England: Basil Blackwell.

Chapter 9

The Use of Children's Literature to Promote Social Justice Issues

Kathy R. Fox

As I talk with classroom teachers about book selection, I experience many wonderful conversations, much like this one:

Interviewer: How do you choose your books for classroom read alouds?

Teacher response: I look for books that show children from different cultures living together and getting along. I want them to see that people might speak a different language or wear different clothes, but they can still get along and be friends. This is important for them to feel as if they can be friends with different people in our classroom and school.

This response was typical of many comments from first-grade teachers when I asked what influenced their choice of books to read aloud in their primary school classrooms (Fox, 2000). Books were used as mediators of social justice lessons, in that they were seen as tools for transformative education. Transformative education employs the critical analysis of curriculum to close the achievement gap and erase established inequalities by

encouraging classroom communities to become forces for critical change (Banks, 1994). Here, in these linguistically, culturally, and academically diverse classrooms, books were seen as
gateways to open conversations regarding social justice issues
across these lines.

Interviewer: How do you use books to teach these [so-
                      cial justice] lessons?

Teacher response: We talk about the book. Sometimes the
                      children write about it in their journals. I ask
                      them, "Can you do this like the character
                      in the book?" They learn that they have
                      more in common with other people than
                      they have differences.

Rather than a textbook script, children's literature offers opportunities for social justice lessons embedded in storyline, illustrations, and/or character representations. By representing
characters of diverse cultural, linguistic, and ability backgrounds
in an empowered stance through literature, teachers felt that
literature validated membership in a particular minority group.

Interviewer: What do you look for in a book for class-
                      room read alouds?

Teacher Response: I look for books that reflect the different
                      languages and cultures in our classroom.
                      This year, I have several children who
                      speak Spanish in their homes, and one child
                      is from South Africa. I look for books that
                      include Spanish words in the text. We did
                      a unit on Africa, and I read several books
                      from Africa.

Introduction

Books are traditionally categorized by literacy associations for their content
and readability levels (Huck, Hepler, Hickman, & Kiefer, 1997; Norton, 2001).
"Multicultural" is sometimes used as a category but is defined differently among

organizations (Norton, 2001; Temple, Martinez, Yokota, & Naylor, 2002). Interestingly, in my research, I found no standard definition of multicultural and/or social justice literature by publishers, reading associates, library associations, and/or booksellers. Instead, my initial findings show that the category of multicultural can mean anything from anthologies of world literature to works on social justice, such as civil rights advocacy or issues of gender equity.

Through a critical analysis of this broad genre of literature, teachers may find appropriate material to introduce themes of racial, religious, and gender prejudice and bias, as well as issues of social justice. As Norton (2001) says, "The best books break down borders," they extend the phrase "like me" to include what the mainstream majority previously characterized as foreign, exotic, and/or strange (p. 2). They may teach mutual respect by emphasizing cultural equality (Baker & Freebody, 1989). Also, literature as a field may be examined critically by students regarding how political and cultural themes are represented in literature and how these issues influence what is published and taught (Banks, 1994). Thus, teacher choice of materials and discussion topics are important in determining what students are exposed to in terms of diverse literacy events (Fehring, 2003a, 2003b). Children learn about individuals different from themselves, which is reflected here as a goal from the teachers' interviews.

In order to make informed choices about the books and other materials a teacher uses in his or her classroom, it is important to recognize that authors and illustrators offer different types of cultural cues and messages through their literature. These different strategies and techniques may be used to emphasize language, culture, and social messages or to analyze from a critical literacy perspective. Looking at books through this sociocultural lens also informs the teacher (*and students*) about the political nature of authorship.

This then brings us to the questions addressed in this chapter. What books are appropriate for a transformative curriculum that would promote critical analysis of culture and society as a force for critical change? How, as teachers, do we best teach a transformative curriculum? Are the teacher's goals, as described here, best met through an embedded lesson, such as discussion and journal response to the story? *Or*, how can we shape lessons to be more effectively taught through explicit lesson strategies?

The Curriculum and Children's Literature

The National Council of Social Studies (NCSS) calls for explicit teaching of 10 identified social studies thematic strands. These strands include dealing with interpersonal, community, and global connections, as well as economic, geographical, and ethnic factors as related to power (NCSS, 1994). The strands are as follows: (1) Culture, (2) Time, Continuity, and Change, (3) People, Places, and Environment, (4) Individual Development and Identity, (5) Individuals, Groups, and Institutions, (6) Power, Authority, and Governance, (7) Production, Distribution, and Consumption, (8) Science, Technology, and Society, (9) Global Connections, and (10) Civic Ideals and Practices (NCSS, 1994). Using powerful multicultural literature as a prompt, teachers can *tap into* family resources and build on background knowledge (Moll & Greenberg, 1990). This methodology then enables the teacher to use curriculum as a way to learn about family literacy practices and places the social studies thematic strands in the context of transformative education. This type of practice echoes Moll and Greenberg's (1990) learning model of "funds of knowledge," that all families have practices and resources useful in ensuring the well-being of the households. Moll and Greenberg (1990) define funds of knowledge as the practices and products of the family operation. Greenberg (1989, as cited in Moll & Greenberg, 1990) states that every family has its own "operations manual of essential information and strategies that households need to maintain their well-being" (p. 217). Moll and Greenberg's work tell us that by learning more about our students and their lives, teachers can develop a curriculum that matches their lives, avoiding a disconnect or mismatch.

All families have resources to be tapped, but that these are not always recognized as mainstream schooling and parenting practices. These funds of knowledge are often traditional, and when brought into the classroom, validate the child's home and culture as a learning site and resource. As discussed in chapter 2, with Derek's Cub Scouts book, when a teacher makes literature a bridge between the home and school, the school and home literacy practices inform each other. This methodology is loosely based on Vygotsky's (1978) social constructivist theory, which views learning as both socially based and integrated, has played a major role in guiding the research in this area. Hence, studies of classroom language and literacy learning generally assume that learning is a social activity; learning integrates both oral and written activities across knowledge areas, and learning requires student interaction in classroom activities.

As a primary teacher for 22 years, I often taught social studies through literature and other language-based methods. Currently, I teach courses in multicultural perspectives in children's literature at a university teacher education program. Obviously, I am not one to degrade or devalue literature's place in an integrated curriculum. What I have come to reject, however, is the oversimplification of social studies and other content-area themes by reliance on teacher read alouds with follow-up discussions. As Palinscar and Magnussan (2000) reported: "Too often the text does not provide a structure for further inquiry along the concept" (p. 472), but rather presents it in storybook form, complete with closure. I call on teachers to make explicit the social studies and other content-area lessons they teach through literature. Rather than gloss over powerful or controversial themes in children's literature, teachers can pull out these themes through role-play activities, character analysis, graphic organizers that lead to character analysis and/or cause and effect, or other methods to push children's reading of a book beyond the surface level. I believe that even young children can question events that take place or what happens to characters in a book. Teacher questions, such as:

- "How could you make this situation better for the character?"
- "How are you like the character in the book?"
- "Has this ever happened to you?"
- "What did you do?"
- "What do you wish you had done?"

push the children to look at literature as sample events…occurrences that they can take part in, even if through transactional reading (Rosenblatt, 1976). Additionally, I challenge all of us who work with children to examine our own teacher bookshelves. What do our book collections tell us about the controlled curriculum we offer our students? What group is represented, and who is left out? Delpit (1999) urges us to challenge racially based societal views of the competence and worthiness of the children and their families, and help them to do the same. One way we can do this is through careful analysis of the books and curriculum we offer our children.

In a study by the author (Fox, 2000), four first-grade teachers and one multigrade (first–third grades) teacher were interviewed regarding their use of multicultural literature as classroom read alouds. Sessions of the teacher reading to the whole class were videotaped, as well as activity and play sessions following the read alouds. The interviews and video tapes were analyzed for teacher's intent for the sessions, what types of books they included, how the material was presented, and how the children responded in both the reading session itself and the follow-up activity time. All five teachers taught in a multiethnic, multilingual Title 1 school. Two of the teachers were bilingual English-Spanish and the other three were monolingual English. The results of the study found teacher and student uses for multicultural literature to be significantly different from other genres. Teachers responded to interview questions regarding the choice of text to be determined by the racial, linguistic, and ethnic backgrounds of their students. Teachers stated that both their mainstream ethnic and linguistic children, as well as those minority-language and ethnicity students, benefited from multicultural literature. The uses of text emerged through an analysis of the interviews and teachers' and children's responses to the texts. The outstanding goal of the teachers for multicultural literature was to help their students to get along with each other by realizing what characteristics they shared and diminishing the effect of their differences. The students' use of the texts were also found in the analysis of their read-aloud and activity sessions. Children used "other language" words to discuss language usage during read-aloud time. Children compared their own cultural practices to those of characters in texts. Children used illustrations from the text to explain cultural differences to each other. Both teachers and children discussed multicultural and linguistic issues, using the texts as mediators and/ or prompts.

One implication of the study was the emphasis put on choice of multicultural texts for social justice lessons in the classroom. Making an informed choice of appropriate texts is a challenge for beginning teachers, but even experienced teachers may benefit from guidelines and suggestions. In analyzing the broad category of multicultural literature, I developed 13 subcategories to aid in text selection and use. These categories are described in the subsequent section on characteristics of multicultural literature.

The Selection of Children's Literature

The careful consideration of children's texts along with concrete, explicit lessons that include the child's own background, are the best ways in which to teach social justice themes, as described in the NCSS strands. Using the "funds of knowledge" approach (Moll & Greenberg, 1994), the teacher discovers what "untapped sources" of knowledge are occurring in the homes and communities of his or her students. It can be challenging in the sense that teachers may come from different language backgrounds, cultural and ethnic histories, and economic and ability levels than their students. However, diversity in the classrooms should be seen as an additive factor in the classroom communities for both minority- and majority-culture children (Banks, 1994; Delpit, 1996; Higgins, 2002; Norton, 2001). Delpit (1993) states, "Teachers must acknowledge and validate students' home language without using it to limit students' potential" (p. 293). Delpit (1999) suggests that the key to reaching all students is to learn about them on their own turf. She urges teachers to use familiar metaphors and experiences from the children's world to connect what they already know to school knowledge. In order to do this, we must discover what their lives are like, including what are their traditional family literacy practices, using some of the suggestions in chapter 5. The easiest assumption is that there are no family literacy practices because these might be different from the mainstream school expectations. In other words, because a child tells a teacher that his mother or father does not read a nightly bedtime story, the teacher may assume that there are no literacy events occurring in the home. By digging a little deeper, the teacher may discover that the dad includes the child in recording baseball scores or the grandmother teaches the child the home language through oral stories and songs. The teacher, by making a point to find out about the resources, or we might say, riches, of the children's home lives, will bridge home and school practices. This reciprocal methodology uses children's literature selections that are thoughtfully selected as mediators or prompts for family discussions, writing, collections, and sharing. The beauty of this gained knowledge, then, is to use it to guide in-text selections and curriculum choices that reflect all our children's lives.

The next two sections offer suggestions on practical analysis and application of children's literature, based on the findings of the study described above (Fox, 2000). The first section suggests a method for analyzing multicultural literature to enable the teacher to choose socially, culturally, and linguistically relevant texts for classroom use. The second section outlines a method for communication through carefully selected children's texts that bridges the home and school, informing each other about the mainstream classroom and the family's traditional literacy practices.

Teacher Perspective in Literature Selection

In a teacher read aloud, it is the teacher who chooses the texts, the follow-up questions and/or activities, and we could say, what is learned (Wilkinson & Silliman, 2001). If transformative education is the goal, to empower students to understand issues of social justice and make changes, classroom reading choices must be examined in all classrooms and groups. Teachers may operate under the misconception that a homogeneous monolingual, monoculture class does not need to be exposed to multicultural literature. However, the objective of transformative education applies to all children in order to affect long-held stereotypes and beliefs (Aldridge & Calhoun, 2000). During read alouds, the teacher is doing the reading; therefore, the readability need not match that of the children, and in fact, is beyond what most of the children may be able to read on their own. Instead, the content match becomes more important as a "fit" for the larger curriculum. The link to background knowledge and/or comprehensibility may be included in the teacher's decision process of choosing a classroom read aloud. Additionally, physical characteristics of the book play a role in its appeal, such as size of illustration, length, and numbers of words per page (Huck et al., 1997). The less obvious descriptors that influence teacher choice are also the more subtle factors. Often, these are social, cultural, and/or linguistic cues embedded within the text. These cues may be represented through illustration, setting, characterization, and/or use of another language or dialect. In the teacher interviews I conducted for the study described earlier, teachers named the representation of multiple cultures and languages as important factors in choosing a read aloud. However, none of the teachers mentioned using guidelines or standards to choose the books. The Council on Interracial Books for Children published *Guidelines for Selecting Bias-Free Textbooks and Storybooks* in 1980 (Derman-Sparks, 1989). The guidelines suggest 10 steps for evaluating children's literature:

1. checking illustrations for stereotypes or tokenism
2. checking the storyline
3. looking at the lifestyles (watching out for the "cute-natives-in-costumes" syndrome, for example)
4. weighing relationships between people
5. noting the heroes
6. considering the effect on a child's self-image
7. considering the author's or illustrator's background
8. examining the author's perspective
9. watching for loaded words
10. checking the copyright date

Author Perspective

In reviewing the literature on author perspective, there is a similarity between what teachers and authors hope to achieve through the use of multicultural literature. Often, the books chosen by the teachers in this study were those that used "other" language in the text. This type of text, which I term as "embedded second language," introduces monolingual speakers to a second language, usually through the narrative or dialogue in the text. This is one way in which authors write to the teachers' goal: Children learn through this technique that it is okay, and even fun, to speak a language of another culture. Children recognize their native language in a text, and their language is then linguistically validated. Authors who write from a multilingual stance often do so purposefully. In other words, it is no accident that a word other than English is embedded in the text of a story about making tamales. The italicization of the word goes further to show it is special and sometimes precedes the definition written in the text (Fox, 2000). Often, informing mainstream children what it feels like to be the "other" and how important it is to know about other cultures, including names, vocabulary, setting, and cultural artifacts, is the goal. The books we select for our classrooms should reflect not only the easily recognizable diversity of the students in the classroom, but also the diverse reality of the world in which we live (Rochman, 1993). Rosalinda Barrera (1992) and colleagues described the context of Mexican-American literature as "literature about the human experience" (p. 231). The author Bobbi Salinas (1998) said that she writes so that Latino children can see themselves validated in print and stereotypes of her culture broken through her books (Fox, 2000). Religious practices and celebrations are a part of culture that may be acknowledged through children's literature. If no books with dreydles and menorahs are read in a classroom when discussing winter holiday celebrations, Jewish children may feel invisible in their own classrooms while, at the same time, depriving non-Jewish children the opportunity to learn about the traditions. Eileen Tway (1989) writes that: "In a country of multicultural heritage, children require books that reflect and illuminate that varied heritage" (p. 109). The purposeful reflection of our own heritage, illuminated in the observation of others, can occur through literature, if not based in personal experience. Just as in bilingual theory of learning a second language, it is through the studying of the "other" that we can learn the most about ourselves.

The Characteristics of Multicultural Literature

In analyzing the broad category of multicultural literature, I analyzed over 150 titles classified as multicultural literature for children and developed 10 subcategories to aid in text selection and use. These categories were developed primarily through representations of cultural and linguistic cues in the literature. These cultural cues include characterizations of skin color, ethnicity, language, economic level, geographic location, and school relationships. The linguistic codes include the use of more than one language in a text, the use of more than one font to emphasize a culturally significant word, the use of font to emphasize a linguistically significant word, a semantic device used to emphasize a cultural and/or linguistically significant word, the naming of character(s), location, and artifacts with cultural or linguistic significance, etc.

Cultural instructive texts are those that have a lesson within the story that tells about a culture. Some of these titles represent cultures as foreign, or the "other." An example of this type of text would be a nonfiction book about Kenya. Others of this type of text show cultures living side-by-side, such as *Everybody Cooks Rice* (Dooley, 1995), a book wherein children can learn about other cultures through the foods they eat as the main character (mainstream majority) goes from house to house and discovers about her neighbor's traditional cultures.

A second category is the linguistic instructive. In this category, other language vocabulary is introduced in the text and then defined. An example of this is the text *Too Many Tamales* by Gary Soto (1993). The italicized Spanish language words embedded in the English text are set off by italics and then defined in a following clause (i.e., "Papa rolled the *masa*, soft white corn dough, in his hands"). The reader is notified by the italics that this is an "other language" word and then given the translation.

A third category is the cultural instructive in illustration. Here, as in the first category, the illustrations give cultural cues embedded in illustrations but not described in the text. The book *Los tres credos/The Three Pigs: Nacho, Tito y Miguel,* by Bobbi Salinas (1998), shows Latino cultural icons through illustrations, that is, Frieda Kahlo's portrait is hanging on the wall as a part of the living room decor in the main character's home.

The fourth category is the bilingual translation text. These texts use more than one language, either placed in a vertical format on the same page or facing horizontally on side-by-side pages. This text makes the text available to a bilingual reader and/or readers of either one of the two languages presented in the text. An example of this type of text is *Gathering the Sun: An Alphabet Book in Spanish and English* by Alma Flor Ada (1997). For each letter of the Spanish alphabet, including those letters that are specific to Spanish, the author gives a description of an object culturally relevant to a Latino child. The direct translation in English is placed directly to the right of the Spanish text.

A fifth category that also incorporates translation is the multilingual translation text, such as *This Is The Way We Go To School* (Baer, 1992). This text juxtaposes English and the direct translation of other languages represented by the culture described on each page.

A sixth category is the bilingual embedded in text, where the use of another language within a text is not set off by italics or comma. The book *The Story of Divaali,* by Jatinder Verma (2002), describes the traditional tale of the Hindu festival Ramayana, using traditional vocabulary embedded in the text to describe the epic tale.

Social instructive texts are those that have a social or moral lesson within the story. This seventh category may define a social characteristic, consequences for not practicing it all embedded within a story. A book that fits in this category is *Chicken Sunday* by Patricia Polacco (1998). In this story, a moral lesson is given by the elder female character as she instructs the children to always make things right, even though in this case, the children were unfairly judged.

An eighth category is distinguished by teaching social lessons in a more subtle way, such as through the outcome of the character's action in the story. This category, embedded social stories, is exemplified with the book *The Legend of the Bluebonnet* by Tomie DePaola (1996). In this Native-American story, a little girl teaches about selflessness when she gives up a prized possession for the greater good of the group.

The ninth category is distinguished by teaching social lessons embedded in illustrations. In *Mufaro's Beautiful Daughter* (Steptoe, 1987), an African Cinderella story, the greed and dishonesty of the characters is shown through the illustrator's depiction of emotion on her face. This book, as most of the titles analyzed, fit into more than one category, but the illustrations here can stand alone to show the storyline.

The tenth category is the comparative culture category. The group of texts compares one culture to another, not specifying any mainstream value system but equally representing various practices as universals. An example of this category is the book *People*, by Peter Spiers (1980), where the author compares how people of different cultures adorn their hair, dress for celebrations, live in houses, etc. Other books represent the universal by using one concept across many cultures. The book *Hats, Hats, Hats* (Morris, 1993) is a part of a series by the author that fit this category.

In my analysis of texts, I discovered that the majority of these books used more than one technique to deliver the message; thus, most books fit into more than one of the categories. Depending on the teacher's and/or reader's "take-up" or use of the material, the lesson could be attained from more than one delivery system in the same book.

Bridges to School and Family Literacy Use: Classroom Connections

With informed choices and explicit lesson objectives, a teacher can use literature to connect school and family cultural practices, thereby validating the child's home as a learning site. One way multicultural children's literature can have an impact is in "grand conversation" or interactive story discussions (Temple, Martinez, Yokota, & Naylor, 2004; Walker, 2004). As the teacher facilitates the "grand conversation" through story, the children relate text to their own background knowledge (Walker, 2004, p. 37).

In the following example, the teacher sits down with a group of first–third grade students, all gathered around her on the rug. She holds up a big book version of the text *Dumpling Soup* (Rattigan, 1993).

Teacher: Today, we're reading a book about a girl and her family at New Year's. What do you think is going to happen in this book?

Child: She's going to eat her lunch. She is Chinese.

Teacher: How do you know? Why do you say that?

Child: Because she has those little sticks. Those sticks are for eating Chinese food.

The children continue to discuss the cover of the book, going on to discuss the soup bowls and the dumplings, which they name as "cookies with notes," or fortune cookies. The teacher closes the discussion of the cover by stating:

Teacher: Now let's read the story and find out what happens when he goes to the cafeteria.

She opens the book and begins the story. By exposing the children to a character much like themselves but whom they can identify having practices and/or traditions different from their own (eating with chopsticks), the children's discussion addresses the goal reflected in the teacher interview above. Helping the children to identify with storybook characters who are from a different cultural and/or linguistic background helps them to be more tolerant and accepting of others, as well as see themselves in a diverse world.

The NCSS encourages teachers to engage in grand conversations about culturally relevant topics for all children. In this example, the teacher leads the children in "grand conversation style" to explore the text further. By asking the children, "What can you do just like the character in the book?", the children now have an opportunity to discuss how they are like the character in the book. During the reading of the text, the teacher points out that the child's mother makes the dumplings with flour and water, patting them with her hands. The teacher provides time for the children to simulate this action with their hands. She then asks, "Have any of you ever done this before?" After a moment, one boy says, "Yes, my grandma makes tortillas like that. Sometimes, she gives me a little bit of flour to pat one for me." Several children then join in, showing and stating how they help to make tortillas at home, all using their hands to simulate the patting of the dough, just as the Hawaiian grandmother is pictured doing in the text. Again, here, the children see themselves and relate to the character in the book (older people teach how to make food) but are able to place themselves as different as well (some make dumplings, others make tortillas).

After story time, the children write in their journals to the prompt, "What can you do just like the character in the book?" "Make tortillas," is a repeated response through both in their text and illustrations. "Share my lunch," and "Eat with chopsticks," are other responses.

A sponge activity after journal time is the free play in the dramatic play area, where a kitchen is set up. Here, two of the same students, as described above, Jose and Alicia, the same boy and girl who participated in the discussion about tortillas, are now acting out the making of tortillas and cooking them over a stove in the dramatic play area. The girl tells the boy that she helped in food preparation for a wedding over the previous weekend, where tamales were served. They then act out the making of the "*masa*," or flour mixture, again patting the "dough" in their hands.

One interesting characteristic of this conversation was that it occurred in Spanish (their home language), the original text was written in English, and the content was about similarities between Hawaiian and Japanese-American food with Mexican-American food (Fox, 2000). The book sponsored the desired type of talk and reflection first mentioned in the teacher interviews above . . . that children would see themselves in the literature selections read aloud in class and understand that there are both similarities and differences among people.

Bridges to School and Family Literacy Use: In Home to School Connections

In the above example, the book *Dumpling Soup* (Rattigan, 1993) became a prompt for a classroom conversation about what children in one classroom and cultural group could do like a child from another culture. In order to gain insights into family practices, or "funds of knowledge" (Moll, Armanti, Neff, & Gonzalez, 1992), a teacher may again use multicultural children's literature as a prompt for conversations between the home and school. One tool for this type of communication is "Story Letters." These one-page communications might be compared to "Book Notes" in *New Yorker Magazine* or "Book Talk" in *Instructor Magazine*. The letters simulate book-group discussion notes, as found in the back of many current novels and on Oprah's Web page. The letters communicate the classroom curriculum, as well as prompting family conversations around literature. Additionally, I use the letters to introduce social, linguistic, and cultural information that may be the same or an "other" to the family. The questions and activities contained in the letter prompt discussions to compare and contrast the information to the family's practices.

Using the child's knowledge of a book, the teacher prepares a Story Letter to prompt family conversations in the home. The book is introduced through classroom read-aloud and follow-up activities, perhaps as a part of a unit to address a social studies or other content-area objective. In the home, with the prompting of the Story Letter, family resources in the form of traditions and practices become a part of the discussion and are valued here as literacy practices. These same resources, when shared in class with the return of the Story Letter, inform the teacher and his or her peers about the child's literacy practices outside of school. As in the classroom, the book serves as the prompt or mediator of cultural information.

Along with regular lesson planning, the teacher completes the Story Letter with the children's literature selection to be used as the lesson's read aloud. A sample Story Letter for *Chicken Sunday* (Polacco, 1998) is included here as Appendix 9:1. The book should be a title that the children will be exposed to more than one time, perhaps as a part of a unit plan. In this example, the teacher makes a copy of the Story Letter for each child to take home as a part of the unit closure. This letter becomes their homework to prompt language and literacy practices but may be seen more as an enrichment rather than "graded" or assessed homework item.

The Story Letter activities emphasize oral language but often include a writing, art, or social studies suggestion as well. The teacher may copy the cover of the book on the back of the Story Letter to help younger children recall elements of the book when discussing it with their families. The families are encouraged to do the Story Letter together. The Story Letters may be returned to class, where children are encouraged to share the results in class. In this way, the family responses are added to the classroom conversation surrounding the book. For the story mentioned earlier, *Dumpling Soup* (Rattigan, 1993), the Story Letter might ask the family to discuss a favorite food that they prepare together. The child, with parents' help, can practice "miming" the making of the food. Upon returning to class, the children can guess what food each child's family enjoys by watching the child's dramatization.

Just as in the previous discussion regarding reviewing a teacher's bookshelf, the Story Letters are a record of a teacher's classroom selections. A year's worth of Story Letters allows a teacher to see the classroom literature offerings at a glance. "What did I tend to emphasize? Were there any gaps?" are some of the questions a teacher can answer through this record of classroom read alouds.

One caution for teachers regarding Story Letters is to be aware of the tendency to ask for conversations or to write activities not accessible to all children. When asked to develop a Story Letter, the education students in my teacher-preparation classes tend to lump families into one income and lifestyle group. For instance, a student in my methods class wrote, as the suggested follow-up to the book *Just Plain Fancy* (Polacco, 1990), "Take your child to a farm." While this is a way to encourage families to go to a petting farm, not all families will have the cultural and/or economic means to drive to a farm. Beginning teachers need to understand that for children, often, what is interesting are the things in their own lives and that visiting a farm is not necessarily more interesting to a child than a discovery walk around one's own backyard. I suggest to my students to instead put the more exotic type of activity as one of the choices in the extension section of the Story Letter. For *Just Plain Fancy* (Polacco, 1994), list a more accessible activity, such as, "Go on a walk around your house or neighborhood. Are there any rocks, shells, leaves that stand out from the others? How?" (By color, size, and texture?) A discussion starter for the family to use with this book would be, "Have you ever found something special? What happened?" Not that all parents will, or should, follow this suggested list, but offering a variety of appealing and authentic suggestions opens up the mindset to explore themes in the books in more culturally relevant ways.

Story Letters communicate about our classroom curriculum, as well as the wealth of fine children's literature available today. Additionally, the letters introduce social, linguistic, and cultural information that may be the same or perceived as an "other" to the family. The questions and activities contained in the letter prompt discussions to compare and contrast the information to the family's practices. Following the teacher and author responses mentioned above, the family resources are included in the exploration of the text as a cultural mediator for understanding one's place in a diverse world.

Conclusion

A common response of first-grade teachers when asked what influenced their choice of books to read aloud in their primary school classrooms was that the books presented students of different social, cultural, and linguistic backgrounds "getting along" (Fox, 2000). In this sense, books were used as mediators for social justice lessons, in that they were seen as tools of transformative education (Banks, 1994). The potential for children's literature to not only be support material, but also to become a tool for pushing an activity, discussion, or response to a more explicit analysis gives teachers groundwork for more powerful content. The range of children's literature makes it possible for teachers to represent characters of diverse cultural, linguistic, and ability backgrounds in an empowered stance. Teachers in this study felt that literature validated membership in diverse groups and provided their students with a sense of belonging and awareness of the "other" at the same time.

While there may be no more pleasant way to find wonderful children's literature than an afternoon in a library or bookstore, there are several Web sites available for exploring a wide array of multicultural literature. I would recommend the two following sites to begin exploration: the Cooperative Children's Book Center, from the University of Wisconsin at Madison, at http://www.education.wisc.edu/ccbc/ and the Multicultural Book Review Home Page at http://www.isomedia.com/homes/jmele/homepage.html.

With informed choices of children's multicultural literature, teachers can present a curriculum that includes explicit teaching of social studies objectives. More than status quo conversations, the teacher's critical analysis of literature lends itself to powerful curriculum, such as a grand conversation prompted by the literature selection. Including the family in the conversations, through communicative tools, such as Story Letters, brings family resources into the classroom. In all classrooms, books can be seen as gateways to open conversations regarding social, linguistic, and cultural factors that can enrich and extend learning opportunities for all children.

References

Ada, A. F. (1997). *Gathering the sun: An alphabet in Spanish and English.* New York: Lothrop, Lee & Shepard Books.

Aldridge, J., & Calhoun, C. (2000). Fifteen misconceptions about multicultural education. *Focus on Elementary*, *12*(3), 1–2.

Baer, E. (1992). *This is the way we go to school.* New York: Scholastic Books.

Baker, C., & Freebody, P. (1989). *Children's first school books: Introductions to the culture of literacy.* New York: B. Blackweed in association with A. Deutsch.

Banks, J. (1994). *Multiethnic education: Theory and practice* (3rd ed.). Boston: Allyn.

Barrerra, R. (1992). In J. J. Higgins. *Multicultural children's literature: Creating and applying an evaluation tool in response to the needs of urban educators.* Online document at: http://www.newhorizons.org Retrieved August, 2006.

Delpit, L. (1993). The politics of teaching literate discourse. In T. Perry & J. W. Fraser (Eds.), *Freedom's plow: Teaching in the multicultural classroom* (pp. 285-295). New York: Routledge.

Delpit, L. (1996). *Other people's children: Cultural conflict in the classroom.* New York: New Press.

Delpit, L. (1999). *Ten factors essential to success in urban schools.* Online document at: http://ces.edgateway.net/lpt/ces_docs/79 Retrieved August, 2006.

DePaola, T. (1996). *The legend of the bluebonnet.* New York: Putnam Juvenile.

Derman-Sparks, L. (1989). *Anti-bias curriculum: Tools for empowering young children* . . . Washington, DC: National Association for the Education of Young Children (ED 305 135).

Dooley, N. (1995). *Everybody cooks rice.* Minneapolis, MN: Carolhoda Books.

Fehring, H. (2003a). Introduction in H. Fehring (Ed.), *Literacy assessment: A collection of articles from the Australian Literacy Educators' Association* (pp. 1–8). Newark, DE: International Reading Association.

Fehring, H. (2003b). Understanding the influences on teachers' judgments in the process of assessing and reporting students' literacy in the classroom. In H. Fehring (Ed.), *Literacy assessment: A collection of articles from the Australian Literacy Educators' Association* (pp. 9–31). Newark, DE: International Reading Association.

Fox, K. (2000). Multicultural literature: Definition, intent, and place in the class-room. *Unpublished master's thesis.* University of California at Santa Barbara.

Higgins, J. J. (2002). *Multicultural children's literature: Creating and applying an evaluation tool in response to the needs of urban educators.* Online document at: http://www.newhorizons.org Retrieved August, 2006.

Huck, C. S., Hepler, S., Hickman, J., & Kiefer, B. (1997). *Children's literature in the elementary school* (6th ed.). Madison, WI: Brown & Benchmark.

Moll, L. C., Armanti, C., Neff, D., & Gonzalez, N. (1992). Funds of knowledge for teaching: Using a qualitative approach to connect homes and classrooms. *Theory into Practice, 31*(2), 132–141.

Moll, L. C., & Greenberg, J. B. (1990). Creating zones of possibilities: Combining social contexts for instruction. In L. Moll (Ed.), *Vygotsky and education: Instructional implications and applications of sociocultural psychology* (pp. 319–348). New York: Cambridge University Press.

Morris, A. (1995). *Hat, hats, hats.* New York: Mulberry Books.

National Council of Social Studies (NCSS). (1994). *Curriculum standards for social studies.* Washington, DC: National Council for the Social Studies.

Norton, D. E. (2001). *Multicultural children's literature: Through the eyes of many children.* Upper Saddle River, NJ: Merrill.

Palinscar, A., & Magnussan, S. (2000). *The interplay of firsthand text-based investigations in a science lesson* (CIERA Report #2, 007.) Ann Arbor, MI: Center for the Improvement of Early Childhood Reading Achievement.

Polacco, P. (1990). *Just Plain Fancy.* New York: Bantam Books.

Polacco, P. (1998). *Chicken Sunday.* New York: Philomel Books.

Rattigan, J. K. (1993). *Dumpling soup.* Boston: Little, Brown.

Rochman, H. (1993). *Against borders: Promoting books for a multicultural world.* Chicago: American Library Association.

Rosenblatt, L. (1976). *The reader, the text, the poem: The transactional theory of the literary work.* Carbondale, IL: Southern Illinois University Press.

Salinas, B. (1998*). Los tres cerdos/The Three Pigs: Nacho, Tito y Miguel.* Houston, TX: Piñata Books.

Soto, G. (1993). *Too many tamales.* New York: Putnam Juvenile.

Spiers, P. (1980). *People.* Garden City, NY: Doubleday.

Steptoe, J. (1987). *Mufaro's beautiful daughter.* New York: Lothrop, Lee & Shepard Books.

Temple, C., Martinez, M., Yokota, J., & Naylor, A. (2002). *Children's books in children's hands: An introduction to their literature.* Boston: Allyn and Bacon.

Tway, E. (1989) Dimensions of multicultural literature for children. In M. K. Rudman (Ed.), *Children's literature: Resource for the classroom* (pp. 109–138). Norwood, MA: Christopher-Gordon.

Verma, J. (2002). *The story of Divaali*. Cambridge, MA: Barefoot Books.

Vygotsky, L. (1978). *Mind in society*. London: Harvard University Press.

Walker, B. (2004). *Diagnostic teaching of reading: Techniques for instruction and assessment*. Upper Saddle River, NJ: Pearson.

Wilkinson, L. C., & Silliman, E. R. (2001). Classroom language and literacy learning. *Reading Online, 4*(7). Online document at: readingonline.org/articles/art_index.asp?HREF=/articles/handbook/wilkinson/index.html   Retrieved August, 2006.

Appendix 9:1 Story Letter Sample

We have been reading: Chicken Sunday

The author is: Patricia Polacco

Please ask me about:

> Why the children in the story want to raise money.
> What do they want to do with the money?

I can also tell you why:

> Mr. Kodinski was angry at the children.
> Why was he mistaken in being angry at them?

> Have you ever been in trouble for something you didn't do? Talk about what you could do to prove it was not your fault [or a mistake].

Suggested at-home activities:

> Look on a calendar for the Easter holiday that the family in the book is celebrating. What other holidays are on the calendar? Are there any special days that your family has added to the calendar?

> *Thank you—*
> *From my teachers and me*

Introduction to Section Three: Reorganizing Schools to Support Literacy Learning for All

In this section, Rodgers and Rodgers explain how individuals and teams of teachers can take ownership and establish a voice in professional development instead of considering professional development as something that is "done" to us.

Jones illustrates how school administrative leaders can cocreate an environment with teachers to better understand and support diverse learners. In this chapter, we meet Kim, a second-grade teacher, who is struggling to address her students' wide range of academic needs. We learn firsthand how Sandy, her principal, supports Kim, and other teachers in their building, by developing trust and staying focused on a vision and mission to support diversity.

We learned about the importance of developing a relationship between administrative leaders and teachers in the first chapter. In the third chapter, the final chapter for this section, Hayes and Hayes use a school example to discuss how a school can "reform itself" through active and ongoing involvement in the change process, with the goal being optimum service for all students. Walters Elementary was so obviously in need of reform that it serves as a powerful example of what is possible.

Chapter 10

Preparing for Diversity: Professional Development for Today's Teachers

Adrian Rodgers and Emily M. Rodgers

I met Maria during the third week of school when she was in first grade. Her family had just arrived in the United States from the Honduras, and Maria spoke only Spanish. On that day, I saw Maria sitting quietly in her classroom, her wide, dark-brown eyes solemnly taking in the activity around her, her stillness a vivid contrast to the busy, chattering classmates who surrounded her. She was present, but she may as well have been invisible for all the attention that her classmates paid her.

I was in the school as a volunteer. Normally, my work as a professor would take me away from teaching young children, but because my university role also included preparing Reading Recovery teacher leaders, I made sure to teach a first-grade student on a daily basis in order to stay grounded in teaching and learning.

This year, I wanted to learn more about teaching students who were learning English. Teachers in my graduate classes were reporting that more and more of their students were coming to school with little or no proficiency with English, and they felt unprepared to teach them. I felt equally unprepared to teach the teachers. I was familiar with theory about learning a second language, but I had never actually taught a student who did not speak English. I knew that I would learn a lot from teaching Maria.

The most valuable part of the experience, as it turned out, was that by working with Maria, I began to uncover and articulate what I did not know. In other words, the gaps in my professional knowledge became apparent. Would it hinder Maria's progress if her mother spoke Spanish at home, or should her mother use English, since she was fluent in the language? Maria's teacher thought it would be better to use English; I thought Spanish, but I wasn't confident. I could only rely on my experiences growing up in Canada, where I saw many children being raised in a bilingual environment (French at home and English at school, and vice versa), and they managed quite well.

Other questions arose. On what basis would I select books for Maria to read? Her Spanish proficiency allowed her to sound out words almost flawlessly. What kinds of books would scaffold Maria as a reader of English? What did she need to learn? I had a good understanding of how children emerge into literacy, but what about a second literacy?

Both Maria's teacher and I were confident that Maria eventually would learn English, but neither one of us really knew how to differentiate our roles to meet her needs. We had a vague sense that the professional development offered by the district had not yet caught up with the current needs of an increasingly more diversified school population. We wondered how we could increase our professional knowledge to support Maria so that we could be more involved in her learning.

Introduction

In the chapters that you have read up to this point, you have read how diversity is defined, and you have learned about the various contexts of diversity and relevant instructional methods. How can a chapter on professional development support you in your work with diverse learners? After all, many of us view professional development as something that is "done" to us. We think that administrators and program directors own the decisions as to the content or focus of workshops that we will attend throughout the school year.

We propose instead that we view professional development as an ongoing support system for our instruction. Since, as educators, we can control how we teach, we can also influence how we develop and refine our instructional skills. For us, then, professional development is a procedure, protocol, or sequence of activities in which we can engage to alter our practice with the aim of enhancing our support of student learning. We can influence, alter, and shape professional development to meet our own needs.

In this chapter, we provide educators with a professional development plan to support their teaching of diverse students. We chose the word "plan" because we are articulating potential future courses of action, not a program with lock-steps or a protocol from which we cannot deviate.

Our plan has three planes, or spaces, that we typically move around in as educators. They are the:

1. school and/or district plane
2. team plane
3. individual plane

We can work along one plane at a time, or all three together, in that one teacher may at one time be entirely consumed with her professional development work with a team of teachers, whereas another teacher may be thinking about professional development work that is being carried out along the district plane, and at the same time, be following individual pursuits to further professional knowledge.

In the first section of this chapter, we describe the school and/or district plane. We discuss how teachers can influence and direct the focus for district- and school-planned professional development initiatives and activities. We provide templates that teachers might take to school or district personnel for professional development at the building and district level. This section will be useful for teachers who seek a voice in their own professional development, and for building- and district-level coaches who seek to foster voice and ownership of teachers over professional development.

In the second section, we discuss how teachers might work as a professional development team to construct learning opportunities tailored to their particular interests around diverse learners. In this chapter, we also provide topics for investigation, related activities, and suggested readings that might guide the work of the team. By team, we mean any group of teachers who are working together on the same problem or with a common purpose. Teams might be horizontal in nature, in that the teachers are working at the same grade level, or vertical in nature, in that they are teachers working in a sequence of grades (such as a group of K, 1, and 2 teachers). Lastly, teams might be multisite in nature, in that the teachers are working in different schools.

In the final section, we propose that professional development might also be conducted by an individual teacher. An individual teacher might undertake this work either because they are working in sites where professional development opportunities at the district, school, or team level are minimal or unavailable, or because they want to augment the professional development work at other levels with work at their own level. Along this individual plane, we discuss formal and informal study that a teacher might undertake. In discussing individual study, we suggest questions for self-directed inquiry and activity that might be undertaken using an action-research approach.

Our intention is that by offering a template for a plan, you will have tools that support you in articulating what work you would like to undertake to support your professional development around your own issues of diversity. It will be challenging work because it involves fundamental changes to teaching. What is important is that we interpret the challenge as an opportunity, rather than a difficult hardship.

School or District Plane

Marie Hughes and several of her colleagues recently conducted a survey of 292 reading/language arts program directors and special education directors from across the United States (Hughes, Cash, Ahwee, & Klingner, 2002). When asked what factors they took into account when planning teacher professional development, 80% or more of the directors most often identified these three influences:

- good fit with the district's reading philosophy
- expectation to increase test scores
- research-based

The fourth most frequently cited factor was "teacher requests," cited by 75% of the directors who completed the survey (Hughes, Cash, Ahwee, & Klingner, 2002, p. 17).

Given our own experience as teachers and our work in professional development, we were not surprised to learn that program directors consider whether a workshop will help raise test scores when planning their professional development. The pressure to increase a school's overall achievement scores often presses down heavily on everybody in the district, particularly those responsible for directing programs. We can't help but be disappointed, however, that increasing test scores mattered more to directors when planning professional development than teacher input. In fact, one quarter of the directors surveyed apparently did not take teacher requests into account at all.

Teachers need to have a voice in planning their professional development because we know that in-service sessions that are grounded in teaching will be most effective (Lyons & Pinnell, 2001), and currently, no topic is more relevant to teachers' daily practice than understanding better how to effectively teach diverse learners.

In this section, we describe how teachers can have a voice so that their requests for professional development are heard at the district level. We describe how to prepare brief proposals for professional development that can be submitted to program coordinators for consideration. The format is simple and can be quickly completed by a group of teachers who share an interest in a particular topic (see Figure 10:1).

Request for Professional Development

Submitted by: _____ **Date:** _____

Contact Information: _____

Hot-Button Topic:

What We Want to Understand Better:

What We Want to Be Able to Do Differently:

A Vignette that Illustrates This Need:

Professional Development Activities Most Preferred for This Topic:

(Number in order of preference, with 1 being the most preferred activity)

_____ Read related articles

_____ Visit another classroom where things are going well

_____ View video of another classroom where things are going well

_____ Hold regular discussion groups to discuss progress of a focus student

_____ Hear an expert in the topic speak on the hot-button issue

_____ Other: _____

Figure 10:1 Request for professional development topic.

The request identifies possible scenarios for professional development as suggestions. It allows you to articulate to your program director or principal the kind of activities that you think would be most helpful in exploring the topic in greater depth. We think the idea of sharing a vignette is a critical piece of the request. It communicates quickly and easily the kind of challenge you are having, and it grounds the issue in a very concrete way.

The next chart (Figure 10:2) shows how Maria's teacher, Deborah, might have completed the form to request professional development in selecting instructional material to scaffold Maria's reading.

Request for Professional Development

Submitted by: Deborah Noseworthy   **Date:** September 11, 2005

Contact Information: 555-292-2922

Hot-Button Topic: English Language Learners

What We Want to Understand Better:
How to teach students who do not speak English.

What We Want to Be Able to Do Differently:
Select and match tradebooks for guided reading that support the student learning to read.

A Vignette that Illustrates This Need:
Maria is in first grade. She just moved here from the Honduras. Her first language is Spanish. She doesn't speak any English yet. I'm used to selecting the right level book based on a student's use of visual information (what known words are in the student's reading vocabulary, does she use initial letters, medial parts of words, or endings to solve a word, does she notice when she substitutes a word for another word in the text). Maria has no problem with visual information – working on that doesn't seem to be meeting her needs. She sounds out words easily and obviously monitors her reading because she is trying to pronounce each word. What should I work on to scaffold her reading?

Professional Development Activities Most Preferred for This Topic:
(Number in order of preference, with 1 being the most preferred activity)
__4__ Read related articles
__1__ Visit another classroom where things are going well
__2__ View video of another classroom where things are going well
__3__ Hold regular discussion groups to discuss progress of a focus student
__5__ Hear an expert in the topic speak on the hot-button issue
_____ Other: _____

Figure 10:2 Sample request for professional development.

School districts must undertake important and significant initiatives to support professional development, and teachers can support these efforts by identifying and articulating their needs so that professional development can be contextualized in classroom efforts and embedded in professional needs. To support teachers in considering needed professional development, some topics we brainstormed are listed below:

- working with parents to support a home–school literacy connection
- fostering reading, writing, and speaking in the languages spoken at home and at school
- using cultural variations as a way to support reading, writing, and speaking
- connecting with families and communities to foster better understandings in the classroom
- building on the strengths that children bring to school: "No oral language? No such thing!"

Team Plane

Chicago Public Schools (CPS) are a part of the Cross City Campaign for Urban School Reform, a consortium of districts and universities that work at school reform. They developed an education plan with nine principles for effective professional development, including the development of "professional communities that work collaboratively" (Cross City Campaign for Urban School Reform, 2005, p. 17).

Teams offer a powerful medium to support professional development for both individual members of the team and the team as a whole. Perhaps one of the reasons for this is because the team falls between the school/district and the individual planes, the team approach to professional development offers strength in numbers and the independence of the individual.

Three Ways Teams Can Work

Three ways in which teams can work are horizontally, vertically, and across multiple sites. By horizontal, we mean that teachers in the same grade in different classrooms work together on an instructional challenge they identify. In this situation, all or some teachers may work together. Teams might also include teachers who are not classroom-based, such as reading, special education, or foreign language teaching staff. In Figure 10:3, we depict 3 of 5 third-grade teachers working with a specialist teacher on an instructional challenge.

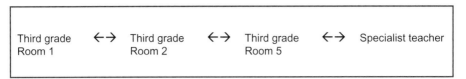

Figure 10:3 Third-grade horizontal approach.

By vertical, we mean that classroom teachers teach in various grade levels. The benefit of this approach is that each teacher can consider the instruction that students encounter in earlier grades and in later grades, because a second-grade teacher might be working with a first- and third-grade teacher. This approach might be especially useful in a school where looping—the practice where a second-grade teacher follows students to third grade the following

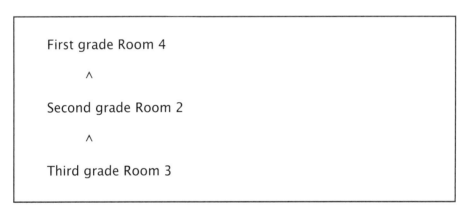

Figure 10:4 First–third grades vertical approach.

year—occurs. In Figure 10:4 below, we depict 3 of at least 9 classroom teachers working together across first through third grades.

By multiple site, we mean that classroom teachers might teach at the same or at various grade levels in different schools. A benefit of this approach is that some teachers have colleagues working on issues very similar to their own but in a different school. By ignoring the artificiality of having to work with colleagues in the same building because of their location in favor of working with colleagues who are working on similar challenges, there is the possibility that professional development might be more robust.

A second benefit is that by working with teachers in different schools, each teacher is exposed to a range of teaching and institutional practices, with the potential of a cross-fertilization of ideas. In Figure 10:5, we depict three classroom teachers across two different grades and three different schools working together.

In the remainder of this section, we will discuss how teams can work together in teams to undertake more robust professional development, characterized by teachers (1) working in close collaboration, (2) over a long period, (3) using changing teaching strategies, (4) with an inquiry-oriented focus on teaching, (5) embedded in a professional development initiative, and (6) in a classroom context (see Rodgers & Keil, in press).

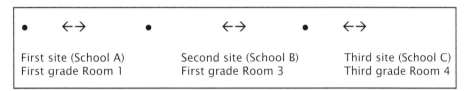

Figure 10:5 First–second grades multiple-site approach.

An Individual with Team Support

One way to get started on the development of a team approach is for one individual to articulate a need to the team and then seek out support. Adrian used this approach extensively in his first 2 years of teaching when he was working with students in a rural, isolated school. On the surface, he struggled with classroom control, but when he looked more deeply, he realized that his assignments and tasks for his students met with little interest. He tried to compensate by creating assignments that provided students with more choice, but that attempt backfired because students interpreted more choice as less structure and, therefore, became what Adrian thought of as more rebellious. Perhaps it's the students, Adrian thought, but he noticed other teachers who typically had more experience did not struggle with the same issues. Observations by administrators were of little help, since the administrators were often out of the content area and quite distanced from recent teaching experience. Additionally, since administrators made contract-renewal decisions based on his ability to manage the class, they did not seem like good choices in which to confide his instructional failings. At midyear, a career in banking was starting to look good!

Based on an off-the-cuff suggestion by one administrator, Adrian decided to observe a class taught by a more established colleague. Adrian went in with a simplistic question—"How do I get control of my classroom back?"—but left the first observation with a plethora of questions, all about instruction. There were questions about procedures, explanations, seat work, and assignment design. There were debriefings when the veteran teachers could spare the time, and Adrian developed his own team of experts. There were teachers in the same content areas, teachers adept at classroom management, teachers in earlier and later grade levels, teachers from different content areas with really cool assignments, teachers who did a great job of coaching students, and teachers who graded similar assignments and who could talk about evaluation and assessment. In short, Adrian developed his own team to support him with instructional challenges. What is important about Adrian's story is that the mentoring he received included:

- observations of other accomplished teachers
- focus around his own questions and quandaries regarding his instruction
- aim at changing his instruction to support student learning needs
- a personal need that drove him to undertake the work

In other words, the work of team members is highly personal and not mandated by a district or school.

In this particular case, Adrian's work was not reciprocal. By that, we mean Adrian watched other teachers to gain insight into teaching and others watched him to provide him with feedback on teaching, but they were not trying to learn from him. That makes sense, since he was a novice, and the other teachers were more established. In other cases, however, we can imagine, and have seen cases where, veteran teachers observe each other's work for the purpose of obtaining professional insights. Even in these cases, the teachers did a couple of things that Adrian did. First, they had a personal goal and some specific questions about their work. Second, they sought colleagues who might act as exemplars. Third, they focused on things that the teacher could control, rather than extraneous factors. Finally, they worked as partners over time.

In the cases that we have observed, we notice that these relationships often grow over time out of a combination of personal and professional relationships. It often seems that grade-level or departmental meetings are taken up with curricular or assessment matters, and that teachers are left to think about instructional issues by forming their own teams or networks. While this may be the case now, educators can support professional development by continuing to think about how we can support teams that focus on instructional questions. Based on these observations, we have formulated a list of some of the characteristics that exist among teams of teachers when they are supporting an individual's effort to refine his teaching practices (see Table 10:1).

The reader can see that in Adrian's case, he was fortunate to have colleagues who displayed the characteristics listed in Table 10:1. When a team of teachers works together to support an individual teacher, the tremendous resources of colleagues can be used to provide professional growth and development. It is fortunate that we work in a profession where resources lie within, and we do not always have to call in an outside "expert."

Table 10:1   Characteristics of Teams Supporting an Individual

> · Start with at least one question about instruction
> · Develop into more sophisticated questions about instruction
> · Include observations of teaching
> · Conduct debriefings
> · Include team members with different strengths
> · Develop out of personal and/or team needs
> · Operate within or outside formalized support system for teachers
> · Aim at changing teaching practices
> · Exist in both reciprocal and one-way relationships
> · Focus on things that the teacher can control
> · Work over time

Using teams to work together

If teachers can identify common ground for an area of inquiry, they can work together scaffolding each other's work to support enhanced teaching (Rodgers & Rodgers, 2004). There are a number of different ways to do this, including the use of teaching observations and discussion groups. As we have discussed, it is very useful to observe the teaching of each other with the goal of changing our teaching practices. To support careful observation, it is useful to start with some focal points so that the participating teacher knows what to observe.

There is one barrier to this approach, and it is that some schools have increasingly arranged their schedule so that all teachers teaching the same grade have a common preparation time. This is a powerful way to support common planning across a grade, but it also means that because all third-grade teachers are free from teaching at the same time, they are also teaching at the same time. What this means is that teachers in the same grade level are often unable to see each other teach, and that their conversations then focus on curriculum and content rather than on instruction. Debriefing with the teacher is also another key component of observing teaching. Since identifying a common time to observe instruction is difficult, videotape offers one way to shift time and make observation more accessible. At the same time, videotape has limitations, since it is like looking at a classroom through a drinking straw.

Discussion Groups

One way to compensate for this is to share common readings that can supplement conversation. There are many powerful and informative texts that may be useful for getting conversations going, such as those by Delpit and Ladson-

Billings. These authors offer one way of grounding our work in classrooms, but there are also other authors who offer other opportunities. Fullan's or Sarason's work offer the possibility of grounding work in school change, while Rodgers', O'Leary's, and Walker's books offer a highly contextualized way of considering instruction. To help get those conversations started, some useful books are listed in Table 10:2 below.

Table 10:2   Useful Books for Discussing Teaching

Lisa Delpit *Other People's Children*

Michael Fullan *Change Forces*

Susan O'Leary *Five Kids*

Adrian Rodgers and Emily M. Rodgers *Scaffolding Literacy Instruction: Strategies for K–4 Classrooms*

Emily M. Rodgers and Gay Su Pinnell *Learning from Teaching in Literacy Education*

Gloria Ladson-Billings *Dreamkeepers: Successful Teachers of African American Children*

Robust Team Approaches

In-person classroom observations, videotaped class sessions, and discussion groups all offer opportunities for team approaches to professional development.

With these possibilities comes an important responsibility. It is important that all teachers own these initiatives and that they not concede ownership to a couple of vocal individuals. We have worked with many teachers who have left the ownership of team projects to vocal peers, and these peers have sometimes created requirements for teaching that have subsequently been endorsed by the school district. Inadvertently, in the effort to work as a team, teachers may give up control of their teaching to a list of requirements designed by zealous peers who may not share the same vision of teaching.

Thus, ownership of the team work is a critical component of professional development. Interestingly, critical theorists have called for increased ownership by students of the curriculum and instruction. An increased emphasis on differentiated instruction and diverse learners is based on the belief that instruction for students should be increasingly customized to individual needs. Although we have made strides in the way teachers think about their students, we have not made the same advances in the way we think about professional development for teachers. We will only have minimal impact on student learning if we deliver professional development initiatives to teachers that are not grounded in the day-to-day practice of teaching. Given the limited resources that educators have at their disposal, it is most likely that quality professional development might be undertaken by having the teachers themselves look carefully at their work through the process of identifying, articulating, and studying their own needs.

Individual Plane

Most schools and school districts conduct some form of professional development, but too often, this professional development is in the form of a "one shot" workshop, a stand-and-deliver activity, where teachers are audience members and are expected to consume, implement, and replicate practice that was exhibited to them after school or on a professional-leave day. Even at professional literacy conferences, such as those sponsored by the International Reading Association or the National Council of Teachers of English, sessions are typically short-lived with many attendees. These sessions are important and valuable, in that they provide teachers with the opportunity to see and hear new ideas and to meet with fellow educators who have researched similar professional challenges.

While these forms of professional development are valuable in disseminating ideas, they are less useful as a form of support for changing our instructional practices. There are many reasons for this, but one main one is that the most difficult challenges that we face are highly contextualized, and, therefore, what we see at a one-shot workshop might not be easily transferable to our context.

Another difficulty is that making changes to our instruction is very hard to do. As busy teachers, we often rely on what we have done before or on what we already know works, albeit not perfectly. We also know that when we do attempt innovations, they are sometimes accompanied by disastrous results.

Lastly, we know from learning theory that we cannot expect to execute a new teaching strategy perfectly the first time, yet when a new effort that we attempt does not initially go well, we often judge ourselves far too harshly. We decide that the "great idea" we learned about in a professional development session "wouldn't work in my classroom," and we revert to the safety of our routines, rather than persevering with a change that we hoped might enhance student learning.

Some of the same problems present themselves when undertaking professional development as a part of a team. Indeed, they might be compounded in the team approach because in some settings, a teacher might have to not only overcome challenges in one's own teaching, but also address challenges being experienced by a fellow team member. Given the constraints posed by some forms of professional development at the district, school, or team level, some teachers might prefer to undertake a professional development effort on their own, either because they feel their own efforts would surpass that of the other efforts, or because they feel work on their own could supplement efforts on other planes. Indeed, since we notice that professional development is often defined in the literature as institutional, we think some of the greatest power might be achieved when an individual begins to undertake their own forms of professional development.

Earlier in this chapter, we defined professional development as any procedure, protocol, or sequence of activities in which we can engage to alter our practice with the aim of enhancing our support of student learning. Professional development activities along the individual plane can be categorized as either formal or informal study. In the remainder of this section, we describe both informal and formal professional development activities that an individual might pursue.

Formal Study

The formal efforts that we might undertake for professional development are already well known and because we frequently engage in them, we will only summarize them here. By formal, we mean institutional efforts that are codified in some way, the most typical one of these being university study. In fact, we often enroll in university courses with the goal of completing a sequence of work that will lead to an endorsement, license, or certificate, such as a reading specialist.

A second set of formal efforts might be some form of study offered by a professional organization, such as the National Board for Professional Teaching Standards (NBPTS). The NBPTS is an organization that seeks to offer an advanced recognition of teaching after a thorough review of a professional portfolio that an in-service teacher develops over time.

What we would like to point out regarding these contexts is that study itself does not constitute professional development. Our definition of professional development claims that the study must be focused on changing teaching practice, and we can really only change teaching practice by looking at our teaching over time. Therefore, the difficulty posed by university courses is that they are typically semester-length, which does not support a long-range view of changing teaching practice. Thus, we would suggest that teachers who view university study as a form of professional development focus on identifying a university program that:

• looks closely at teaching

• allows examination of teaching over a sequence of courses in the program

- allows continuity of instruction so that a faculty member knows the teacher over time
- offers choice so that the teacher can select course work that will support professional development efforts
- employs faculty researching and writing in an area of professional development of interest to the teacher

The NBPTS offers another viable option for formal study. Since the NBPTS uses a portfolio approach, the study of the teacher is highly contextualized within one's own classroom. Although NBPTS study is costly, it offers a highly desirable form of professional development that addresses many of the concerns we identified above.

Informal Study: The Action Research Project

Now that we have summarized formal opportunities, let's consider the informal possibilities more thoroughly. The benefit of informal study is that, since the teacher is undertaking work purely for his or her own professional development, there is freedom to pursue any reasonable effort with the view to changing instructional practices. Work can be grounded in classroom and teaching dilemmas. The teacher is free to pick up and drop initiatives as appropriate, and importantly, efforts can be less stressful, since the work is not being judged by an outside authority, such as a university faculty member or an NBPTS assessor.

While there are many benefits to self-study, there are also many factors that threaten a teacher's attempts to change teaching practices through informal self-study. One difficulty is that there is no model to follow nor presenter to emulate. At the point of difficulty when undertaking a new strategy, there is no one to scaffold a teacher's efforts. Thus, we must be cautious in attempting informal self-study, mindful of the possibilities offered by a potent form of professional development but wary of the risks that might lead to the derailment of our efforts.

Action Research as Self-Study

A useful procedure for initiating a self-study is to use an action-research approach. Sprinthall, Reiman, and Thies-Sprinthall (1996) explain that educators frame action research as:

"... inquiry done by practitioners with the help of a consultant. ...

They attribute four characteristics to action research: (1) It is

collaborative, (2) It addresses practical classroom problems, (3) It
bolsters professional development, and (4) It requires a specialized
structure to ensure both time and support for the research initiative"
(p. 694).

Teachers carrying out action research in their classrooms typically engage
in the process depicted in Table 10:3.

Action research uses these four steps and then repeats them in a cyclical
manner, so that with each cycle, a teacher can make decisions with the goal of
changing their instruction to better support student learning.

To better illustrate the action-research approach, we will discuss some teaching that Emily undertook when she worked with Maria. As we described in the
vignette, Maria's family spoke Spanish as their first language. Her mother spoke
English in the workplace in Honduras, and the previous year, when Maria was
in kindergarten, her mother enrolled her in a school run by German mission-
aries. As a result, Maria had a working knowledge of conversational German.
Despite Maria's expansive linguistic knowledge, when the family moved to the
United States and she started first grade, she stopped speaking German, did
not write in Spanish, could not speak in English, and only spoke Spanish to
family members.

Table 10:3 Steps in Action Research

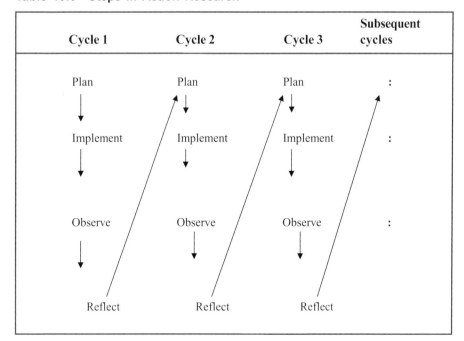

Planning

Faced with these challenges, Emily began the first step in the action-research approach process. She began to plan how she could teach Maria to read and write in English. This was complicated, since Emily is fluent in English and has a working knowledge of French but no knowledge of Spanish. To begin her planning, Emily thought about Maria's strengths and needs. She also made plans for teaching. Her planning notes are recorded in Table 10:4.

We would like to point out a couple of features about Table 10:4. First, Emily has worked to identify some item knowledge (knows "cat") but also to make observations that might help Emily in thinking about reasons that would support her teaching decisions. For example, because Maria is accustomed to a literate environment that includes text and other forms, Emily uses both teacher-made books and Polaroid photos. The second feature of Table 10:4 that we would like to point out is that the right column should be notes regarding how Emily will change her teaching. In this case, Emily has not taught Maria before, but she does know some of the strategies used by Maria's classroom teacher. Thus, in this first cycle, Emily selects choices that she thinks will lead to new student learning that are different than what Maria has encountered before.

Table 10:4 Plan of Action for Teaching Maria

Analyze strengths	Look at what the student cannot do	Activate teaching
• Speaks two languages • Can write her name • Can read/write 'is' & 'the' • understands how print works • Can locate letters in words • Sounds out words	• Speak phrases or sentences in English • understands directions in English	• Write 1 sentence stories • Take photos/ describe photos • Make books with known words • Responded to mom's question by suggesting she speak to Maria only in Spanish at home

Note. Table developed by Mary Fried.

Implementing

Now that Emily has completed her plan, she implements her instruction. In this case, she uses the strategies for about a 2-week period for about 30 minutes a day. She uses each of the strategies on most days and focuses on building a positive working relationship with Maria. Emily videotaped her lessons with Maria to observe later.

Observing

The next step in the action-research approach is to observe one's intervention. In action research, the teacher observes her work as she implements it. Emily had a number of different options to do this. On some days, she wrote notes to herself while teaching. In this way, she kept "one eye on the child" and "one eye on instruction." She also viewed videotapes of her instruction at the end of each day. At the end of the 2-week cycle, Emily conducted a final observation by taking a running record of Maria reading aloud several familiar books.

Reflecting

Once the teacher has conducted her observation, she can use these observations for reflection. In reflection, the teacher studies her observations with the goal of changing her teaching (or implementation) for the second cycle of the action research. In this case, Emily read her notes, observed videos, and collected her thoughts. Emily noted, for example, that she really wasn't sure how much English Maria understood. For example, in response to a Polaroid photo that Emily took of Maria reading, Maria wrote "I am here." It seemed to be an existential insight but not the more obvious "Maria is reading" that Emily had anticipated! Emily also noticed that many of Maria's responses were one word: Yes. Based on her observations, Emily reflected that she needed to:

- ask more open-ended questions that would require more than a "yes" response from Maria

- be sensitive to times when Maria appeared to understand what was said but really didn't

- continue to provide writing opportunities because Maria could read what she had written

Cycle Two

After Emily completed her first action-research approach cycle, she tried to use her first round of planning, implementing, observing, and reflecting to generate plans for a second round of teaching. As before, the essential element of Emily's planning was to change her teaching to better support student learning. Emily was able to do this because she closely followed and learned from her student, knew her student's strengths, and knew what her student could do. Based on this intensive professional work that Emily had undertaken, in the second action-research cycle, she planned to build on Maria's success with letter-sound relationships. Since Maria had difficulty understanding Emily's directions, Emily conferenced with Maria's mother and learned Spanish phrases for a number of key prompts, such as "Do you hear the letter?" Emily also planned to support her mom's reading by using commercially available books for the first time, focusing on books that had words that Maria knew. In addition to this, Emily identified and used books with strong picture support.

Emily implemented these lessons over the period of about a couple of weeks, again gathering her observations both during the lessons, after the lessons, and after a couple of weeks. We won't go into detail regarding how Emily planned her second and subsequent rounds, since the details of what Emily did are not the main point of our chapter. In fact, while Emily has some expertise in literacy, she has no background in second-language acquisition. We do not hold Emily's choice of strategies out as a model, as much as we hold out the process Emily engaged in as a process for inquiring into our teaching. A second point that we would make about the action-research approach is that to make progress in one's teaching, we suggest that a teacher would need to undertake at least three action-research cycles. Significant shifts in teaching occur between each cycle because observations of the student, together with teacher reflection, combine to "activate" or change teaching to better support student learning.

Conclusion

In this chapter, we offered the suggestion that professional development is something that is not "done" to teachers, but rather is an aspect of teaching in which teachers can take active ownership. We considered this ownership from three perspectives that we called professional development planes. Teachers work along one or more of these planes and each is riddled with challenge and opportunity that pull in different directions. We depict some of these factors in Table 10:5.

Table 10:5 Competing Factors in Teacher Ownership of Professional Development

Plane	Threats	Supports
School/District	· Top-down delivery of professional development	· Increased desire by leaders to solicit teacher input
Team	· Focus on district priorities · Difficulty to obtain concensus · Different classroom contexts	· Ability for teachers to articulate need · Like-minded colleagues · Power in numbers · Focus on similar problems
Individual	· Focus on factors beyond teacher control · Difficult to articulate how to change teaching practices	· Ability to narrow focus to classroom context · Can "know" the student

In the school and district plane, we proposed that teachers take a more active role in planning the activities of the school or district, primarily by writing proposals for professional development opportunities. Thus, competition at this level lies between the district and school needs to implement development efforts, and teacher efforts to obtain support for instructional supports. Unlike the district or school level, at the team level, we may be able to identify the need for professional development on one topic, but since classroom contexts vary, even within the same building, and because team members may have different perspectives on the challenge, there can be difficulties in knowing how to proceed. Lastly, at the individual level, the teacher does not have to be concerned about working in harmony with other individuals or agencies but must challenge him- or herself to arrive at new perspectives in the effort to develop pedagogy.

For many years, scholars have called for increased ownership by students of the curriculum and instruction. An increased emphasis on differentiated instruction and diverse learners is based on the belief that instruction for students should be increasingly customized to individual needs. The same is true of professional development for teachers. There will only be minimal impact on student learning when we deliver professional development initiatives to teachers but have not visited their classrooms to know what they are doing and how they approach their teaching.

If teachers can best teach by looking closely at the student, teachers can best develop their teaching through the support of those that look closely at their teaching. Given the limited resources that educators have at their disposal, it is most likely that quality professional development might be undertaken by having the teachers themselves look carefully at their work through the process of identifying, articulating, and studying their own needs.

References

Cross City Campaign for Urban School Reform. (2005). *A delicate balance: District policies and classroom practice.* Chicago: Author.

Hughes, M. T., Cash, M. M., Ahwee, S., & Klingner, J. (2002). A national overview of professional development programs in reading. In A. Rodgers & E. Rodgers (Eds.), *Strategies for scaffolding literacy instruction in K–4 classrooms* (pp. 9–28). Portsmouth, NH: Heinemann.

Lyons, C., & Pinnell, G. S. (2001). *Systems for change in literacy education: A guide to professional development.* Portsmouth, NH: Heinemann.

Rodgers, E. M., & Pinnell, G. S. (2002). *Learning from teaching in literacy education: New perspectives on professional development.* Portsmouth, NH: Heinemann.

Rodgers, A., & Rodgers, E. M. (Eds.). (2004). *Scaffolding literacy instruction: Strategies for K–4 classrooms.* Portsmouth, NH: Heinemann.

Rodgers, A., & Keil, V. L. (in press). Restructuring a traditional student teacher supervision model: Fostering enhanced professional development and mentoring within a professional development school context. *Teaching and Teacher Education.*

Sprinthall, N. A., Reiman, A. J., & Thies-Sprinthall, L. (1996). Teacher professional development. *Handbook of research on teacher education* (pp. 666–703). New York: McMillan.

Chapter 11

The Task of Leaders for Building Capacity in Support of Academic Diversity

Saundra Parker-Jones

One afternoon shortly after school started, one of my new teachers, Kim, stopped by my office to talk about her new class of students. She began by telling me she had just finished each student's reading assessments and had found that her students' achievement ranged from low to very high. "I'm not sure how to deal with so many levels of reading. Last year's class didn't seem as diverse in their achievement levels. I'm wondering how I can teach all of them when it seems they are all so different and come from different places in their learning backgrounds," Kim said. Kim and I talked a while longer and decided that I would visit her classroom the following day during her literacy block. We agreed to talk the afternoon of the following day about what I observed and see if we could develop a plan to address the many learning needs of her students.

I visited Kim's second-grade class the following morning. Students were engaged in a prereading activity with Kim reading aloud and modeling a think aloud as she read.

Following this, students went to their seats to work on a story-related worksheet, and Kim and her assistant, Brenda, monitored the activity. Both the teacher and the assistant helped the children, giving some individual help. I saw immediately where Kim's concern was coming from as I observed her 22 students. She had 3 students who spoke fair, but inadequate, English. They were identified as English as a Second Language (ESL) students and had a resource time in the afternoon to work with the ESL teacher. I recognized 2 students who had been identified for our Exceptional Children's program, 2 others who received speech services, 5 students who wanted help from Kim and Brenda during the entire activity time, and 1 who could not sit still. Several seemed to be grasping the task and getting along fine with it. Four finished the assignment very quickly and asked to go to the listening center and the science center. The class came together to discuss their worksheet, although 3 students did not get entirely finished. Students were called on to read and respond to the activity's questions, then Kim introduced five new vocabulary words from the new story they would read the next day. The students copied the five words on their paper, then, working in pairs, made up sentences using the new words. The teacher assistant collected the papers, and the children got ready to go to art class.

Introduction

The challenge of addressing academic diversity in today's complex classrooms is as important a challenge as any we have before us. The role of the leadership team that fosters attention to academic diversity is both demanding and complex. There is no easy path, nor is it a short-term project. Leaders are driven by a vision of what diverse classrooms could be in order to meet the needs of all learners. This vision fuels the drive to create learning environments responsive to all students and all features of their academic diversity. Classrooms responsive to academic diversity will not happen at random, by default, or haphazardly (Tomlinson, 1999). It will only happen with the kind of leadership that can articulate a vision for change, a purpose for changing, and a coherent rational as to why change is imperative to the establishment of academically diverse classrooms where all students' learning needs are met. The leadership team shares the vision with the school's community of teachers and staff and asks that they respond to its efficacy. It becomes reality when the faculty and staff embrace the vision and proceed to study ways to bring about change in support of academic diversity.

Leadership Stance

Promoting academic diversity requires a leader with a vision who can articulate that vision, based on moral and professional purposes. Morally, leaders are obligated to consider what is fair and equitable for all children in schools. That means a recognition that everyone in the school community must do all they can to meet a range of student needs. We did not become educators to educate only a few. We chose, by choosing education as a lifelong work, to do what is fair and right for all. A leader's vision is driven by a professional purpose. That purpose is to seek the means and ways to deliver high-quality education to all students, regardless of their differences. Purpose promotes broad-scale quality and extends over time. Professional purpose extends from the leader to teachers who become teacher-leaders and sustain the vision and purpose.

The principal and the leadership team work to bring others on board (Fahey, 2000). Teachers are at different places in their thinking about academically diverse classrooms. Some believe that change won't work. "We tried that before, and it didn't work." The response to this statement then becomes, "Try, try, again" (Wilcox, 2003). Convincing others to support different ways of perceiving teaching and learning creates tension and conflict. It creates uncertainty and resistance. Change disrupts a sense of comfort, disturbs routines, and requires work. Leaders help others to realize that teaching to students' academically diverse needs engages all students, not just a few.

In order for leaders to gain the support and commitment of others, they must help teachers develop knowledge and skills necessary for change (Tomlinson, 1999). Internalizing and applying new ways of thinking and responding is a slow process. Unlearning old ways and embracing new ways of thinking and teaching is often even more difficult. A leader inspires others to think and act along with him or her. Together, they adopt a "can do" attitude. Keeping the vision alive is the leader's role. Those who commit early need support all along the way. That support and positive vision must continue to strengthen and sustain all of the participants. This is the beginning of the "leadership team." The principal along with teacher-leaders ignite the vision for others, and the cycle of vision, support, and commitment comes full circle and starts again (see Figure 11:1) (Tomlinson, 1999).

With the leadership team in place, the leaders listen to the ideas of others and incorporate them into the vision as appropriate. Valuing and recognizing

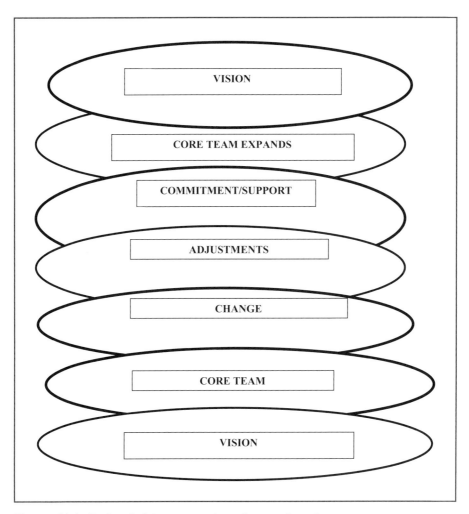

Figure 11:1 Cycle of vision, support, and commitment.

the impact from team members gives the vision life's blood. As the saying goes, "There's no limit to how far you can go, if you don't care who gets the credit." It is the team's individual and collective ideas that, when listened to and acted upon, will benefit the community of learners it was designed to help. Support of academic diversity requires creative ideas and clearly "thinking out of the box." The leader who listens and supports those ideas will clear a path for implementing academic diversity.

Supporting Changes in Thinking

A school does not become attuned and responsive to academic diversity overnight. It requires transformation of thinking. In today's world, change is a constant. The most difficult task for any educator is to change, or lead a change movement. Researchers, such as Lezotte and Pepper (2004) and Schlechty (1997), have written extensively about school change and research supporting change. It is up to the responsive and responsible leadership to help others work through the difficult passages of change. How is this accomplished? The leadership team collaboratively shares a vision and carries the message to others. Teacher-leaders are cheerleaders and coaches. Small gains are celebrated, and high fives become part of the celebration scene. Small gains form the groundwork for greater gains, and the cycle continues. When some cannot go on or see less hope, the leadership team steps in to shore up the weak side and reconstitute the teachers to keep on trying. If teachers are to learn to develop more academically responsive classrooms, leaders must understand change and getting though the difficult passages of change have no end date (Sergiovanni, 2004).

The leadership team focuses on maintaining a sense of direction over an extended period of time. Ironically, staying the course supports change. Often, we have abandoned the ship before it ever leaves the dock. Leaders must stay the course; take the time to stick with the plan. This is a phenomenal time in education. Federal legislation and state initiatives are requiring leaders to look at what we do in our schools and school districts and rethink every aspect of our efforts to reach all students. With the *No Child Left Behind* Act of 2001, all school subgroups are to be addressed. By acknowledging these subgroups, we automatically identify diversity. That is the easy part.

Leaders convince others that teaching to students' academic diversity will work. The question begging an answer is, "How?" There are ways to answer the question. First, there are data reported through research. Numerous studies found in refereed journals support the gains attributed to diversity through differentiation. In a study by Vygotsky (1986), students were more successful when taught in ways that were responsive to their readiness levels. Csikszentmihalyi (1997) conducted a study where learning based on students' interests provided evidence of success. Sternberg, Torff, and Grigorenko (1998) differentiated instruction based on learning profiles and reported significant gains in learning for their students.

To move toward thinking about differentiated instruction requires changes in the way we think about students and learning. Convincing others requires more than research reports. A firsthand view of schools similar to the school in the change process, and engaged in addressing learning in an academically diverse environment, can go a long way in convincing others that academic diversity can be addressed successfully. Teaching students who are academically diverse can be accomplished through differentiation of instruction, and differentiation can be accomplished with training, a paradigm shift in the way we think about teaching and learning, and a resolute commitment from teachers that it is worth the effort to make differentiation work for all students. Teachers must operate from a plan to address academic diversity that differentiates instruction across grade level and content. Determining the plan, leaders and teachers must stick with it over time. Nothing, however, is more convincing than the enthusiasm engendered when teachers see students succeed in classrooms where instruction becomes tailored to match student needs.

As the change agents for academically diverse schools, the principal and the teachers are all responsible for the reforms that need to be implemented to meet the needs of all learners. Whether there are small or large gains as a result of the reform, the message is clear; stay the course, and take responsibility to work to make it better.

Functions of Leadership

The leaders of an academically diverse school perform the following functions (Tomlinson, 1999):

- establish the vision for meeting the needs of all students as a daily reality
- coach teachers through change
- accomplish change through developing trust and commitment with others
- involve teachers in self-study of their own performance and needs, and in the processes of goal-setting and strategic planning
- foster and support self-reflection and self-evaluation
- promote risk taking by creating safe and fear-free settings
- understand theories and best practices about teaching and learning in order to assist teachers with professional development plans

The leadership team makes the vision for meeting the needs of all students through academic diversity a daily reality in the context of the school and classrooms. The team can inspire others to look at individual learners and to understand their possibilities and needs and to craft classrooms well suited to addressing multiple needs. Leaders insure that day-to-day actions toward effective differentiation become the norm for the school and its community of learners. In the continued vignette, Kim looked at her students as individual learners and found ways to meet each student's needs.

That afternoon, Kim came by and we talked about what I observed. First of all, Kim is a good teacher and will become a great teacher in time. She knows that whole-group instruction is good some of the time but not all of the time, and she is trying to introduce more small-group work as she goes along. "Kim, I enjoyed the lesson and thought things were going well; however, I don't think you had enough time to get into the lesson as much as I would have liked to see happen," I said. "I agree," Kim replied. "Three days a week, my reading time is only 75 minutes, and I know that a longer block of time would give me more opportunity to work with my students. I think the lesson was OK today, but I am sure Juan and Jose were having trouble, and Brian was not concentrating during the question-and-answer period." We talked at length about several issues that afternoon, the most important being a way for Kim to spend more time in the small groups working on specific activities related to the needs of the groups. In order to be more specific about the individual needs of the students, Kim wanted to do more assessments with certain students to help her develop small groups for instruction, focused toward specific learning needs. We also decided that she would work with guided reading groups and small groups with specific instructional needs. By working with small groups, she could give concentrated time to specific needs. The groups would rotate to her. While she worked with small groups, her assistant would work with the rest of the class until it came their time to go to a small group. Also, we decided to change Kim's schedule, so that 4 days out of 5, she would have a 90-minute literacy block. We agreed that I would visit again in 3 weeks.

Academically diverse schools must be coached through changes. The responsive leader must understand why teachers practice as they do, not merely attempt to change practices without regard for the beliefs of others. Opportunities to reflect on, and discuss, ones beliefs need to occur at the faculty level and at the individual level. Beliefs need to be examined. The process is not always a comfortable one. Many beliefs have been rooted in classroom practices that research no longer supports. Yet, because of the comfort of what is familiar, those practices are still used in many classrooms in this country. For example, some kindergarten classes will implement spelling words early in the school year. We know that this is developmentally inappropriate, for those children generally have not mastered the sound-symbol relationship of letters and sounds. A visionary leader asks others to expose their beliefs and to understand why they believe as they do. The hard question becomes, "Can you set aside these beliefs in order to try a different approach to learning?" This is a delicate question, and teachers may feel threatened. It is the job of compassionate leaders to encourage educators to explore new classroom practices and to use these new practices as new ways for looking at students. Old beliefs must give way to new practices, and it is the role of leaders to encourage new practices in such a manner that new beliefs evolve without educators feeling their previous beliefs were compromised or considered unworthy (Almack, 1970).

Three weeks later, I returned to Kim's class. Today, she was working with a guided reading group consisting of 2 ESL students, 2 more typical children, and a child receiving speech services. The story was from a basal reader. The students did a picture walk with the teacher and each predicted what he or she thought would happen. They silently read the first page. After reading, they worked on summarizing, clarifying, asking and answering questions, evaluating, and then predicting what would happen in the next reading section. I watched Kim work with this group and then rotate with the other two groups, changing the focus of the guided reading to match the needs of the students. During this time, in small groups, the students also worked with content vocabulary from the story. I asked Kim to stop by after school to discuss what I observed and to get her reactions to changes she had implemented.

School leaders function on many levels. One of those levels is to serve as confidants for teachers and other building-level educators. There is no way to accomplish this without trust and commitment. Trust and commitment to change the classroom and school inspires others to confide in responsive leaders. The trust placed in an administrator or a school's teacher-leaders cannot be minimized in the change process. This trust creates opportunities for teachers and administrators to build a sense of community. Ideas are shared, concerns—even objectives—are shared, and problems are voiced without fear of reprisal.

The effective leader never reacts with a "good guy" (compiler) "bad guy" (noncompiler) mentality. This would derail any drive toward trust. The visionary listens and responds to all issues professed by others and keeps those conversations private as trust dictates. The trust and respect the faculty and staff hold for the school's leadership and each other serves as the bedrock on which the school builds an environment that responds to academic diversity. The leadership treats each teacher professionally wherever that individual is professionally and nurtures the growth and professionalism of that person.

That afternoon, I praised Kim for the way her students worked together and how it was clear they understood how to rotate in and out of their different groups when it was time to work with her. I also commented on the baskets of books on each table and how her students used those for reading after they finished the assignment and were waiting for their time to work with her. "I'm pleased with the small groups," Kim confided. "Doing additional assessments helped me to understand specific student needs and to develop small groups around those needs. With my groups, I'm actually able to spend more focused time with each student. I can give direct help to students, and I can keep everyone focused in small groups." She also said that the ESL teacher was coming in 3 days a week to specifically coach her Hispanic children on class activities during the same time other students were working, thus avoiding a pull-out later in the day. Kim asked if there were funds to purchase a classroom library. She had found a set of leveled readers offered by our basal publisher that paralleled the basal stories but at different levels. She also asked to attend a state conference on learning styles. She agreed to come back and share information from the workshop with other teachers and assistants. "I feel like I am reaching more of the diverse needs of my students much better with the changes I have implemented," Kim observed. A colleague of Kim's, Mrs. Brayboy, had noticed the changes Kim had implemented in her classroom and asked to observe Kim's class to see how she was doing instructional groups and guided reading groups, with the idea that she, too, might try similar applications in her classroom.

Leaders need to give teachers an opportunity to assess their own level of expertise and collaborate on a plan that both the teachers and the leaders feel will provide professional growth. In this way, teachers are involved in self-study of their own performance and needs, and in their processes of goal-setting and strategic planning. Good leaders respond to the requests of teachers who want to take advantage of a learning opportunity. It is the leader's job to recognize where teachers are in their own professional growth cycle, listen to them, and assist in finding ways to help them identify their needs and use professional development as an opportunity for growth. In the case of Mrs. Brayboy, that is exactly what happened.

> Mrs. Brayboy visited Kim's class on several occasions. Since both were second-grade teachers, they began to plan collaboratively for their classes. Mrs. Brayboy asked one of our teacher-leaders, Mrs. McGuinesss, and Kim to observe her first class, where she developed her instruction and instructional materials around the academically diverse needs of her students. They met later to give feedback and shared ideas about the lesson. Both teachers supported Mrs. Brayboy and gave her the opportunity to reflect on the lesson and generate additional strategies for reaching her diverse learners. I did not attend this meeting because I knew that recognized "experts" were at work.

As change agents, the principal, along with teacher-leaders, promotes risk taking by creating safe and fear-free settings. Before an observation, a teacher should know prior to that visit what the observation's focus would be. This can be discussed prior to the visit in a mutually respectful conversation. There should be no surprises and no "gottchas" during an observation. After an observation and during the postconference is a time to share and encourage the teacher to self-reflect on how she saw the lesson unfold. Here is a time to point out the teacher's strengths. Not only does this build confidence and self-esteem for the teacher, but it continues to strengthen the bond of trust that is being built between the teacher and principal. The postconference is also the appropriate time to make suggestions about changes that might improve the learning opportunities and ways those changes could come about. Through mutual respect and an open dialogue, most teachers return to the classroom and attempt those "suggestions" without a fear of reprimand or negativism. This is just one way to create a safe and fear-free setting. There are ways for a teacher to maintain his or her dignity, even if the lesson has many areas for improvement. It is the sensitive leader who can help that teacher change and improve without destroying the teacher's potential. The leader has to be seen as a helper and a source for ideas and resources. A leader who is viewed as a threat will never grow trust between herself and her faculty and will never become a change agent. Coaching teachers is a vital part of the leader's efforts to make good things happen in the classroom, and it is a bond for trust. Supporting and coaching Kim led to a positive change in the way she managed her classroom and conducted learning experiences for each student. Teacher-leaders who develop creative learning opportunities in their classrooms are excellent coaches for other faculty members. These teachers take pride in what they do, knowing it is based on sound learning theory. They may be eager to share their ideas and coach others. Encouraging teacher-leaders to model and share their creative ideas is one of the most important jobs a building-level principal can do.

An administrator affecting change facilitates a satisfying learning process for teachers to continually expand their capacities. A learning process starts with contributions from all participants and an administrator who will recognize that individuals have different levels of expertise needing support in different ways. Leaders encourage teachers to determine specifically what professional learning experience they need to be even more successful teachers and leaders. Ways to accomplish this might be as simple as having a conversation with each teacher and noting areas where he or she feels greater expertise is needed. This reflection time would allow a teacher to step back and assess her teaching beliefs, knowledge, and methodology for instruction. The question posed is, "How can I be a better teacher and develop a greater capacity for reaching all of my students?" In order for this self-assessment to be successful, several things must take place. First, the administrator and teacher must have a trust relationship. The principal must trust each teacher to recognize his or her strengths and weaknesses. Second, the principal must be knowledgeable about teaching and learning in order to offer suggestions to guide educators in a direction that will promote professional growth. Third, there must be resources to carry out learning opportunities in the form of time, money, and energy. Fourth, and possibly most importantly, it must be a shared experience. It is important for all members to share their individual learning plans. In this way, there is focus and direction added to the capacity to learn and develop (Sergiovanni, 2004). It will possibly become apparent that several teachers are pursuing professional development in similar areas. For example, if a group of teachers wants to learn more about brain research as it applies to student learning, then this is a perfect way to provide training for this group, either by arranging attendance at workshops, forming a study group, or viewing videos on the common and desired topic for learning and growth.

The school leadership team may recommend that the whole faculty could benefit from an annual learning project. An example of this would be the development of curriculum maps across grades and content areas. This becomes a collaborative event allowing for an exchange of information that teachers need and want to share. The process is nonthreatening and helps teachers realize where greater emphasis should be placed on skills and training. For example, at one school, teachers engaged in this process and quickly realized that the geometry strand in their math curriculum needed greater emphasis across all grade levels. As a result, they began to look at ways to introduce geometry earlier in the curriculum and opportunities for students to apply geometric concepts through relevant activities and assignments. Teachers began to notice that students were taking a greater interest in geometry when they could identify concepts with real-world application. Regardless of the process or project, the engagement of highly qualified teachers is a powerful incentive toward promoting a collective change movement. The leadership in a school recognizes the power of increasing learning capacity through individual assessment, group discussions, and whole-faculty activities. Leaders make this all possible, thus laying another building block into the change model.

Success Acknowledged

In addition to promoting the opportunity to expand learning capacities, a leader for change builds opportunities for teacher success and recognizes that success. Knowing one's faculty and recognizing where strengths lie is one way to build opportunities for success (Fahey, 2000). In one school, there was a teacher who is exceptionally motivated when it comes to studying and developing science studies for her children. She has been given the lead-teacher assignment for developing an elementary science lab for our school. While this is a major project demanding extra time, she embraced the project because she sees this as an opportunity to promote and develop science goals for all of the children in our school. Recognizing her interests and facilitating opportunities for her success continues to be rewarding for her personally and professionally. She understands what an important role she is filling in igniting a greater interest in science for elementary students. As a teacher-leader, she is encouraging others to follow her example and have students participate more fully in science instruction.

An educational leader allows teachers the opportunity for their own vision to grow through collaboration with others. As in the example of the teacher taking the lead in promoting science education, the teacher has a vision for her school and its children. The principal's role is to support her vision and facilitate collaboration with others. Time becomes a crucial factor in this process.

Providing time for the teacher-leader to meet with others can happen when the principal provides opportunities in teachers' schedules, enabling them to work together. Scheduling common planning or release time supports collaboration and sends a clear message that this project is important and efforts will be made to allow collaboration for its success. Providing the teacher-leader time to conduct discussion groups and share outside workshop/conference information speaks volumes about leader support and puts added value into the endeavor. No one wants to engage in a process that has no support, either from the school's leadership team or teachers. The best way to ensure that a clear message of support is heard is to declare that support through actions and follow through with the process (Blokker, Simpson, & Whittier, 2002).

Kim continued to make progress with her class and was feeling a lot better about how they were achieving with literacy activities. She continued to do ongoing assessment with all of her students and adjust learning to meet their diverse needs. In addition to Mrs. Brayboy, two teachers from first grade also invested more time into assessment and, using this information, began to group and diversify their lessons in a manner more in keeping with their students' needs. As this whole concept of addressing academically diverse learners spread, teachers began to ask more questions and collaborate with their colleagues within their professional school community.

Creative Problem Solving

Change is messy. It has loose ends that never get secured, but the process of bringing about change can be exhilarating if school leaders are behind it 100% and keep the vision alive and the process on track.

At times, we all want someone to solve our problems for us, but in truth, we are the ones most capable of solving those problems. Promoting creative problem solving is a leader's task and is part of the change process. Instead of someone telling teachers what to do, the leader establishes an environment where several work creatively to solve problems that are acceptable and owned by the stakeholders. "Two heads are better than one." Teachers are good thinkers; they just need to be guided and encouraged to exercise that opportunity and not settle for a "one size fits all" solution, such as purchasing a commercially prepared program. As problems arise as part of change, the combined energy and thinking power of those involved will bring about creative solutions that all can feel they helped to bring about. The key is providing an opportunity for creative problem solving. Leaders of change do not tell others what to do. Leaders for change create environments that allow others to work together to use a tremendous amount of talent to benefit learning for all children. Leaders must encourage thinking in another way, and teachers must understand they have the liberty to do just that and see their ideas put into practice (Wilcox, 2003).

Administering for Change

Thus far, this discussion has focused on the leadership requirement for change and how to support change in a school with a community of learners. However, a leader also has the task for administering change (Willis & Mann, 2000). Often, administering change is a behind-the-scenes process that smoothes the way for creative endeavors by teachers as they work through the process of change. The administrator lays the foundation for change by making plans to ensure that the change visions become reality. The plan must be introduced and evidence provided to support the change. The administrator must be knowledgeable about the topic and present elements supporting it, such as current research.

Change in a school environment affects everything that can promote or inhibit it. The school budget effects change, and it is up to the leaders to take care of the budget. For example, where funds were once spent at random or on an as-needed basis, the leader uses change as the budget's focus. What is necessary for change will require funds to support it. It is up to the school leadership to plan for expenditures that will support change, rather than use funds randomly and without a purpose. Funds once used to buy workbooks may need to be encumbered for professional development needs, which support training related to the change plan. Funds for furniture may be better spent on purchasing classroom libraries.

Just as budgets get serious scrutiny as part of the change process, so do class schedules and teacher planning time. Teachers need time to plan individually and collaboratively. They need time to discuss and reflect, and they need time to work on the change process as it unfolds. The administrator's job is to plan the use of school time wisely so that change can be accomplished between, and among, the school's teachers. The principal or a teacher-leader needs to have access to materials and knowledge as a part of her role in implementing change. The World Wide Web puts materials, resources, and knowledge at our fingertips. It is up to the school's leadership team to research materials and sources of knowledge and provide those sources for teachers. An important part of a principal's day may be spent looking for evidence-based research to support the school's initiative or searching for Web sites, which support classroom instruction. Another use of the Internet is finding materials at a lesser cost, or finding professional development conferences that are offered to teachers. These are just a few ways an administrator can help teachers implement change. These efforts say, "This project is important for our educational family, and I am supporting you by finding these resources." Again, actions speak louder than words, and the message of change gains momentum.

> By February, Kim had converted her math time into guided instruction with math centers. Materials were bought to support the second-grade math curriculum and develop appropriate centers. Word spread fast, and second-grade teachers came to ask for a common planning and meeting time. They had already figured out how minor changes to the schedule would accomplish this. They presented their ideas, and I readily agree it was what we needed to continue to develop and support our beliefs about student learning and academic diversity.

Often, a school can have a lot of resources that are not being used simply because they are not organized for easy access. For example, students need access to all different kinds of books and books at multiple levels. Organizing those resources, so teachers have access to them either permanently in their classrooms or through the media center, book rooms, computer labs, or other areas, is important for students and teachers. Perhaps the media specialist and her assistants could inventory materials and organize them so teachers are not hindered in gaining access. Teachers may not realize all of the computer programs that are available unless the principal requests the lab assistant to publish a list of materials, content, and age appropriateness. Usually, it is up to the principal to designate these job responsibilities. But these are actions, which build capacity and support for the school's vision of academically diverse learners. It sends a message: The leadership will provide the resources for teachers to initiate change in creating classrooms for academically diverse learners.

A great way for an administrator to support change is by anticipating teachers' needs. If they need math manipulatives, provide them. If they need maps for social studies, provide them; or if they need materials for centers, provide them even before teachers ask. When teachers begin to talk about what they want to do and what they need to accomplish their plans, a good administrator will hear that expression of need and provide for it to be filled. Sometimes, teachers are hesitant to ask for things. The administrator can convey a receptive attitude to teachers by offering to provide for needs that are asked for, or not asked for but needed. The change process gets promoted by helping teachers get what they need to do their jobs without feeling they have to do battle to get books, paper, or technology to help students. The judicious use, and equitable distribution of, resources and materials is the administrator's duty.

> We have already started making plans for the summer and next year, which will more specifically meet the needs of all academically diverse learners. The fourth-grade teachers wrote a grant, and as a result, the entire staff will receive 3 days of training in learning styles and developmentally appropriate practices. Our media specialist will purchase books for next year, which reflect the thematic units of the basal series we adopted, and our Parent Teacher Organization (PTO) raised $5,000 to purchase classroom libraries.

Assessing the Impact of Change

In this day of accountability, a school leader and the leadership team must formally assess both the process of change and its outcomes. Change has to have an accountability component for several valid reasons. The way information is gathered for assessment purposes is also very important for valid reasons.

Consider first the reasons for assessing change. The goal of change is to increase student engagement in learning, student understanding, and student capacity to apply what has been learned to settings inside and outside the classroom (Tomlinson, 1999). In order to achieve this goal, the leadership team needs to determine if change is working. Is student achievement improving as a result of the change process implemented? In other words, is the change successful? Is it successful for a few, some, or all students? Does the plan need some modifications to be even more effective? The school leaders must know what is working for whom and to what degree. They must also determine if the change process is not working and then why it is not working. If leaders can see the benefits of change through academic growth, behavior, and attendance, for example, then the process needs to be continued. If change cannot be ob-served as helping students, then the school leadership and its teachers must rethink the entire process and determine how it can be corrected to promote the goal of increased achievement for all students. The reason for assessing change is to determine if the change project was successful and how to proceed once that determination is made.

That leads to the next question. How do we assess change? This is a more complex question and one with several possible answers. They involve:

- assessment of teacher growth through both formal and informal observation
- self-regulation and reflection by the entire faculty and administration
- formal and informal assessment of students

These areas for assessing change have to be discussed individually, but they are intertwined in terms of their usefulness.

Those who are to be evaluated have to have a role in determining how assessment will be done. Most school districts require a formal assessment of teachers annually. New teachers are usually required to have more formal assessments. Administrators must be equipped to recognize activities in a class-room that have been brought about as a result of change—for example, a teacher, who as part of the change process, has implemented centers within her classroom where, before, these were not part of her classroom environment. Not only must the school leaders recognize change activities, they must con-sider the effectiveness and appropriateness of the activities and be able to sug-gest alternative strategies, as necessary. The formal evaluation instrument should provide high-quality feedback to the teacher; however, this is only one way to assess change and provide feedback. A strong leader will consult with teachers on a regular basis, allowing time for sharing how plans are working or voicing concerns about activities that may not be as effective and offering guidance and support through the change project (Sergiovanni, 2004).

Another way to assess change is by reviewing student achievement. Infor-mally assessing student growth with observations, anecdotal records, and port-folios gives strong feedback to the leader and teachers about the effectiveness of change. The leader and teacher leaders help others examine indicators of growth, reflect on the meaning of evidence, and determine implications for both school and individual practice.

Leaders for change understand that efforts to promote change cannot stop at the schoolhouse door. Effective leaders communicate with parents and com-munity leaders, letting them know about activities in the change process that will affect the lives of their children (Tomlinson, 2000). Parents want to know that their children are being treated fairly and equitably, and that they are getting the best education possible. Keeping the general public and parents informed about the "world of school" gives stakeholders a sense of confidence in what is being done, and in doing so, generates support from parents and leaders in the community. Leaders have a responsibility to keep parents informed about their children's education, so that parents can help support teachers' efforts at home. Parents want their children to be successful and open communication with the school, and understanding all of the many facets to a child's education can help parents learn about ways to help their children. For example, reading is emphasized at one particular elementary school. Teachers frequently sent home progress reports and suggested ways they could help their children foster a love of reading at home to parents. At the end of this school year, they will send home a grade-level-appropriate reading list to parents so they can help and encourage their children to continue to read during this summer. Teachers have not done this in previous years. It is a change whereby the school's leadership and teachers will need to stress the importance to parents of having their children continue to read during the summer. This change effort will only be successful with the help of parents who understand how this change project will help their children. The school leaders must help parents understand the concept of change and how this experience benefits their own children (Tomlinson, 2003), and that the change being implemented is educationally sound.

As a leader for change, the principal must also carry the news to the district level. District leaders need to know about efforts at the school level to bring about positive change in student growth and achievement. Communicating with the district office lets them know that their help and support is needed, if positive change is to take place. Commitment from the district leaders in the form of time and resources provides just two ways the district can support change at the school. However, if the district office is not aware of the change efforts, then they are in no position to help. The change leader communicates with everyone, from teachers to the district superintendent to community leaders and board members, in order for them to understand special efforts that are being put forth to advance all children in positive ways.

Conclusion

School change is complex and never-ending. There can never be real closure to school change. Think of change efforts as an uphill climb. After the struggle to the pinnacle, leaders assess, regroup, and start the climb to the next level. Referring to the spiral pictured earlier in the chapter, as the leadership team commits to change, support must be at every step along the way. The vision of purposeful change is enlivened through support and commitment by all participants and continues as others join the team. There must be no time constraints on the spiral of change as it adjusts to the learning needs of students. Making change the centerpiece of planning is important. Helping teachers to change practices in significant ways takes a long time. That length of time will vary from teacher to teacher (Tomlinson, 1999).

Change is not short term, even though some will see it only as a fad, and it, too, will pass. The leadership team and teachers must embrace change as if it were a newborn child, needing lots of attention, and nurturing to help it grow and bloom. As long as student populations are academically diverse, then addressing change to meet the needs of the academically diverse has to be the focus for every aspect of school life, including working with a faculty, planning for professional growth, assessing their effectiveness, adjusting schedules, and monitoring expenditures of funds. As every diverse learner enters school, there must be leaders there to recognize that diversity and initiate strategies to meet their needs.

Finally, as leaders in schools, celebrate the small steps of change, because they will lead to more steps, both small and large.

Stay focused, and never lose sight of the goal to improve student achievement by meeting individual needs and moving each child from where he or she is to as far as he or she can possibly travel.

> My teachers and I have 471 students who are academically diverse learners. Additional initiatives to reach, and teach, all of our diverse learners are being considered. We know we are headed in the right direction.

References

Almack, J. (1970). *Modern school administration* (rev. ed.) Freeport, NY: Books for Libraries Press.

Blokker, B., Simpson, A., & Whittier, P. (2002). Schoolwide literacy: The principal's role in schoolwide literacy. Online document at: www.naesp.org

Csikszentmihalyi, M. (1997). Finding flow: The psychology of engagement with everyday life. New York: Basic Books.

Fahey, J. A. (2000). Who wants to differentiate instruction? We did . . . *Education Leadership, 58*(1).

Lezotte, L., & Pepper, J. (2004). *Instructional leadership: What the effective schools research says.* Okemos, MI: Effective Schools Products, Ltd.

Schlechty, P. (1997). *Inventing better schools: An action plan for educational reform.* San Francisco: Jossey-Bass.

Sergiovanni, T. J. (2004). *The principalship: A reflective practice perspective* (5th ed.). Boston: Allyn and Bacon.

Sternberg, R. J., Torff, B., & Grigorenko, E. L. (1998). Teaching triarchically improves student achievement. *Journal of Educational Psychology, 90*(3), 374–384 (EJ 576 492).

Tomlinson, C. (1995). How *to differentiate instruction in mixed-ability classrooms.* Alexandria, VA: Association for Supervision and Curriculum Development (ED386 301).

Tomlinson, C. (1999). *The differentiated classroom: Responding to the needs of all learners.* Alexandria, VA: Association for Supervision and Curriculum Development (ED 429 944).

Tomlinson, C., & Allan, S. (2000). *Leadership for differentiating schools and classrooms.* Alexandria, VA: Association for Supervision and Curriculum Development.

Tomlinson, C. (2003). *Fulfilling the promise of the differentiated classroom.* Alexandria, VA: Association for Supervision and Curriculum Development.

Wilcox, B. L. (2003). Leadership and professional development. *English Leadership Quarterly, 25*(3), 1–2.

Willis, S., & Mann, L. (2000). *Differentiating instruction: Finding manageable ways to meet individual needs.* Alexandria, VA: Association for Curriculum Supervision and Development.

Vygotsky, L. (1986). *Thought and language.* Cambridge, MA: MIT Press.

Chapter 12

Reform of Schools to Support Diverse Learners

Hathia A. Hayes and Andrew E. Hayes

The following description is of a real school that made significant changes to improve instruction and student learning. This is an extreme example of both diverse student groups and need for reform, but it should illustrate that conditions such as these could not have been addressed successfully by teachers acting alone or in groups.

Walters Elementary School was located in a run-down former high school building in a run-down part of a small town near the largest metropolitan area of the state. Students in prekindergarten through fifth grade attending the school were among the most needy and lowest performing in the school district. About 45% of students were black and about 40% were Latino (mainly Mexican) and the remainder were white (non-Latino and other groups). About 95% of the students were receiving free or reduced-price lunch. The school was a "dumping ground" for the school district—principals and teachers who were not successful in other schools had been "dumped" here. Furniture, equipment, and materials were mainly hand-me-downs from other schools, and the building and grounds were in near-condemnation state of repair and upkeep. There was regular turnover of principals and teachers—they moved from the school as quickly as they either gave up or could get positions in other schools or districts. As a result, many of the position vacancies in the district were in this school, so there was a high percentage of beginning teachers among the staff and there had been several new principals assigned to the school over the past few years. Teaching and leadership was novice, at best, and ineffective, for the most part. Issues relating to misbehavior, low achievement, low attendance, frequent illness, low parental engagement, and transience among students were pervasive. The image of the school in the community was consistent with its actual state—awful!

From of a variety of community-based events and conditions, including some coming from extreme black–white racial tension in the area of town where the school was located, the school district began actions to improve the school.

First, came an experienced principal who had led another school to Blue Ribbon status. He was given authority to "purge" the faculty and recruit capable and dedicated teachers. The result was almost 90% new teachers in 2 years. Added initially were experienced and capable lead teachers, one for each grade and one for reading and one for math, who worked with the teachers as coaches to improve instruction to meet new school-adopted standards. Two experienced, energetic teachers were assigned full-time positions as curriculum specialists to lead a 3-year reform initiative, including adopting a whole-school reform model under a Comprehensive School Reform (CSR) grant. Regular, high-intensity coaching and professional development became part of every workday for teachers. Also came several teacher–team meetings each week to review their own work, to review student performance and issues, and to seek ways to improve their instruction and to deal with student learning needs.

The building and grounds were cleaned, painted, and polished; and the interior of the old, three-story building actually was pleasing, especially when bright colors, art prints, and student work were installed all over the building. It became clear, from even a brief walk down a hall, that students and teachers had begun to engage in serious work in this school.

At the beginning of the reform initiative, the percentage of Latino students was higher than among most other elementary schools in the region. The number continued to increase over the 3 years of the reform initiative, reaching close to 50%— even while the other students remained enrolled and others moved in, giving an increase in overall enrollment. To respond to this large number and continuing increase in Latino students, a variety of changes were made, including: special classes added, as needed, to serve the students; all communications with parents, including newsletters and all reports, were in both English and Spanish; translators were added to the staff to work with parents and communicate with them; and special training was given to all teachers. By then, the school had become an active place, with parents routinely visiting and working. The community relations and image improved to the point that this was among the most desirable schools in the community.

During the third year of reform, this school moved into a beautiful new building on the outskirts of town. That new building was organized into "villages" for each grade level, with colored hallways and markers leading from the inviting entrance hall to each village. Teachers in each "village" worked as a team to serve the students "living there." Norms for behavior and responsibility were developed and adopted, and all students and faculty adopted those norms and the responsibility to communicate them.

Walters became one of the most consistently successful schools in the state in gains in student performance on the state testing programs. To illustrate those gains, from 2000 through 2005, the percentage of students performing at the level of "proficient" or above on the state end-of-grade tests were: 35.5%, 39.8%, 51.6%, 61.7%, 78.1%, and 82.3%, respectively.

These changes in school quality came about by making massive changes in the school culture and in the school as an organization and as a system of services to support teachers and classroom instruction. Those school-level changes paralleled

> changes made in teacher capability, in the professional quality of teaching, and in the degree of focus on learning for all students, regardless of their characteristics or needs.

Introduction

This chapter is intended to illustrate a need for working with diverse student groups and to illustrate that teachers cannot address differences among diverse student groups successfully in a school, either individually or collectively. It also will demonstrate that, while teachers have responsibility to implement programs to meet needs of diverse learners, the responsibility for serving diverse students well rests at the organization levels—system and school. An overarching position taken by the authors is that the organization must adopt learning goals for students, and those goals may be either differentiated or common among students. If the goals are differentiated, then services must be differentiated to reflect those different goals. On the other hand, if goals common among students are adopted, then educational services must differ significantly to achieve the same goals for people who are markedly different at the beginning.

Whichever approach to goal-setting is used, once those goals are adopted, the organization has the responsibility to adopt instructional systems that are appropriate for achieving those goals. Furthermore, the organization has the responsibility to adopt systems and processes that enable teachers to implement those instructional systems. Mismatches between the adopted instructional systems and the organization will, almost without exception, create significant barriers to effective implementation by those who must provide the instruction.

Furthermore, this chapter describes general methods for reforming schools and some barriers to reform and some unsuccessful practices and conditions that were observed in over 150 schools studied by the authors as they were attempting to achieve schoolwide reforms.

The Need for Schoolwide Reform to Serve Diverse Students

In the school described above, changes were made in all aspects of the organization and its services, including:

- leadership and management
- teacher accountability, support, and retention
- curricula and instruction
- assessment of student characteristics and learning
- student support
- management and involvement of parents and community in the schooling of children
- professional development
- use of external support and assistance
- evaluation
- use of computers throughout the school operations, including instruction
- acquisition and use of resources toward a single purpose

The reform was led by a dedicated and experienced principal who used a variety of staff and faculty positions to serve roles in designing, implementing, and managing the change initiative. Their work focused directly on ensuring that needs for all students were met through the new instructional and support services. Their commitment to serving all children effectively guided the reform efforts and resulted in a set of programs and services that met that standard.

It is unlikely that such significant and sustained improvements as those achieved could have been made at the instructional level by teachers working either individually or collectively. This example describes how a "dumping ground" school that clearly needed improvement was transformed into one that was serving diverse students well and achieving high levels of student learning. Fortunately, most schools are not so obviously in need of reform. The story does not give the details about how this reform dealt with serving diverse student groups, nor does it address why schools must reform if they are to be successful in serving diverse learners. But, as a "dumping ground," this school was serving the "neediest" students. Then came the "normal" and high-performing students as the image improved in the community. The resulting mix of students was one that represented a wide range of histories of education and prior achievement before coming to this school.

A one-size-fits-all instructional system could not have worked to serve the children enrolled in this school. Therefore, a variety of instructional approaches were put into place through the changes that were made; and most of the changes in the school organization were made because they were essential to support those instructional approaches. That is, significant changes were made in the instructional system to serve effectively the complex needs and conditions of the students. But those changes required a complex set of changes in the school organization to support the changes made in instruction.

But in making such reforms, there are at least four major issues that impact both the reform processes and the probable success that can be expected from such an effort to change. Those issues listed here, and addressed in the sections that follow, are:

1. conflicting political and policy demands both for serving diverse student needs effectively and increasing demands for rigor and common standards for all students

2. conflicts between the commonly held images of the way schools are supposed to be and the demands that schools change to produce different results

3. conflicting views among the general public, policy makers, and even among some people in educational positions, about teaching and leading as craft occupations (skilled workers) rather than as professional occupations (skillful practices based on judgment made using technical and theoretical knowledge)

4. the complexity of the task of providing optimum educational services for diverse students within a social and political context in which there are many conditions and other factors impacting both what can be done by schools and how effective that work will be

Issue: The Pressures for Schools to Serve Diverse Students

The recent political and professional demands to "bridge the gap" among various subgroups of students is one important illustration of a concern for diverse student groups. However, at the same time, other political and social actions present strong demands that we not deal with diversity by using a variety of means that might be effective or even essential. Particularly, there are powerful demands in public policy and in accountability systems to "strengthen standards" and "increase rigor." That focus on standards and rigor is expressed in the form of increased demands for offering advanced or higher level courses, elimination of remediation programs, or having more testing and meeting higher score standards that hold schools accountable for ensuring that all significant subgroups of students meet the same content and performance standards. In other words, there are increasing demands on schools for both differentiation and standardization—along with the expectations that both of these demands are met.

Under these competing demands, schools and teachers are being pressured both to "differentiate instruction" to "meet the needs of diverse learners" and to "ensure that all students meet the same high curricular and performance standards." No small matter, and almost certainly not possible unless the school organization is designed to serve those multiple demands and operates to support these complex needs and demands while it supports the complex systems of services that are essential to achieve that end.

Issue: Pressure to Change amid Pressure to Remain the Same

Schools and schooling are traits of U.S. culture, just as they are in almost all other national cultures. Furthermore, these traits in U.S. culture differ markedly from those in other countries, just as other traits differ, such as language, foods, dress, and norms, among others. These and other culture traits are very difficult to change because, "That's the way it's supposed to be."

Among the characteristics of schools and schooling that are embedded in U.S. culture are special school-related language, positions, role of student, role of teacher, curriculum expectations, organization, and even the notion of school as place (a building) that has certain styles and forms of construction and design. When attempts are made to change, these specific school-related traits have the same tenacity as any other cultural trait—language, gender roles, body piercing, tattoos, clothing styles, hats, foods, and more. Imagine what is required to make change in general culture traits through deliberate actions. School and schooling traits that are elements of culture are no different, especially when those traits have also been adopted within education as "the way it is supposed to be."

Consider, for example, the content we teach in the different grades. Why do we teach the social studies, literature, or science content at the different grade levels in which we generally find them? To illustrate: state history in fourth grade, cursive writing in third grade, and so on.

Suppose you want to stop using the notion of "grades" for grouping students for instruction—that is, change to nongraded schools. Forget about it! Some parents wouldn't know the age of their child. (How old is your child? Third grade.) They would have little way to know whether their child was making "normal" progress in schooling.

Or, consider the adoption of letter grades commonly used in schools as a common way to make summary judgments in society (What grade would you give the president on his performance?) or the generalization of the percentage-correct grade scale (90, 80, 70, 60, etc.) to almost any form of tests, testing, or performances. To illustrate, suppose you took a 100-item, multiple-choice test and the number of correct answers you made is 38. What are your immediate thoughts about making that raw score? Actually, that score is meaningless without some referent for interpretation, but the common response is, "I failed!"—primarily because of the assumption that the percent-correct grade scale should apply to this test and score just as it does to classroom testing in which tests or the scoring systems are commonly constructed to correspond (more or less) to that standard.

Mind images are powerful consequences of the adoption of culture traits. For example, suppose you ask typical adults in your community to think about schools and describe what they "see." Most likely, the descriptions would include an entrance with the principal's office just inside, hallways with classrooms on each side, a teacher, and a group of children in each classroom, desks arranged in rows or some other teacher-determined pattern, the teacher "teaching" and students following the directions and attending to the content, and a particular subject area is being addressed. Of course, you might get some different responses from a particular individual; but more likely, some version of this culturally specific convention would be described. Indeed, that image of school has been converted into state and local policy in most states. Teachers are allocated to schools based on the number of students, and the maximum number of students in each class is prescribed; the minimum number of minutes per day that math, reading, or other subjects must be taught are prescribed, or textbooks are prescribed (or even the amount of "homework").

Look further into this cultural image of schooling, and each classroom probably will have whole-class teaching, with all students addressing the same instructional content and the same tasks. That is, in that mind image, there will be little, if any, differentiation or mechanisms for addressing diversity! Yet, we are expected to differentiate instruction to serve diverse student learners—a conflict with that cultural image of classroom and, perhaps, even with the image of "classroom" that is held among educators.

Think about the role of the student in U.S. schooling. Using popular humor and comics as illustrations, "Schooling is something we do to students while they resist." Schools and educators "own" the goal of becoming educated. There is little in our culture that communicates expectations that, in grade schools, the parents own these goals or that students are expected to adopt the goals as their own. Consider the almost-daily depiction of "Little Jughead" in the comics, any of the other students in comic strips, or the numerous cartoons in each monthly issue of *Kappan* as examples to the contrary. Yet, this is quite different from the role of the student in other nations. The energy and attention given over to managing pupil behavior in some of the schools the authors visit is pervasive, with little likelihood that most of the students will take the goal of becoming an educated, responsible person while they are students.

Of course, one teacher in a school (or even a few teachers) could attempt to change instruction, classroom organization, and roles of the student and teacher from the cultural and common images, even if the remainder of the school did not. But addressing these culturally linked expectations of schools and schooling will require concerted efforts, even by schools or school systems, if they are to be countered successfully. Teachers almost certainly cannot make these changes alone or by working only among themselves. We are reminded here of Sancho's line in *Man of LaMancha:* "It doesn't matter whether the pitcher hits the stone or the stone hits the pitcher, it's going to be bad for the pitcher."

Issue: Teaching Is Not a Professional Field of Practice

As those cultural images of schools and schooling are being addressed, we also should deal with another cultural notion about teaching—teaching is not viewed as a professional field of practice. In the visual image of classrooms held by members of the general community, do they see teachers doing anything they do not think they could do if only they knew the content and had the patience to deal with the students? Do they consider the teacher as able to do something they don't know how to do (other than know content and deal with students)? On the other hand, if they imagine walking down the hall of a hospital, would they expect nurses to be doing something they don't know how to do, or to know how to do things they don't know how to do? . . . or, an electrician? . . . or an engineer?

The notion that teaching is not a profession is pervasive in current policy relating to public education—and the authors think that view has been adopted glibly within education even while teachers proclaim that, "We are professionals." That public view of teaching mainly as "communication of content" to students is an important cultural barrier to change. However, when that view is also held among teachers and school leaders, along with their general resistance to learning and using generalized technical and theoretical information as the foundation for their practice, a formidable barrier to reform to address diversity is created.

Among the distinguishing characteristics of a profession are that: (1) People occupying positions have discretion over certain classes of decisions; and (2) A body of specialized technical and theoretical knowledge is recognized, known, and used by practitioners for making those decisions. But among teachers, there is a tendency to celebrate "practical" knowledge and to eschew general principles and "theoretical" knowledge. Furthermore, there continues to be arguments in education policy making and leadership about whether (or how) decision-making autonomy should be distributed to the lowest level in the organization at which the decision is appropriate to be made.

This failure to recognize teaching (and also leading) as professional fields is reflected in the continuing demands among policy makers and some in education to "find the one best approach and then use it"; for example, to find the one best approach to teach reading (even though advocates probably would not agree, the current "gold standard" for research—experimental design—reflects assumptions that we can find a "best practice"). This best-practice assumption about education is common among leaders in business and industry and in educational policy making who might ask, "Why can't you tell me the best way to teach a child to read?" or to teach whatever? When those of us who understand the complexity of the task and the various conditions that must be considered to select appropriate instruction say, "It depends on . . ." a common response, often made in disgust, is, "There you go! You educators don't even know the best way to teach reading."

In several settings while addressing business and political leaders, one of the authors has turned this around to ask an attorney, for example, "Tell me the best way to defend a client." Or to an architect, "Tell me the best way to design a house." Of course, they respond by saying, "It depends on . . .", to which he responds, "No, no, no! You wouldn't let me describe the variety of conditions on which best methods for teaching reading depend, so you can't do that either." He continues, asking, "Do you think the mind of a child is less complex than representing a client or designing a house?"

This response to people outside of education illustrates the intended point here—the answer to the question about "best practices" for teaching anything must always be, "It depends upon . . ." The practices must fit the particular learning that is intended and the characteristics of the particular students for whom that learning is intended.

Therefore, teaching fits the task requirements for a profession—a complex task that requires the application of specialized knowledge to make choices about which practices (methods and materials) to use in a given situation. However, if teachers are to work as professionals, first and foremost, they must come to recognize and know the appropriate bodies of technical and theoretical information to use in instructional decision making and then become skillful in deciding about practices that match the particular intended learnings and student characteristics. Next, they must become skillful in using the practices they select.

How does this notion of teacher-as-professional relate to school reform to meet the needs of diverse learners? Successful use of the professional knowledge and skills for teaching requires organizational conditions that enable their use—the teachers must have the appropriate decision-making autonomy and the conditions in which they can make the decisions without unnecessary constraints. School organizations that demand the use of, for example, particular instructional practices, classroom organizational arrangements, instructional materials, roles and responsibilities of students, curriculum sequences and schedules, or working arrangements among teachers, without regard to whether they match the particular students or intended learnings, place serious restrictions on, or prevent the use of, sound professional practice. Teachers cannot meet the needs of diverse learners under constraints on their practices such as those.

Issue: The Dilemma of Complexity of the Task of Schooling

Reflect here on the complex set of tasks faced by Walters Elementary School as it changed from a "dumping ground" to one of the most desirable and successful schools in the state—all within a high-stakes state accountability system. Remember, they made changes in all aspects of the organization and its services, including: leadership and management; teacher accountability, support, and retention; curricula and instruction; assessment of student characteristics and learning; student support; management and involvement of parents and community in the schooling of children; professional development; use of external support and assistance; evaluation; use of computers throughout the school operations, including instruction; and acquisition and use of resources toward a single purpose.

A further anecdote relating to the diversity among students in classes faced by contemporary teachers is captured in the following story told to the authors recently by a colleague who was returning from a visit to the classroom of a first-year teacher. Students in the middle school class varied widely on cultural, socioeconomic, developmental, and learning characteristics. But they also reflected some of the worst of contemporary societal problems. Within a few days prior to the visit to the class, students in that one classroom had experienced:

· mother being beaten by her boyfriend
· parent arrested for criminal activities
· father incapacitated from drug and alcohol use
· parents and all adults absent from the home
· staying with grandparents because parents were sent to rehabilitation
· a parent murdered
· visiting parent in prisons
· severe physical abuse

Our colleague asked rhetorically, "How do new teachers deal with these demands as they try to apply what they have learned in college?" She went on to say, "Veteran teachers find that it becomes increasingly difficult to use good instructional practices, focus on the state curriculum, and relate that curriculum content in a meaningful way to the students who seem to be growing up in a world most teachers do not understand themselves."

Yet, while the range of student and family issues facing the schools increase, the external demands for change and for higher levels and more pervasive student achievement also continue. Just a few of those issues and expected changes, among many others, are listed below:

- adopting a common set of expectations for all students
- effectively addressing the needs of all students, irrespective of their home and family context, of their prior experiences with schools and schooling, or of the community resources available to support the schools, students, or families
- accommodating the frequent changes in national, state, and local mandates that may be made without regard to whether the schools have the capacity to respond in meaningful or timely ways
- responding to long-term needs or goals while addressing demands for improvements in short-term results
- finding, employing, and retaining "highly qualified" teachers in all fields, but especially in fields with current shortages, such as math, science, or exceptional children
- supporting inexperienced leaders and teachers who are new in their positions
- making changes in schools and schooling practices that are based on culture traits but clearly need changing (A superintendent in a rural school district said to the Board of Education, "None of you would even think of raising corn the way you did 40 years ago; but, you expect me to run schools the way we did 40 years ago.)
- engaging parents and the larger community in the schooling of children
- building relationships across cultures within the school and community
- accommodating the prescribed materials and methods mandated in federal and state grants or programs
- integrating the use of computers and computer-based applications into instructional systems

- using assessment data meaningfully and appropriately
- developing the capacity of teachers and others in schools to work effectively as professionals in their respective positions

However, as they attempt reforms, whether because of their own choices or in response to any of the variety of external demands, teachers and school leaders face the challenge of understanding, selecting, and using a wide range of information about, among other things: complex and changing community demographics; diverse student characteristics and performances; various school organizational alternatives, demands, and constraints; and to a wide variety of other internal needs and external demands.

The complexity of the tasks facing educators as they attempt to respond to all of those expectations is complicated even further by the tensions between lack of consistency in school expectations and practices (coming from sources such as frequent changes in local, state, and national policies, processes, and expectations and frequent turnover of school leaders and other professional staff and turnovers among policy makers) and the increasing expectations that educational practices should improve dramatically to reflect some new, but yet unclear, vision of schooling.

Addressing most of these issues and challenges effectively will require school or school district responsibility and leadership. Teachers cannot do it alone. However, it may not be so clear that each one of these issues and challenges is linked, in one way or another, to serving diverse student groups. Furthermore, for most schools, addressing this broad range of issues and expectations successfully will require significant changes—even reform—and, once changes are made, will make significant improvements in their ability to serve diverse students.

Another Perspective on the Need for School-Level Reform: Applying Organization Theory to Schools

If we assume that all students are alike on all characteristics that are related to learning or engagement in the learning process, and, furthermore, we assume the intended learning is clearly known, then we can design instruction explicitly so that it is appropriate for producing the learning by all of the students. That is, a single instructional approach can be designed and prescribed to result in the learning for all students. The student group can be considered simple (all alike, not diverse or complex), and the instructional task can be planned as a routine to follow. If we have these conditions, teachers can be trained to implement the instructional routine, and they can be effective teachers for all students without having to make discretionary decisions throughout the process (assuming that the routine is designed appropriately for the students and intended learnings and then implemented as designed). As an example, if we want to teach a particular reading skill and all students in the group are essentially homogeneous on their prerequisite skills and willingness to engage in learning, then we can design and prescribe a particular instructional practice that has a high probability of resulting in the learning by the students.

However, most people who work in the school business do not expect all students in an instructional group to be alike in their prior learnings, values or beliefs, willingness to engage in the instructional processes, or in their capacity to learn or engage in the instruction. Therefore, even if we assume a relatively homogeneous group of students, some modifications in well-designed instructional routines will need to be made by the teacher as the instruction occurs—responding to the variety of conditions as they arise, sometimes each moment. And the more students differ, the more adjustments and modifications will be needed in a general design, if the instruction is to be effective for all or most of the students. As the differences among the students become more profound and complex, the less the teacher can rely solely on a preplanned instruction for effective student learning. Indeed, at some point of complexity of the students, ongoing professional judgment applied continuously within a general plan will be required to serve the instructional purposes well.

The description in the preceding paragraphs, which is intended to be intuitively apparent, represents a well-grounded proposition in general organization theory. Perrow (1967, 1970) and Woodward (1965) claim that for an organization to be effective, the more complex the "raw materials," the more complex must be the methods for transforming those raw materials into the desired results. Harkin (1972) and Harkin and Hayes (1973) translated that proposition to educational applications and claimed that for schools to be effective, the more complex the group of students (the raw materials), the more complex must be the instructional system. That is, the greater the student diversity on factors affecting learning, the more flexibility and variability there must be in the instructional system.

Considering the example above of the homogeneous group learning the reading skill. If the students vary significantly in their prior learnings, values or beliefs, willingness to engage in the instructional processes, or in their capacity to learn or engage in the instruction, then significant variation will be required in the instruction if all students are to acquire the skill. While the teacher may work within a general plan for instruction, a great deal of variation will be needed "on the fly" to accommodate effectively the many questions, barriers, and difficulties that will be encountered.

But if the essential flexibility and variations in instruction are to be implemented effectively, teachers must have both the capability and the discretion to make the essential accommodations whenever they are needed to effect student learning. The more complex the student needs and characteristics, the more variability there must be in instruction and the more discretion the teachers must have to make those accommodations. This is an almost endless cycle, limited only by the variations among students that are assumed within the school to be important to take into account in making instructional variations.

As the complexity of needs increase within an instructional setting, there is more potential for an instructional system that matches those needs to be incompatible with the current school processes, roles, norms, expectations, or other systems of control and coordination. If there should be significant incompatibilities between the instructional system that is required to serve the diverse student needs and the school conditions, then changes must be made in the school, if instruction is to be provided that is appropriate for serving the diverse learners effectively (see Figure 12:1 for a depiction of this relationship).

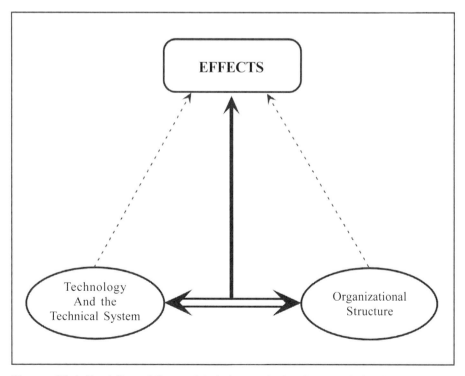

Figure 12:1 Depiction of the match between technology and structure as a major influence over organizational effects.

Again, we ask readers to remember the wide range of school-level changes that were made in Walters Elementary School to support the changes in instruction that were needed—teacher teams, regular team meetings and processes, special assistants for teachers, ongoing training and coaching, and more.

In the Perrow (1970) and Woodward (1965) conceptualizations of appropriate organizational conditions for effectiveness (depicted in Figure 12:1), neither the organizational structures nor the methods, tools, and materials alone is sufficient for effectiveness. Rather, it is the match between the organization and the methods and materials that determine effectiveness—simple methods, tools, and materials can be used effectively in centralized and simple organizations—if the task is simple; complex methods, tools, and materials require decentralized and complex organizations—if the task is complex. For example, if we assume that for methods to be appropriate, they require integration of instruction across teams of teachers, then the organization must enable the work of the team as they plan and implement the instruction. Or, if appropriate instruction requires varying the schedule of learning among the students within a group, the supervisory and assessment systems for teaching must allow teachers to make those variations and those systems must enable teachers to make the variations in instruction among students that reflect those assumptions. (For example, it would be inappropriate to expect teachers to make instructional accommodations in the schedule of objectives among students and also demand use of a single pacing guide by having inspectors checking to see if all teachers and students are on the same page on any given day.)

Thus, from the perspective of theory, if an organization assumes that it has complex tasks—more complex than can be established as routines—then a "professional" system of services will be required. Teachers must have discretion over certain classes of decisions, and the organization will be designed and managed to enable those professional practices. Most schools experienced by the authors over the past several years will require important changes, or even comprehensive reform, to meet the conditions needed to support instruction that is appropriate for a highly diverse student group. (Recall the supervision of instruction in Walters. There were teacher teams that met several times each week to review student cases, and instructional problems were addressed and plans for instruction were made for each child who was being considered in that meeting. The specialists participated in those assessment and planning meetings and provided coaching to help the teachers implement the plans.)

Reforming Schools

Even with all the task complexity and difficulty described in the section above, it is clear to the authors that teachers and leaders in schools are attempting to respond to the variety of demands for them to produce more student learning for all students. Most are working hard and in good faith toward that end, even with large odds against them. Other writers agree. For example, Risko and Bromley (2001) claim that when elementary school educators are asked, they make a positive response to a question, such as, Can all students in today's widely diverse classrooms—regardless of difference in language, learning style, culture, ethnicity, race, socioeconomic background, ability, or age—achieve literacy goals that will allow them to become contributing, satisfied citizens?

While the responses made by these educators may have been influenced by social desirability in responding (a form of systematic error that is expected for questions such as this one), practices observed by the authors in over 150 schools over the past 6 years reveal a general willingness to try to serve the needs of children enrolled in their classes—whether or not they are successful.

However, an objective answer to this question should go beyond the personal beliefs of teachers and leaders and reflect a serious consideration of the capacity of schools within districts, states, and the nation to reform so they can serve those diverse learning needs. The history of attempts to reform schools has not been impressive because of the successes. Of the over 150 schools studied by the authors over the past 6 years that were attempting comprehensive reform, no more than 10% made significant progress toward reform and even fewer sustained those changes over time. It is clear to the authors that teachers, whether working individually or collectively, cannot ensure a positive answer to that question above. That requires appropriate organizational responses and significant reforms.

The Nature of Reform

All reform requires some amount of changes of various types. For example, Garratt (1987) described first- and second-order change. First-order change of schools does not affect the essence of the educational experience—the underlying characteristics of the instructional system and related learning. Second-order change, on the other hand, results in qualitatively different educational experiences for students by changing the fundamental assumptions underlying school organization and instructional practices. Similarly, the authors make a distinction between improvement and reform. Improvement makes changes in the practices and relationships of the school and instructional system that are important for some reason. Seldom would they involve changes in the fundamental assumptions underlying what is done, why it is done, or how it is done. Reform, on the other hand, does require changes in the foundations for what, why, and how work is done. While improvements may be important for meeting the complex needs of students enrolled in schools, shifting teaching to the level of professional practice will require significant reform of schools.

But the first question to be answered when dealing with reform of schools is, "Reform what?"

Answering that question might result in a list, such as:

- organizational structures—the patterns of relationships among organizational components (systems of communications, coordination, and control among positions, roles, and responsibilities)

- goals and goal structures—the curriculum and curriculum organization; what we expect students to learn, and in what sequence

- knowledge bases or assumptions about how to do work effectively (referred to in organization theory as "technology")

- the technical system—the tools, materials, and methods to use in instruction

- culture traits—especially those linked to education, schools, and schooling

- norms—the group assumptions about how people behave and relate

- behaviors of individuals

- values held by individuals

- skills or proficiencies of workers

Some of these "whats" may be more difficult to change than others. For example, changing personal values might be less complex and less difficult to change than group norms; and group norms may be more prone to change than culture traits. Also, they may actually prefer changing ways to coordinate work among colleagues and, thus, easy to change—especially if the methods adopted by the school are ones they prefer and also require these working relationships. The various factors that might need to be changed must be considered in the process of reform and given the attention that is required to affect the particular type of change. Remember, here, that some of the elements of schooling that need to be changed may be culture traits and extremely resistant to change. Others may be straightforward and require little time or effort.

Surely, there are many barriers to reform, some of which were described in sections above. But among the most pervasive barriers may be a variety of myths about reform. They are formidable barriers simply because they are myths and "we all know they are true." For just two examples, everyone knows that, "No one likes change, except a wet baby." Also, everyone knows that, "Successful change is difficult and takes a long time." However, both of these statements reflect mythic thinking about change and reform. Let's consider why.

Probably a more appropriate, and presumably probabilistic, statement than "no one likes change" would be, "People are afraid of uncertainty and insecurity." Another way of stating that new proposition might be, "People will avoid uncertainties and will act to protect themselves, if they perceive their security to be threatened." Consider the implications of the original and latter versions of this statement. The first—no one likes change—provides little understanding about how to approach the reform initiative. So, no one likes change; what can we do about that? On the other hand, the latter of these statements reflects an understanding that for reform to be successful, uncertainty and insecurity must be prevented, or at least minimized. But this condition could be addressed effectively if only we had, "A clear and shared vision of the reforms to be made"—the most frequently claimed factor in reform success and the one condition found missing among the 150 schools studied by the authors.

Furthermore, most examples of change reported to these authors and described by people working within them as "needing more time" actually failed because there were serious and apparent flaws in the designs and processes for change. In our judgment, more time would not have helped. Usually, what was being expressed was, "If I had another chance, I think I could make this work next time." Real change can be made in short periods of time—if managed carefully and authentically and done by using what is known about reform; especially, about the importance of clarity and precision of descriptions of planned changes and dealing with change at the level of particulars.

Conceptualizing Reform

In order to conceptualize a reform and the nature of the changes attempted, it is essential, first, to know what is currently in place. Therein lies double trouble. Generally, education leaders and teachers do not use a common technical and professional language or set of analytic models for thinking about the school as an organization, the instructional system, the curriculum, the student characteristics, or learning. Thus, it is difficult, if not impossible, for them to describe what actually is in place at the outset of a reform initiative or to describe in any operational or technical language what will be in place if the reform is successful.

Among the over 150 schools studied by us as they were attempting reform during the past 6 years, none of the leaders were able to describe in any operationally meaningful way what was being changed or what it was to become. Common descriptions were, "become more student centered," "all the students will be engaged in meaningful learning," "focus more on higher order learning," "accommodate different learning styles," or some other such statements that have equally indefinite meaning. With such indefinite language for talking about current and intended states of the school, it is not likely that, "a clear and shared vision of the reformed school" will be achieved. Much more explicit meaning is needed to guide a reform initiative.

Again, we refer to Walters, in which teachers, specialists, and coaches adopted common language to use by teams in assessment, analysis of teaching and learning problems, planning instruction, and coaching to ensure high-quality implementation.

A Framework for Providing a Common Technical Language

One approach for defining what is in place now, and for defining the desired organization, instructional system, and curriculum, is to think in terms of "a model" and try to define the current "model" (or models) that represent the school. But first, refer again to the notions of Perrow (1970) and Woodward (1965), who provided a framework that can be used for assessing the general characteristics of an educational organization, its components, and issues related to probable effectiveness. In their conceptualization, the organization has structures (the patterns of relations among organizational components) and technology (the knowledge and assumptions about how to produce work). In an effective organization, the technology and structure match (see Figure 12:1 again as a depiction of their assumptions). Of course, there is a further assumption here that the technology and resulting technical manifestations in the form of a system of methods, tools, and materials are appropriate for producing the intended learnings for the particular students for whom it is intended to be used.

Using this depiction as an overall starting point, one might begin by defining any one of the three parts: (1) the current effects; (2) the current technology and related technical system; or (3) the current organizational structures. For that purpose, a general conceptual framework and related graphic device can be used for defining and documenting the current model.

But first, what is an educational model, and what are the characteristics of a good model? As an overarching set of standards, an educational model must be:

- Coherent—It must be based on a set of design standards that are internally consistent. The methods, tools, and materials must all be consistent with the underlying design principles and assumptions;

- Comprehensive—It must cover the full range of students and curriculum areas for which it is intended; and

- Valid by design for producing the desired results for the target groups of students—based on sound evidence (it should be research-based).

Defining this concept of model further, any educational program or system of practices has several components that can be used to define the program "model" and to assess its validity. Those components are:

- a curriculum—the organized set of intended learnings from the program and the framework for defining the effects
- a "technology"—the knowledge bases and assumptions that are used to produce work
- a "technical system"—the materials, tools, and methods used in work— the material and procedural manifestations of the technology
- an organization—the system of structures for coordination and control of work
- an information system—the measures and measurement tools and the related systems for analysis and reporting of results

The three overall standards, and each of the five components listed above, have specialized and technical language and knowledge foundations in the literature in their respective fields. For example, there are various frameworks for analyzing and describing curriculum within that field and there are frameworks for analysis of organizational structures in the field of organization theory. However, without having to go to the foundational literature in those various fields, there can be an intermediate beginning point to defining the current model and the anticipated model that does not require engaging in intensive study of those foundations for each component and general standard. For this alternative approach for defining a model, consider the graphic illustration of a Knowledge V in Figure 12:2.

To use this Knowledge V, it is important, first, to recognize that the part labeled "technology" is the same as in the Perrow (1970) depiction of organizational effectiveness. Furthermore, the "technical system" in this V is the set of tools, materials, and methods that are the manifestations of the technology. The primary difficulty in preparing a description of the current model may come from limitations in the language to express the knowledge and assumptions used to determine how to do work; for example, limitations on language for stating the philosophical or ideological views held or the theories or generalizations that are being used.

To provide a set of materials and language for that task of defining the technology, the authors reviewed the models for comprehensive reform included in the NWREL (Northwest Regional Educational Lab) (1999) handbook of approved school reform models, key literature on characteristics of effective models of schooling, and state standard courses of study. From that review, they prepared lists of "standards" for effective schools that were found consistently across all of the references.

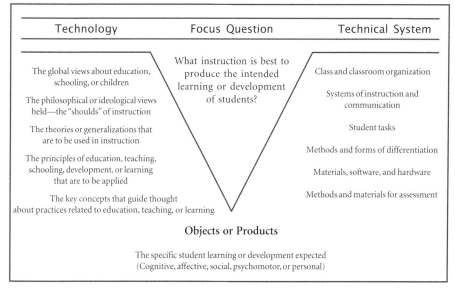

Figure 12:2 The Knowledge V—a framework for defining an instructional system model. Developed by Andrew Hayes, Department of Specialty Studies, Donald R. Watson School of Education, University of North Carolina at Wilmington, from the Knowledge Vee by Bob Gowin and published in Joseph D. Novak and D. Bob Gowin, *Learning How to Learn.* Cambridge, MA: Cambridge University Press, 1986.

Those standards are organized into sections relating to (1) the school organization, (2) the curricula and instructional systems, (3) the methods for engaging parents and community in the schooling of students, and (4) the student outcome goals and benchmarks. (These standards are available from the authors without cost. They will be sent as an e-mail attachment upon receiving an e-mail request.)

To use these standards to make an assessment of the current model, each standard can be entered into the V under "Technology" and then, corresponding to it under the Technical System, list all current school practices that address that standard.

To design the model, as it will be after reform, make another V form with the standards listed. In this form, rather than listing what practices currently are in place to address each standard, list the technical system (the tools, materials, and methods) the school will have in place at the end of the reform initiative. The reform task, then, is to make the change for each standard from the current "technical system" to the desired one. Of course, if you should decide that one or more of these standards are not appropriate for your school, then leave those out of your analyses and plans for reform. Also, if you identify some that you think are important but are not included, then add them to your set.

Examples of these standards for each of the four components of a school are listed below for illustrative purposes:

1. Leaders and professional staff adopt and communicate a common set of expectations for student achievement and responsibility;

2. The curricula are comprehensive and challenging and allow for acceleration of learning by any student;

3. There is agreement among parents, community members, and school personnel about a core set of purposes of schooling, responsibility for student achievement, and student achievement that is expected; and

4. The student-assessment system is comprehensive in its coverage of all goals and benchmarks: academic, personal, and social.

Planning for Reform

The tasks in planning for reform are illustrated in Figure 12:3. In this figure, the current system is producing the current results. To know whether change is needed, the current results must be known—the full set of results, not merely global test scores, such as those produced by testing programs for accountability purposes. If those results are what are desired for all significant subgroups of students, then no change is necessary. If they are not, then apparently some changes are needed. However, responsible planning for change cannot begin immediately after knowing the current results by asking the question, "What should we do differently?" Rather, the first task is to determine what there is about the current system of materials, tools, practices, and relationships that are producing the current results—determine what is causing the current results to be what they are. Only after that causal determination is made should planning continue to the next task, which is to determine the results that are desired—set the goals for desired outcomes. Those must be clarified before planning for action begins.

Once goal-setting is completed, then the task of designing the new system can begin. The authors recommend that this system design be done for each of the program standards (from the lists for each of the four components available from the authors) and by careful consideration of the overall standards for a model—coherence, comprehensiveness, and validity. Special attention should be given to ensuring that there is clear research-based evidence

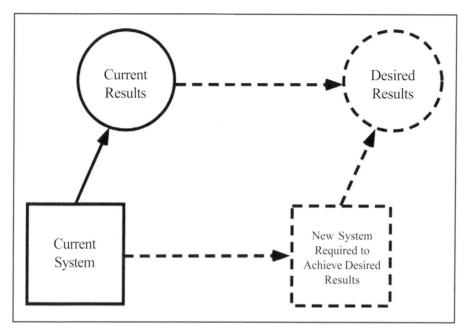

Figure 12:3 Depiction of the task in planning for reform.

that supports adoption of any particular materials, tools, methods, or relationships.

Once the desired system is designed, then the change process can be determined. Remember, a model is in place now. So, getting the desired model in place requires making changes that are essential to get all the current materials, tools, practices, and relationships to become the ones that are designed into the desired model. To be successful in reform, these changes cannot be left to chance, nor can they be treated in any way that results in staff uncertainty or insecurity. Otherwise, the reform managers should expect resistance to the changes. Furthermore, the processes that will be used to achieve the change must reflect the nature and expected difficulty of the changes that are being attempted.

It may appear that performing an assessment of current conditions of the school for all of these standards and then determining what technical system is needed to meet the standards is a daunting and overwhelming task. It may be; but doing so could result in a comprehensive plan for reform. Then, making those changes for all standards could result in a reformed school—a major transformation.

However, if a comprehensive reform is neither needed nor desired, then a reduced version of the planning and change processes can be used. The same approaches are recommended, however, beginning with a review of the standards, to determine the ones for which bridging the gaps between current conditions standards probably are most important for achieving the results that are most desired. Using those selected standards, plans can be made by:

- clarifying the gaps in achievement that will be given priority attention
- selecting standards that are the most important to meet
- clarifying the meaning of the standards
- identifying the current practices that are consistent with the standards, if there are any
- identifying the current practices that are not consistent with the standards, if there are any
- identifying gaps in full coverage of the standards by the current practices
- determining any improvements in current practices that might be needed to meet the standards
- determining methods, tools, materials, or relationships to be adopted to meet the standards
- developing plans for making the changes needed to adopt the new practices, tools, materials, or relationships

To ensure that the school is able to address the differences among its students, as plans for selecting or designing an instructional system are being made, it is essential to answer the following questions:

- What are the characteristics of learners that we think make a difference in instruction and learning?
- Which student characteristics—for example, prior learning, motivation to learn, language barriers, or exceptionalities—are currently taken into account by the instructional system for most of the students? Which will be addressed in the reformed system?
- Which differences among students is the school most unable to address?
- How much difference among students makes a difference? —that is, how much difference is required before instructional accommodations need to be made?
- Is there an expectation that all students will ultimately achieve a common set of skills? If so, what are those skills? If not, what variations will be allowed?

Once those questions are answered and the assessment of the current school model is completed, the planners can determine the overall guidelines they will use for selecting new model components. For example, considering these differences to be accommodated in the new instructional system, there may be a need to have several different technical systems to serve the variety of student needs and characteristics. Variations within one primary system may not be enough. That decision should be made by taking into account the purposes to be served and the range of student needs that will be considered. Marie Clay (1998) claims that if the intent of the reform and the new instructional system is to serve all students optimally, then the resulting technical systems must differ, as must the support systems that are needed for full implementation of the system. This may mean that quite different instructional tools, materials, and methods will be used for different students and purposes but within a coherent vision of schooling.

More Factors to Consider in Planning for Reform

The literature on comprehensive school reform, and the federal policy covering such funded reform initiatives, identifies 11 components of an effective reform. Four of those components cover the areas of a school for which reforms might be needed. Those are:

- research-based school organization model
- research-based curricula and instructional model
- system to engage parents and community in the schooling of children
- comprehensive goals and benchmarks for student achievement

In addition to those four areas in which reform will be needed, some other task areas or conditions, also referred to in the literature on school reform as "components," must be addressed to ensure reform success. Those remaining components are:

- professional development—a sound system to prepare people to make the changes from the current to new practices and to develop skills to adopt the new ones
- assessment—a comprehensive information system that effectively and efficiently serves both formative and summative decision making
- technical assistance—an effective and efficient system of external assistance to facilitate the change process and to provide specialized skills required for the change
- resources—resources that are required for the change, available when and in the amount and forms needed, along with overall resource allocations that do not create significant distractions to the vision and initiative of reform

- support within the school—support from the participants that is sufficient for them to engage readily in the change process and to make changes that are needed

- organizational support—support from the organization so that anyone who has a job to do can do it without interference from the organization and support by designing and adopting all organizational structures that are needed to support the technical system that is adopted

Meeting the conditions for these components requires the school organization to be both effective and efficient. To meet those conditions, the school must have a clear and shared vision of the current organization and its curricula and instructional systems, the desired organization and the desired curricula and instructional systems, and the current and desired effects. The design of the planned system should be consistent with the set of beliefs and principles set out in the related Knowledge V for the design, and it should have tools, methods, and materials that support those beliefs and principles. In other words, the design should conform to the standards for congruence set out in the Perrow (1970) framework—organization and technology should match.

As the case was made in sections above, to meet the conditions for serving diverse learners, schools cannot focus attention mainly on the curriculum and instruction in the classroom. The school structures and functions, and the parent and community engagement, must also reflect the school's adopted assumptions and practices. When seen as a whole, all other components of the reform—professional development, participant support, use of resources, and technical assistance—serve the purpose of implementing the intended program model within the school programs so that it is able to meet the needs of diverse learners. In reference to literacy programs, Booth and Rowsell (2002) claim that the coherence or consistency among all program components is key to implementing a literacy initiative effectively.

While that point may be intuitively clear and appear to be an "of course," the authors have not found that degree of coherence in most of the schools studied while they were attempting comprehensive school reform. More commonly, they find a variety of forms of "shotgun approaches" that were selected and implemented in piecemeal fashion because they were thought at the time to be appropriate for addressing some particular need for some particular group of students. However, when taken as a whole, seldom were these "assemblages" either coherent or comprehensive.

A revealing experience for the authors has come from interviews with several hundred teachers in schools attempting comprehensive school reform. The topic of discussion in the interviews was their adoption of their literacy model, whether Success for All (SFA), Direct Instruction, or others. As an outcome of the interview, we usually listed all of the literacy programs, approaches, or materials that teachers mentioned or that we observed being used in classrooms and in the school. Rarely did schools have literacy programs that matched some overarching design principles. Commonly, the programs for English as a Second Language (ESL) students, exceptional children, and students receiving remediation, and the various motivational and tutoring programs were selected by using very different beliefs about literacy and instruction. In some schools, there was no understanding demonstrated that there should be coherence among the various literacy programs and practices.

One approach to reform used by some schools is to select a nationally validated school-reform model. These models should already meet the general conditions for coherence (at least they were designed to be and have been reviewed for validation). Examples of validated literacy programs, among others, are: SFA, Direct Instruction, and Literacy Collaborative. Though quite different in designs and guiding assumptions, they have practices in their literacy programs that are consistent with their assumptions. These models include recommended instructional and assessment methods and provide professional development options. They also offer both external and internal support services for teachers and leaders as they learn to use the model and adopt it into the system of services in the school. Materials provided are also consistent with the design principles.

These program designs give attention to key areas in the literacy curriculum and are examples of programs that reflect recommendations from the professional literature about program design to ensure capacity to serve diverse learners. Among those recommendations by Rodgers and Pinnell (2002) are for core programs that provide an organized and balanced array of whole-class, small-group, and individual instruction to ensure that all of the children make acceptable progress as they develop individually. Furthermore, they claim that instruction must account for those different paths and do so within the parameters of the school day and group teaching. Or, stated differently by Dorothy Strickland (2005), "Get a good plan, so you can differentiate."

Organization and education studies over the past 50 years and more have focused on theory building and produced a wide range of models and principles for analysis, design, and management of different forms of organizations and their processes, including schools. Among those findings, are the importance of:

- clear and shared vision of the desired organization or effects
- matching the degree of task structure with the characteristics of the group

- transforming a selected design to fit the particular characteristics of the adopting organization

- achieving commitment to the design before training

- matching instruction and assessment with the type of learning that is intended from the instruction

The quality of an educational program depends upon the overall quality of the school. All aspects of programs reflect the values, assumptions, and practices that guide the school organization, relationships, and ability to change. There is a strong knowledge foundation for assessing and designing programs and for planning and guiding reform initiatives. Those knowledge bases should become part of the common knowledge recognized and used in schools as the leaders and professional staff go about reform to serve diverse learners. If the authors' experiences with over 150 schools attempting reform are a good indicator, failure to do so almost certainly will result in failure to make significant reforms.

Implementation and Management of Reforms: Preparing the Professional Staff

"Restructuring requires that all who participate in the life of the school unlearn many things that have been taught in the past and learn new skills and abilities" Schlechty (1990, p. 11). In order to achieve school reform, leaders and faculties of schools must focus their attention on how *they* must change and not so much on how students (or their parents) should change. That difference in focus among the schools proved to be an important indicator of successful reform or improvement in the schools experienced by the authors. Ultimately, anyone who was successful in change had to recognize that *they* must change. Most did not reach that point of recognition, especially the teachers in the secondary academic subjects.

Preparing for reform requires building the capacity of the faculty to understand and accept the knowledge and assumptions about schooling that are to be the foundation for the program model that will be implemented. In addition, there are some other key understandings about reform that must be developed and accepted. Among those are:

1. The professional knowledge and the assumptions serving as the foundation for the program model must be the same or compatible;

2. Clear visions of the old model, the new model, and the reforming process must serve as the referents for all reform events;

3. The vision for the school and its implications for the social, emotional, and learning behaviors of students should be built upon the expectations for the adults who will work with those students;

4. The knowledge bases for designing a new model and for planning a reform initiative should come more from studying research findings and less from the collective experiences and judgments of the faculty and leaders. Professionals recognize and value the essential nature of research-based information and recognize the limitations on experiential learning. The reformed school will be a place that has studied itself and knows how to reform itself;

5. Reform of a school cannot happen without external support. The school system has to support the school and change along with the school in any ways that are needed to support the changes made in the school. The Local Education Agency (LEA) should consider the school reform initiative as part of its own reform or improvement;

6. Reform depends on a focused plan of professional development of teachers, other professional staff, and school leaders to prepare them for all aspects of the reform;

7. The current systems for "doing school" are not good enough to support reform—only improvements are possible within current practices;

8. Reform is complex, fluid, contextualized, and continuous;

9. Appropriate data that are understood well are the best tools for guiding discussions about reform;

10. Fullan (2001) claims that the need for external intervention is inversely proportional to how well the school is progressing—the less progress and the less capacity, the greater the need for external assistance. He continues to claim that over the long term, internal capacity building is the best approach to lasting reform; and

11. Fullan (2001) also suggests that, when the focus remains on changing things that are not significant, fundamental, instructional reform will not happen.

Few schools experienced by the authors appear to be approaching improvement or reform by adopting an explicit and coherent set of principles or practices to build a program model that serves diverse learners and high-priority needs. However, the probability of success in reforming current models of schooling is low, unless there is careful and consistent use of important principles of change and principles and practices of strong organizations.

Preventing Failures in Reform: Findings from the North Carolina Comprehensive School Reform Initiative

The sections of this chapter presented above lay out conceptual frameworks for thinking about how to serve diverse learners and how to analyze program models to determine what they are and why they work the way they do. Much of that presentation has dealt with organizational factors and the essential match between those organizational factors and the instructional systems. These foundations, and many others, have been documented well in the general literature on general organization theory and applications to schools as organizations and in the literature on reform of schools.

For example, almost any research report dealing with organizational effectiveness makes a strong case for the importance of a clear vision of the achievements that are being attempted. We have all kinds of clichés about that—"If you don't know where you are going, any road will get you there," etc. Nevertheless, the authors found that most reforms that were attempted were not guided by clear visions, nor were most of the other known foundational principles of reform being applied. The following section gives some of the common findings from analyses of the North Carolina reform attempts as a way to give warning to others not to follow these paths.

There is a wide range of barriers or traps facing particular schools and a wide range of the effects of these barriers. The conditions that were judged most powerful in resisting reform in the schools attempting reform are:

1. In most schools, there was an incomplete translation of the principles and general practices of the selected models to particular operational systems and practices that matched the particular school. A key task in reform is to translate the general model design into an operational plan that matches the details of the particular school. That task was neither attempted nor accomplished in most schools. Details, details, details! The reform "devil" is in the details, and they must be addressed;

2. There was an overall weakness in clarity and completeness of the plans for reform. The plans for the initiative were not clear enough to communicate what changes were intended or through what means;

3. The pressures were high for student-performance accountability on some schools that serve primarily students who had histories of low aspirations, low engagement in schooling, and low achievement. That focus on improving test scores became a major detractor from the focus on reform;

4. There were wide differences among the faculty, in most schools, on teaching practices used and in the proficiency in teaching and readiness to engage in the reform. These differences required differentiating the reform strategies, just as we expect to differentiate instruction for diverse students, but that was not done in any systematic way, either within or across schools;

5. There was a general lack of vision of a reformed school with the selected model central to that vision in all schools. The school leaders were not able to describe how either the school as an organization or the curricula and instructional systems would be different at some specified time in the future—such as at the end of this year—even when asked about particular classrooms or particular school processes;

6. Leadership generally was not focused on reform—there was a general absence of reform vision and lack of apparent commitment to reform, even though there may have been a high degree of focus on student test preparation. Leaders could not envision change processes by taking a particular needed change and telling what would have to change to get that new practice in place—they could not perform a task analysis of the change to determine the essential subordinate changes, neither in school processes nor in student learning outcomes, and they could not identify the benchmark accomplishments;

7. Leadership for the reform initiative was often delegated to teachers or other staff who did not have either the specialized leadership skills or the time allocation required to provide the leadership needed for success;

8. There was a general view among the schools that the comprehensive school reform initiative is "a *project* to be implemented" rather than work to transform the school in some fundamental ways. Events in the schools tended to be treated "as events" rather than as methods leading to reform. This view was reflected even more strongly among the schools that used external consultants for writing plans and impact reports. Leaders in these schools frequently referred to (and resisted) the state focus on clear, coherent, and comprehensive plans and reports as "paperwork" rather than as project planning and evaluation;

9. There was a general lack of clear, precise, and coherent technical assistance and training from some model providers, especially considering the high levels of structure needed by some schools. The models for dissemination of the program designs were not complete and did not provide the full range of technical assistance and training needed to put the models into place in most of the schools; and

10. There was a pervasive focus of evaluation on student performance and on analysis of student test data for use in instructional planning and for grouping or regrouping of students. Few schools systematically monitored and managed the reform initiative through assessment of the reform processes and the results from efforts to change school or classroom practices. There was a general inability among the leaders to analyze the planning processes or practices and then devise ways to know the degree to which they were in place as designed.

From those and other similar findings, one might reasonably assume that the reform initiatives were not successful. Indeed, most were not. However, most of the schools did improve; but sustaining those improvements tended to be elusive. The authors found little among the schools that prevented success other than an absence of dedicated and capable leadership that was focused on reform and sustained that focus over the 3-year time given to the initiatives.

Of course, there were wide variations in the collective capacity of the teachers among the schools. But that capacity was not a clear distinguishing factor in success. In low-capacity schools, good leaders created conditions and expectations that enabled those teachers to be successful. On the other hand, poor leaders in high-capacity schools accomplished little. Seemingly, the knowledge bases for sound leadership for reform are readily available but not known by many in leadership positions. When this knowledge base is used well, reform can, and does, occur. If schools are to be successful in dealing with diverse students, sound leadership must guide the initiatives to reform the schools to ones that support an instructional system with the complexity needed to serve the students well.

Walters Elementary School is a case in point. The knowledge foundations for reform were used there, whether explicitly or not. The experienced and capable principal provided the organizational conditions for reform to occur and provided ongoing direction to ensure that all aspects of the design were working.

Conclusion

We close by referring again to the descriptions of schooling as a culture trait, to the essential need for the organization to match the instructional system, to the need for a common technical and professional language and knowledge base on which decisions are made, to the limits on the capacity of teachers to effect reform (either individually or collectively), and to the essential role of sound leadership in reform success, and turn to Schlechty (2001, pp. 8–9), who stated the need for a match between the technical system and organization structures in another way. He stated that:

"If *restructuring* and *systemic change* do not mean changing the conditions that make it difficult or impossible to do what needs to be done to improve the schools, then the words have no meaning. If teachers do not have the time to engage in significant dialogue with colleagues, then it is necessary to reconfigure rules, roles, and relationships so that teachers do have this time and students do get more attention."

Reference

Booth, D. & Rowsell, J. (2002). *The literacy principal: Leading, supporting, and assessing reading and writing initiatives.* Markham, Ontario, Canada: Pembroke.

Clay, M. (1998). *By different paths to common outcomes.* York, ME: Stenhouse.

Fullan, M. (2001). *Leading in a culture of change.* San Francisco: Jossey-Bass.

Garratt, B. (1987). In L. Stoll & D. Fink (2001), *Changing our schools* (p. 151). Philadelphia: Open University Press.

Harkin, R. E. (1972). *Educational technology, organizational structure, and teacher perceptions of effectiveness.* Final Report, USOE grant.

Harkin, R. E., & Hayes, A. E. (1973). Educational technology, organizational structure, and teacher perceptions of effectiveness. Unpublished paper presented during the Annual Conference, AASA, February 20, 1973, Atlantic City, NJ.

North Central Regional Education Lab (NCREL). (1999). *Changing by design: Comprehensive school reform.* Oakbrook, IL: Organization.

Novak, J. D., & Gowan, D. B. (1986). *Learning how to learn.* Cambridge, MA: Cambridge University Press.

Perrow, C. (1967). A framework for the comparative analysis of organizations. *American Psychological Review, 32,* 194–208.

Perrow, C. (1970). *Organizational analysis: A sociological view.* Belmont, CA: Brooks/Cole.

Risko, V. J., & Bromley, K. (Eds.). (2001). In *Collaboration for diverse learners: Viewpoints and practices.* Newark, DE: International Reading Association.

Rodgers, E., & Pinnell, G. S. (Eds.). (2002). In *Learning from teaching in literacy education: New perspectives on professional development.* Portsmouth, NH: Heinemann.

Schlechty, P. C. (1990). *Schools for the 21st century: Leadership imperatives for educational reform.* San Francisco: Jossey-Bass.

Schlechty, P. C. (2001). *Shaking up the schoolhouse: How to support and sustain educational innovation.* San Francisco: Jossey-Bass.

Strickland, D. (2005). Statement made in an address to the National Conference on Family Literacy, March 21, 2005. [unpublished presentation] Louisville, KY.

Woodward, J. (1965). *Industrial organization.* London: Oxford University Press.

Editors' Biographies

Barbara Honchell

Barbara Honchell has worked as a primary-grade classroom teacher and reading specialist in the public schools of Indiana, Michigan, and North Carolina for over 30 years, most recently as a Reading Recovery Teacher Leader. She earned a PhD. in Special Education and Literacy from the University of North Carolina (UNC) Chapel Hill in 2001. Most recently, Barbara serves as assistant professor at UNC Wilmington as Director of the Reading Recovery University Training Center, where she continues to teach first-grade children. Her interests include early literacy, at-risk readers, and the design of comprehensive literacy programs.

Melissa Schulz

Melissa Schulz began her work with diverse learners when she taught for 10 years in Ohio. As an elementary teacher, she taught second and third grade and gifted education with fourth- through sixth-grade students. Most recently, she worked with struggling readers and writers in first grade. Her research focuses on diverse literacy learners, family literacy, and home–school relationships. She has a Ph.D. in Language, Literacy, and Culture from The Ohio State Uni-

versity. Melissa currently is an assistant professor in Early Childhood Education at the University of Cincinnati in Cincinnati, Ohio, where her work focuses on teacher preparation and professional development for teachers regarding the reading and writing development of diverse literacy learners.

Contributors' Biographies

Maria Luiza Dantas

Maria Luiza (Malu) Dantas is an assistant professor in the Department of Learning and Teaching in the School of Leadership and Education Sciences at the University of San Diego. Her research focuses on sociocultural influences on early literacy learning, teaching/curriculum, and assessment processes—in particular, family/community literacy and cultural practices, home–school relationships, and the nature of culturally responsive teaching. Her current work also examines ways to build teacher competence to work with diverse learners in the context of international education.

Vickie Ellison

Vickie Ellison is an assistant professor of Spanish Pedagogy at Kent State University in Kent, Ohio. She earned her Ph.D. in Foreign Language from The Ohio State University. Her research interests are teacher knowledge and Spanish heritage language learners. She became interested in Spanish heritage language learners when she taught high school in central California and noted that many of the comments made about these students were made about African-American students in Ohio. This sparked her interest in teacher knowledge and what types of knowledge teachers need in the classroom to become effective teachers and also how teacher attitudes toward students of color affected their teaching.

Kathy R. Fox

Kathy R. Fox has spent her career working with language-minority children and families as a classroom teacher and teacher educator. She taught kindergarten and first grade for over 20 years and now teaches courses in language and literacy at the University of North Carolina Wilmington. As a North Carolina native, she is interested in language and literacy practices in the diverse family structures and backgrounds in the state, particularly in the growing immigrant populations and their nonschool-based literacy practices, such as oral stories, family histories, and native language maintenance practices.

Andrew E. Hayes

Andrew E. Hayes has worked for 44 years in education, as a teacher and assistant principal and as member of the faculty at the University of Georgia, University of North Carolina (UNC) Chapel Hill, and UNC Wilmington. His teaching areas include mathematics, educational administration, research, computer applications, instructional design, project design and management, and evaluation, among others. He directed an educational research lab, provided technical assistance to state- and federally funded projects on education of exceptional children, provided evaluation services for numerous funded programs, and served as director of research for the National Center for Family Literacy, where he is now a member of the Board of Directors. He and Hathia A. Hayes developed a model for assessment of teaching that can be used for summative evaluation or for continuous improvement. Since 1999, he worked with Hathia to evaluate comprehensive school reform initiatives in their state, a program including over 170 schools.

Hathia A. Hayes

Hathia A. Hayes is an associate professor at the University of North Carolina Wilmington. She teaches graduate courses in language and literacy education, one specifically related to literacy programs and practices. For the past 36 years, she has served in a variety of leadership roles at public school and university levels, in which new programs were designed, old programs changed, and reforms made that was based on the best theories and practices that were known in the field. She has been involved in literacy program development and implementation as a district-level literacy educator, as a state department consultant for elementary and literacy education, as a college professor responsible for designing and implementing a professional development system, and as a coevaluator with Andrew for North Carolina Comprehensive School Reform projects for 6 years.

Sandra Parker Jones

Sandra Parker Jones is recently retired from the North Carolina Public Schools, with over 30 years of experience. While serving in the public schools, she worked as a teacher, an elementary school principal, a director of personnel, and a curriculum and instruction specialist for elementary and middle schools. Immediately upon retirement, she was named the Chairman of the Department of Education at St. Andrews Presbyterian College in Laurinburg, North Carolina. Additionally, she teaches graduate courses in reading and educational leadership at the University of North Carolina at Pembroke. Dr. Jones received an earned Doctorate from Virginia Polytechnic Institute and State University. Her dissertation was awarded "Dissertation of the Year" honors by the North Carolina Association for Supervision and Curriculum Development in 1990. Her interests include designing literacy environments that teach and reach all students regardless of their diversities, and working with adolescent African-American males who struggle with literacy issues.

Rebecca Kantor

Rebecca Kantor joined The Ohio State University faculty in 1983, after receiving a B.A. degree from the University of Rochester in Developmental Psychology and Linguistics, and both a Masters in Early Childhood Education, and a Doctorate in Education and Applied Developmental Psycholinguistics from Boston University. Dr. Kantor's research, scholarship, and publication record are centered within the field of early childhood development and education, and are concerned broadly with how children's language, literacy, social growth, and development can be supported and extended within educational settings using ethnographic methodology. Dr. Kantor teaches a variety of early childhood and core courses in both the Masters and Doctoral programs. She is also involved in the M.Ed. program leading to the early childhood license.

Hengameh Kermani

Hengameh Kermani is an associate professor of education at University of North Carolina Wilmington. She teaches courses in the Early Childhood Education Program. A native of Iran, she has worked as a classroom teacher with young children, as well their families, in a multicultural context. Her research interests focus on maternal scaffolding strategies and their impact on children's problem-solving abilities, family literacy, peer-tutoring, and impact of technology on learning and teaching.

Denise N. Morgan

Denise N. Morgan is a former elementary teacher who worked with diverse learners in kindergarten, second, and fourth grade in Alabama and Illinois. She earned her Ph.D. in Language, Literacy, and Culture from The Ohio State University. Denise currently is an Assistant Professor of Early Literacy Education at Kent State University in Kent, Ohio, where she studies the reading and writing development of young learners and professional development of teachers.

Emily M. Rodgers

Emily M. Rodgers first began her work with diverse learners when she taught for 10 years in Newfoundland. She continued this work by focusing on young, struggling readers and writers when she joined the faculty of The Ohio State University as an assistant professor in the College of Education. Her research focuses on the professional development of teachers and the nature of effective scaffolding of literacy learning. She received the National Reading Conference Outstanding Student Research Award in 1999. Emily is coeditor of *Learning from Teaching in Literacy Education* and *Scaffolding Literacy Instruction: Strategies for K–4 Classrooms*, published by Heinemann.

Adrian Rodgers

Adrian Rodgers first began his work with diverse learners 20 years ago as a junior and senior high school teacher in Labrador and then continued it at the college level in Ohio. He has a Ph.D. in Educational Studies, with a specialization in literacy and teacher education from The Ohio State University. He is currently assistant professor in teacher education at The Ohio State University in Newark, Ohio, where his work focuses on teacher preparation and professional development for pre- and in-service teachers. Rodgers views scaffolding as a useful tool for thinking about the teaching of diverse learners and has edited *Scaffolding Literacy Instruction: Strategies for K–4 Classrooms*, published by Heinemann. He is currently completing a coauthored book on literacy coaching for Teachers College Press.

Bradford L. Walker

Dr. Bradford L. Walker is an associate professor at the University of North Carolina (UNC) Wilmington. He received a B.S. degree in Elementary Education from Brigham Young University in 1974, a M.Ed. degree in Curriculum and Instruction with a concentration in reading from Brigham Young University in 1981, and an Ed.D. degree in Reading Education from Indiana University in 1988. His professional experience includes teaching third, fourth, and fifth grades for 10 years, as well as working as an elementary school principal for a year. He has been at UNC Wilmington for the past 17 years. One of his assignments during his first year of teaching was to work with the fourth-grade students at his school who were identified as struggling readers. This experience sparked an interest that grew into a passionate focus for his work—researching what is needed to most effectively support diverse learners in their literacy growth.

Index

Response. *See also Cambourne, Brian.*
  feedback, importance of, 81–82
Responsibility. *See also Cambourne, Brian.*
  discussions of learners and, 77–78
Rodgers and Rodgers
  teaching, team support to enhance, 227–229
Rogoff and Wertsch. *See also Scaffolding.*
  scaffolding, variations on, 116–117

S

Scaffolding (of instruction). *See also Rogoff and Wertsch.*
  defined, 11
  development of reading strategies and, 41, 116
  support of enhanced teaching and, 227–228
Schlechty, P. C.
  restructuring and systemic change, 291
  school reform, requirements of, 287–288
Schunk, D. S. *See also Bandura, A., and Zimmerman, B. J.*
  self-efficacy and strategy development, 42–43, 46
Searching and checking
  use of, 51–52
  teacher attention to, 56, 57–59
Self-correction. *See also Clay, Marie.*
  as a framework for the decision process, 45
  as a strategy for successful readers, 46
  successful rate of, 52–53
  teacher attention to, 57–59
  use and interpretation of, example, 57–59
Sergiovanni, T. J.
  academic leaders and change, 243

individual learning plans, sharing of, 249
  leadership and teacher consultation, 255–256
Smith, Frank
  approximation, consequences of, 79
  learning community, notion of, 91–93
  and learning environment, 100–102
Smitherman, G.
  linguistic patterns, characteristics of, 117–120
Story Letter. *See also Read aloud(s).*
  caution for teachers regarding, 210
  as communicative tool, 212
  preparation of, 209
  purpose and usefulness of, 210–211

T

Teale, W. H.
  questioning notions of reading readiness, 112
Thalp and Gallimore. *See also Scaffolding.*
  development of reading strategies, 41
Title 1 (reading services), 1, 37, 89, 201
Tomlinson, C.
  academic diversity, leadership for, 240–241
  communication as essential for, 255–256
  functions of, listed, 244
  teacher knowledge for, 241–242
  vignette on, 245, 246, 247, 248, 251, 253, 254
  change, goal of, 254–255
  adjustment for teachers, 257
  benefits of for children, 256